Missional Life
in Practice and Theory

Missional Life in Practice and Theory

Essays in Honor of Gailyn Van Rheenen

Edited by
CHRISTOPHER L. FLANDERS
and GREG MCKINZIE

Foreword by
MONTE COX

PICKWICK *Publications* • Eugene, Oregon

MISSIONAL LIFE IN PRACTICE AND THEORY
Essays in Honor of Gailyn Van Rheenen

Copyright © 2024 Wipf and Stock Publishers. All rights reserved. Except for brief quotations in critical publications or reviews, no part of this book may be reproduced in any manner without prior written permission from the publisher. Write: Permissions, Wipf and Stock Publishers, 199 W. 8th Ave., Suite 3, Eugene, OR 97401.

Pickwick Publications
An Imprint of Wipf and Stock Publishers
199 W. 8th Ave., Suite 3
Eugene, OR 97401

www.wipfandstock.com

PAPERBACK ISBN: 978-1-6667-3560-4
HARDCOVER ISBN: 978-1-6667-9284-3
EBOOK ISBN: 978-1-6667-9285-0

Cataloging-in-Publication data:

Names: Flanders, Christopher L., editor. | McKinzie, Greg, editor. | Cox, Monte, foreword.
Title: Missional life in practice and theory : essays in honor of Gailyn Van Rheenen / edited by Christopher L. Flanders and Greg McKinzie; foreword by Monte Cox.
Description: Eugene, OR : Pickwick Publications, 2024. | Includes bibliographical references.
Identifiers: ISBN 978-1-6667-3560-4 (paperback) | ISBN 978-1-6667-9284-3 (hardcover) | ISBN 978-1-6667-9285-0 (ebook)
Subjects: LCSH: van Rheenen, Gailyn, 1946–. | Missions—Theory. | Missions—Practice. | Missions—Africa.
Classification: BR127 .M6 2024 (print). | BR127 (epub).

Table of Contents

List of Contributors vii

Foreword ix
Monte Cox

Introduction: A Biographical Sketch and Bibliography xiii
Christopher L. Flanders

CHAPTER 1: Mission between Theory and Practice 1
Greg McKinzie

CHAPTER 2: The Conversion Process in the Stone-Campbell Movement Churches in Southern Africa (1914–1927): An Historical Analysis 33
Paul S. Chimhungwe

CHAPTER 3: Van Rheenen's Incarnational Model for Tribal Africa and Watson's Church Planting Movement Model: How Different Are They? 49
Anthony B. Parker

CHAPTER 4: They Call Him Father: The Metaphoric Image of God as Father among Modern Shona in Zimbabwe 69
Linda F. Whitmer

CHAPTER 5: From Missions to Missional: Preparing a Royal Priesthood 87
Earl Lavender

TABLE OF CONTENTS

CHAPTER 6: Let My People Go!
Diaspora Mission in the North American Context 99
Daniel A. Rodriguez

CHAPTER 7: Understanding by Movement: Seeking Sensible Interdependence for Latino and Hispanic Missionaries 109
J. Omar Palafox

CHAPTER 8: Love, Joy, and Grace:
Formation Together in the Life of God 128
P. Kent Smith

CHAPTER 9: Contemplative Mission: The Interplay between Spirituality and Missional Practice in Mission Alive Church Planters 142
Tod K. Vogt and Charles Kiser

CHAPTER 10: The Impact of Diaspora Mission and the Shift to a Mission Paradigm in the North American Church 164
Jared Looney

Bibliography 179

List of Contributors

Dr. Paul S. Chimhungwe—Vice Principal, Kgolagano College of Theological Education, Gaborone, Botswana

Dr. Monte Cox—Dean of the College of Bible and Ministry, Harding University, Searcy, Arkansas

Dr. Christopher L. Flanders—Professor of Missions, Graduate School of Theology, Abilene Christian University, Abilene, Texas

Dr. Charles Kiser—Pastor and theologian, Storyline Christian Community, Dallas, Texas

Dr. Earl Lavender—Professor of Bible, Lipscomb University, Nashville, Tennessee

Dr. Jared Looney—Executive Director, Global City Missions Initiative, Orlando, Florida

Dr. Greg McKinzie—Executive Editor, *Missio Dei: A Journal of Missional Theology and Praxis* and Affiliate Assistant Professor, Fuller Theological Seminary, Pasadena, California

Dr. Anthony B. Parker—Global Partnerships Officer, Pioneer Bible Translators, Dallas, Texas

Dr. J. Omar Palafox—Assistant Professor of Missions, Abilene Christian University, Abilene, Texas

List of Contributors

Dr. Daniel A. Rodriguez—Professor of Religion and Hispanic Studies and Dean, Religion and Philosophy Division, Seaver College, Pepperdine University, Malibu, California

Dr. P. Kent Smith—Chair of the Eden Center for Regenerative Culture, Abilene, Texas

Dr. Tod K. Vogt—Executive Director, Mission Alive, McKinney, Texas

Dr. Linda F. Whitmer—Dean, School of Intercultural Studies, Johnson University, Knoxville, Tennessee

Foreword

Monte Cox

If you know Gailyn Van Rheenen, you will appreciate just how manifestly he embodies the title of this volume, written in his honor, *Missional Life in Practice and Theory*. I have known Gailyn for more than four decades. In that time, I have come to know him as a consummate practitioner who grounds his missional life in profound theological reflection. His genius was made known to me before I ever even formally met Gailyn, and long before I used words like *missional* or *theological reflection*.

During my freshman year at Harding University, Gailyn Van Rheenen served as a visiting professor of missions and my girlfriend was taking his New Testament Survey course. It was there that she (and everyone else in Gailyn's orbit) first learned of the Kipsigis, the largest of the Kalenjin-speaking tribes of Kenya in East Africa. Surveying the New Testament gave Gailyn the opportunity to connect the dots between the ancient biblical text and its relevance for the world we students knew at the time. As a professor, Gailyn expanded his students' horizons by showing how the gospel impacted these people we'd never heard of who lived on the other side of the globe. Photographs cast onto the classroom wall by a slide projector testified to the way God was drawing many Kipsigis to Jesus and how their lives were being transformed. During the semester, my girlfriend (now my wife), a little weary of references to tribes as opposed to locations in Africa, declared, "If there is one place in the world I will never go, it is to the Kipsigis." Five years later, after that same girlfriend had become my wife, we boarded a plane and began planting churches among—you guessed it—the other Kalenjin-speaking peoples of Kenya. To Gailyn, the gospel was not simply theory. The New Testament was not theory. A survey of the New Testament was a review of God's own account of how the Word becomes

FOREWORD

flesh and dwells among people. In his classes, students (like my wife) saw evidence that the Word was becoming flesh once again and making a home among the Kipsigis. God used Gailyn Van Rheenen and his wife Becky to inspire a generation of missionaries who followed in their steps.

Gailyn was always a strategic thinker to his core. In the 1970s and eighties, the church growth movement was *the* way to do missions, but Gailyn didn't embrace it without recognizing its areas of weakness. He and his colleagues wrestled with the implications of the "homogeneous unit principle." They tweaked the movement's leadership training models, the "three selves," and the "euthanasia of mission." Gailyn continued strategizing out loud in his early publications *Church Planting in Uganda* (1976) and *Biblically Anchored Missions* (1983). In what may seem at first to be an unrelated anecdote, a group of us missionaries was playing poker in a cabin in a Kipsigis forest during a break from fishing when Gailyn, frustrated with a game he had not played before, exclaimed, "I just don't have a construct for this game." The room erupted in laughter. But it was true. Gailyn *needed* a construct for the game; he needed a construct for everything he did. He could not pursue something—even a frivolous game—for very long without some basic understanding of "how this works." He eventually felt compelled to collect his missiological conceptions and express them in print. From his construct-seeking mind eventually emerged the missional helix.

Gailyn was intentional about mobilizing students for foreign missions. In the summer, interns would shadow Gailyn and his teammates for a few weeks. Then, intrepid as he was, he would take them to neighboring countries like Tanzania or Uganda, where the Van Rheenens and their coworkers had actually begun their ministry in 1971 before Idi Amin forced them out. Gailyn cast a vision for raising up harvesters for the less-evangelized people groups of East Africa, then invested the time and energy by showing prospective missionaries those fields firsthand. Driving through the Sukuma land in Northern Tanzania, it was easier to picture how future Sukuma-speaking church planters could settle there, sow seeds of the gospel in that fertile soil, and replicate the fruitful work of incarnational ministry they observed in Kenya. When Gailyn and Becky left Kenya, I and others took up that mantle. The teams of workers that arrived in the decades that followed were a tribute to Gailyn's vision.

At Abilene Christian University, Gailyn and Becky once again found themselves in a receptive field. Some of his former students from his time at ACU have contributed to this volume. Many, many more of them have participated in the expansion of God's kingdom in powerful ways. After his fruitful time at ACU came Mission Alive, which he founded in search of innovative ways to communicate the gospel to unreached peoples in the US.

Borrowing a phrase from the apostle Paul, God endowed Gailyn Van Rheenen with the gifts and skills of "an expert builder" (1 Cor 3:10). Now, by God's grace, those of us who gleaned from Gailyn's wisdom and experience will continue to build atop the solid foundation that is Christ. May the Lord use the contents of this book to bless other builders with that same Spirit-filled, Spirit-led expertise that Gailyn exemplified so well.

Introduction
A Biographical Sketch and Bibliography[1]

Christopher L. Flanders

Those who know Gailyn Van Rheenen know this about him—he has consistently demonstrated a missional practice that is theologically grounded and a missiology that aims at practical embodiment. That is to say, Gailyn has always labored to be a *theory-informed practitioner* and a *practice-focused theoretician*. While a church planter in Uganda and Kenya, Gailyn was a voracious learner and was one of a rare breed—a cross-cultural church planter that actively published. When he had transitioned to become a professor in an academic institution, he continued to write and mentor for active participation in the ongoing mission of God. And, when in his later years Gailyn and his wife initiated a church-planting organization, he continued to infuse his recruiting, training, and mentoring with theologically informed missional resources.

Thus, whether as cross-cultural church planter, missiologist and professor, or a leader of a mission organization, Gailyn Van Rheenen represents an exceptional example of missional praxis that holds in creative tension practical engagement with theoretical reflection. Where many tend to polarize and then lean into one end of the theory-practice polarity, Gailyn has successfully lived into this tension, representing the type of missionary theologian that Greg McKenzie argues for in his chapter in this volume. He wonderfully embodies the title of this work—a missional life in practice and theory.

---

1. Much of the information for this biographical sketch comes from a personal interview I conducted with Gailyn and Becky Van Rheenen on October 25, 2021.

Introduction

It is surely the case that Gailyn has been as influential a figure for missiology in Churches of Christ as any other single individual. His influence is expansive, due not only to the substantial number of missionaries and church planters he helped train, but also his extensive publication career, including his blogging work on missiology.com and missiology.org (domain names he purchased in the 1990s, presciently aware of the growing significance of the internet and digital communication).

Gailyn was born and spent his early years on a farm in Tracy, Iowa, a small farming community just outside of Pella, which was begun by Dutch immigrants seeking religious freedom. Gailyn did not grow up around missionaries, though he recalls when quite young saying to his older sister "I want to be a missionary!" In retrospect, this probably came out of his familiarity with the book of Acts and Paul.

It was there in southeastern Iowa the Van Rheenen family came in contact with the Church of Christ. Upon switching denominational affiliation, the family experienced ostracization by the strongly homogenous Dutch Reformed community. Gailyn's parents felt the need to move. On a campus visit to Harding University in Searcy, Arkansas, the Van Rheenens learned through a "chance" conversation at a gas station about Crowley's Ridge, a Christian academy in Paragould, Arkansas. In Gailyn's' own words, "we checked it out and stayed." This move to Arkansas would be important to his evolving mission consciousness.

The Van Rheenen family moved to Paragould where Gailyn began his 8th grade. He would eventually graduate from Crowley's Ridge Academy in 1964. In his senior high school yearbook, under his senior picture was a brief tag. It read "Wants to be a missionary." Church planting became a part of his life in Paragould when the main Church of Christ congregation at which the Van Rheenen family worshiped and served, planted a new congregation in Paragould. The Van Rheenens became a part of that new church plant. It was also in Paragould where Gailyn would meet his future wife, Becky.

Gailyn eventually attended Harding College, was the 1966 Sophomore Class president, and was Student body Vice President in 1968. There he pursued a degree in Bible and organized and took part in weekend and Spring Break outreach short-term mission trips. But it was through the influence of his Bible professors there at Harding College that his missions passion continued to grow.

Introduction

Soon after graduation, Gailyn became campus minister at Northeast State College in Tahlequah, Oklahoma, working there from 1969 to 1971. During his ministry there, he began a master's degree in missions at Abilene Christian College which, at the time, was the only graduate missions program in Church of Christ schools. Gailyn eventually completed his degree in 1974. It was during this time that Dr. George Gurganus, professor of missions at ACC, planted the seeds of Africa in Gailyn's missional imagination. Gurganus informed the Van Rheenens that ACC had put together a mission team and Gurganus suggested Uganda. Gailyn and Becky would go to Africa, where they would ultimately spend the next decade and a half!

The Van Rheenens went to Uganda, to work among the Bakonjo, an unreached people group. Gailyn finished writing his master's thesis while there. As Gailyn noted, writing his thesis while planting churches in Africa was for him a demonstration of critical learning while active in practice. In Uganda, they planted one church but were soon advised by the US government to leave due to the rising dangers from the Idi Amin administration. They journeyed across the border to neighboring Kenya, thinking they would return to Uganda in a few months. But, as God would have it, they stayed for much longer.

The Van Rheenens would remain in Kenya for a decade and a half, working among the Kipsigis, a Kalenjin people group in Kenya. These years in Kenya were challenging, with language and culture learning, adaptation, and raising a family. During it all, this effort would grow from an initial plant and become a thriving movement of over 150 churches. Numerical growth was not the only cause for celebration. With their culturally-aware approach, Van Rheenen and his team learned Kipsigis culture and language and witnessed Jesus emerge in a new cultural form, that of Kipsigis culture, which included culturally appropriate leadership, worship forms, and hymnology.

During his work in Africa, Gailyn returned two times as visiting missionary to his alma mater, Harding, in the academic years of 1977-78 and 1982-83. During these two stints, he continued to teach, mobilize students, and grow in his missiological understanding. He eventually entered the doctorate of missiology program at Trinity Evangelical Seminary and studied toward its completion while still working as a church-planting missionary in Kenya. It was during his time at Trinity that mentoring friendships with senior missiologists David Hesselgrave and Paul Hiebert significantly impacted Gailyn. At this prominent evangelical seminary, Gailyn was

INTRODUCTION

stretched in his theological and missiological understandings. The greatest change in his theological life was moving from a sectarian, proof-texting Christianity to a narrative-centered story of God approach. This time at Trinity would assist greatly in his personal growth. As Gailyn would note, the experiences at Trinity helped "move me from being a fan of the 'church of Christ' to being a fan of Christ."

Additionally, though Gurganus and his earlier experiences at ACC significantly impacted Gailyn's missiology and mission practice in Africa, still, the "Church of Christ did not have the training at that point to help me be an incarnational missionary." This would form later, through the influence of these thoughtful missiologists at Trinity who influenced Gailyn's missional theology. In particular, this change consisted of Gailyn adopting a core theology that was *incarnational*—the theological doctrine of incarnation now became the grounds for how to become the Word-in-flesh dwelling among people. John 1:14 became a central text for his developing incarnational missiology.

One of the hallmarks of Gailyn's impact among Churches of Christ has been his strong connections with the evangelical missiological community. Developing collaborative friendships with missiologists such as Michael Pocock, Doug McConnell, Scott Moreau, and Steve Strauss, a circle of friends with whom Gailyn had extensive dialogue, significantly helped him broaden his own viewpoints. Because of this, Gailyn became an influential voice in the Evangelical Missiological Society. Later, when Gailyn was engaged in training church planters for North America in his work with Mission Alive, he became conversation partners with Mike Breen and Alan Hirsch. Historically, Churches of Christ have leaned toward sectarianism, hesitant to engage with the broader Christian community. Gailyn rejected that sectarian tendency as his consistently broad ecumenism gave him a significant voice in the evangelical missiological community and helped many among the Churches of Christ (especially among the Church of Christ missiological guild) to learn to engage with and appreciate Churches outside their own ecclesial "tribe."

One thing that becomes clear by examining Gailyn's life is how he has always been an inveterate learner. "I have always been a student." This humble, always-hungry learning posture is clear in several ways. During two furloughs, he always made it a practice to take a graduate course. While in Kenya, he learned through correspondence courses from Fuller

Introduction

Theological Seminary. Even in his earlier "sectarian" mode, Gailyn made a point to continue learning from the best missiological resources.

This learner orientation also shows up in his relationships. As I interviewed Gailyn for this introduction, he was quick to point out the incredible significance of his mentors of the past and those from whom he continues to learn. His named list of significant personal influences demonstrates how Gailyn learned from older mentors who have shaped him through the years but also those younger. He noted as important influences those from whom he has and continues to learn. George Gurganus showed him the concept of the Indigenous Church. Donald McGavran taught him cultural analysis. Paul Hiebert exemplified how to engage "paradigms of thinking." David Hesselgrave taught him the integration of disciplines. Leonard Allen and Randy Harris provided models of simple, practical, portable theology. Tod Vogt demonstrated how to ask questions and seek deep discernment. Don McLaughlin showed Gailyn racial reconciliation and provided an example of the movement from theology to practice (practical theology) at its best. He also referenced the considerable influence of Greg McKinzie, a contributor to this festschrift and current editor of *Missio Dei Journal*. Finally, Gailyn noted his wife Becky, whom he called "my personal and spiritual mentor in more ways than she can understand. Of all humans, she has been my greatest mentor because of how she listens to God."

As I reflect on Gailyn's life and career, several things stand out. First, Gailyn has always possessed an incredible drive and commitment to God's calling. As I spoke to him about his missiological impact, Gailyn noted that despite lifelong struggles with dyslexia, he was "not a quitter." Self-confessedly, he admitted that "many have talents that I do not have but perhaps not the drive, even the calling. I felt in my heart and soul the calling as a missionary." Gailyn only over time did learn how to inhabit fully that calling as both missionary and missiologist. His relentless determinism is a significant part of his missiological legacy.

Second, his missiological impact on Churches of Christ and the broader evangelical world has been immense. His two texts, *Missions: Biblical Foundations and Contemporary Strategies*, (now in its second printing and one of the most used introductory missions texts in evangelical missions circles) along with his earlier work, *Communicating Christ in Animistic Contexts* (a seminal work in this area as one of the earliest North American missiological treatments on cultural power dynamics among folk religionists) remain incredibly influential.

xvii

Introduction

Third, Gailyn and his wife Becky have always been passionate about close, personal mentoring as a primary vehicle for missional training. Though his publications and classroom teaching have been monumental in influence, it was also the countless missions meeting where people came into the Van Rheenen home where he purposefully cast a vision for a generation of cross-cultural servants. I was a student of his while at Abilene Christian University and also his graduate assistant for three years while pursuing my master's degree in missiology. I not only personally benefited from this mentoring but saw his powerful mentoring work among students time and time again. It is impossible to overstate how much impact Gailyn has had on the global church through his powerful mentoring.

Along with the chapters of this volume, we offer a bibliography of Gailyn's missiological publications. This list demonstrates what I have already remarked above—his broad and influential scholarship. Those of us who have benefited directly from his formative influence dedicate this volume with gratitude to a man whose life has ably proven the creative missional impact of holding theory and practice together in the same life and career. Here's to Gailyn Van Rheenen, the missional practitioner par excellence! His is indeed a missional life in theory and practice.

Books and Book Chapters

Kenya Mission Team. *Church Planting, Watering, and Increasing in Kenya.* Austin, TX: Firm Foundation, 1980.

———. "Introducing the Kenya Church Growth Philosophy." In *Church Planting, Watering, and Increasing in Kenya*, 5–10. Austin, TX: Firm Foundation, 1980.

———. "God's Increase in Kipsigis." In *Church Planting, Watering, and Increasing in Kenya*, 81–91. Austin, TX: Firm Foundation, 1980.

Pocock, Michael, et al. *The Changing Face of World Mission: Engaging Contemporary Issues and Trends.* Encountering Mission. Grand Rapids: Baker Academic, 2005.

Towns, Elmer, et al. "Reformist View: Gailyn Van Rheenen." In *Evaluating the Church Growth Movement: 5 Views*, edited by Gary L. McIntosh and Paul E. Ingel, 165–206. Counterpoints. Grand Rapids: Zondervan, 2004.

Van Rheenen, Gailyn. "Archery, Dentures, and Eagles: Missionary Metaphors of Wendell Broom." In *100 Years of African Missions: Essays in Honor of Wendell Broom*, edited by Stanley E. Granberg, 49–60. Abilene, TX: Abilene Christian University Press, 2001.

———. *Biblically Anchored Missions: Perspectives on Church Growth.* Austin, TX: Firm Foundation, 1983.

———. *Church Planting in Uganda: A Comparative Study.* South Pasadena: William Carey Library, 1976.

———. *Communicating Christ in Animistic Contexts.* Grand Rapids: Baker, 1991.

———. *Contextualization and Syncretism: Navigating Cultural Currents.* Evangelical Missiological Society Series 13. Pasadena: William Carey Library, 2006.

———. *Mission Alive! Revitalizing Missions in Churches of Christ.* Abilene, TX: Abilene Christian University Press, 1994.

———. *Missions: Biblical Foundations and Contemporary Strategies.* 1st ed. Grand Rapids: Zondervan, 1996.

———. *Missions: Biblical Foundations and Contemporary Strategies.* 2nd ed. Grand Rapids: Zondervan, 2014.

———. "Modern and Postmodern Syncretism in Theology and Missions." In *The Holy Spirit and Mission Dynamics*, edited by C. Douglas McConnell, 164–207. Evangelical Missiological Society Series 5. Pasadena: William Carey Library, 1997.

———. "Reformist View: Gailyn Van Rheenen." In *Evaluating the Church Growth Movement: 5 Views*, edited by Gary L. McIntosh and Paul E. Ingel, 165–206. Grand Rapids: Zondervan, 2004.

———. "Syncretism and Contextualization: The Church on a Journey Defining Itself." In *Contextualization and Syncretism: Navigating Cultural Currents*, 1–25. Evangelical Missiological Society Series 13. Pasadena: William Carey Library, 2006.

Van Rheenen, Gailyn, and Bob Waldron. *The Status of Missions in Churches of Christ: A Nationwide Survey of Churches of Christ.* Abilene, TX: Abilene Christian University Press, 2002.

Introduction

Articles and Reviews

"Leadership Training among the Kipsigis of Kenya." Mission Strategy Bulletin 4 (September–October 1976) n.p.

"Introducing the Kenya Church Growth Philosophy." In *Church Planting, Watering, and Increasing in Kenya*, edited by Kenya Mission Team, 5–10. Austin, TX: Firm Foundation, 1980.

"A Biblical Perspective on Church Growth." In *God's Increase among the Kipsigis*, 3:37–69. Self-published, The Kipsigis Team, 1982.

"Introducing God's Work in Kipsigis." In *God's Increase among the Kipsigis*, 3:1–7. Self-published, The Kipsigis Team, 1982.

"Leadership Training." In *Church Growth among the Kipsigis of Southwest Kenya: A Statistical Picture of the Church of Christ among the Kipsigis in Southwest Kenya*, 4:37–55. Self-published, The Kipsigis Team, 1983.

"A Balance between Maturing Churches and Training Leaders." *Mission Strategy Bulletin* 11 (April–June 1984) n.p.

"Vernacular or Trade Language." *Mission Strategy Bulletin* 12 (January–March 1985) n.p.

"Cultural Conceptions of Power in Biblical Perspective." *Missiology* 21 (1993) 41–53.

"Animism, Secularism and Theism: Developing a Tripartite Model for Understanding World Cultures." *International Journal of Frontier Missions* 10 (1993) 169–71.

"The Unique and Complementary Role in Training: First Response." *International Journal of Frontier Missions* 11 (1994) 51–52.

"Training for the Frontiers—Who Does What? Response by Gailyn Van Rheenen." *International Journal of Frontier Missions* 11 (1994) 51–52.

"A Theology of Culture: Desecularizing Anthropology." *International Journal of Frontier Missions* 14.1 (January 1997) 33–38.

"Animistic and Western Perspectives of Illness and Healing." *International Journal of Frontier Missions* 15 (1998) 83–86.

"Learning . . . Growing . . . Collaborating . . . Phasing Out." *Evangelical Missions Quarterly* 36 (2000) 34–67.

"Theology of Power." In *Evangelical Dictionary of World Missions*, edited by Scott A. Moreau, 776–78. Grand Rapids: Baker, 2000.

"Using Money in Missions: The Good, the Bad and the Ugly." *Evangelical Missions Quarterly* 38 (2002) 38–45.

"A Theology of Power." *Evangelical Missions Quarterly* 41 (2005) 32–38.

"Contrasting Missional and Church Growth Perspectives." *Restoration Quarterly* 48 (2006) 25–32.

"From Theology to Practice: Participating in the Missio Dei." *Missio Dei Journal* 1 (August 2010) n.p.

"Is Missional a Fad?" *Missio Dei Journal* 7 (Summer–Fall 2016) n.p.

"The Essence of Renewal; The Anatomy of Decline: Ten Priority Questions for Renewal." *Missio Dei Journal* 9 (Summer–Fall 2018) n.p.

"The Logic of Evangelism." Review of *The Logic of Evangelism*, by William J. Abraham. *Restoration Quarterly* 34 (1992) 191–92.

"Transforming Culture: A Challenge for Christian Mission." Review of *Transforming Culture: A Challenge for Christian Mission*, by Sherwood G. Lingenfelter. *Restoration Quarterly* 35 (1993) 127–28.

Introduction

"War and Anti-War: Survival at the Dawn of the 21st Century." Review of *War and Anti-War: Survival at the Dawn of the 21st Century*, by Alvin Toffler. *Missiology* 23 (1995) 488–89.

"Yearbook of American and Canadian Churches: Religious Pluralism in the New Millennium." Review of *Yearbook of American and Canadian Churches: Religious Pluralism in the New Millennium*, by Eileen Lindner. *Missiology: An International Review* 29 (2001) 253.

"Church Planting Movements." Review of *Church Planting Movements*, by David Garrison. *Restoration Quarterly* 44 (2002) 128.

"Quest for Power: Guidelines for Communicating the Gospel to Animists." Review of *Quest for Power: Guidelines for Communicating the Gospel to Animists*, by Robert C. Blaschke. *Evangelical Missions Quarterly* 39 (2003) 118–20.

Editorial Work

Missionary Anthropology. Edited with Fielden Allison and Richard Chowning. Vol. 1.1 (January 1985)–vol. 1.3 (November 1987). Self-published, The Kipsigis Team.

Kipsigis Kommunique: A Quarterly Statement of the Team's Culturally Relevant Methods in Communicating Christ to the Kipsigis of Kenya. Coeditor with Fielden Allison and Richard Chowning. Self-published, The Kipsigis Team. Vol. 1.1 (October 1982)–vol. 7.1 (January 1988).

Blogs

"Celebrating God's Work." *Missional Church Planting—A Mission Alive Blog*, Oct 8, 2012. https://missionalchurchplanting.org/2012/10.

"Back to Africa." *Missional Church Planting—A Mission Alive Blog*, Sep 8, 2014. https://missionalchurchplanting.org/2014/09.

"Church Planting: A Calling." *Missional Church Planting—A Mission Alive Blog*, Aug 11, 2021. https://missionalchurchplanting.org/2021/08/11/church-planting-a-calling.

"Four Competing Worldviews You Can't Escape." *Missio Alliance* (blog), Aug 8, 2016. https://www.missioalliance.org/four-competing-worldviews-cant-escape.

"The Art of Church Planting." *Missional Church Planting—A Mission Alive Blog*, Jun 2, 2014. https://missionalchurchplanting.org/tag/the-art-of-church-planting.

"Before and After: The Homewood Story." *Missiology.com* (blog), Jan 1, 2000. http://www.missiology.org/blog/MR-1-Before-and-After-The-Homewood-Story.

"Money and Mi$$ion$." *Missiology.com* (blog), Feb 9, 2000. http://www.missiology.org/blog/GVR-MR-2-Money-and-Miion.

"Why Missionaries Fail." *Missiology.com* (blog), Mar 19, 2000. http://www.missiology.org/blog/GVR-MR-3-Why-Missionaries-Fall.

"Missionaries: Pastors or Apostles? (Part 1)." *Missiology.com* (blog), Apr 10, 2000. http://www.missiology.org/blog/GVR-MR-4-Missionaries-Pastors-or-Apostles-Part-1.

"Missionaries: Pastors or Apostles? (Part 2)." *Missiology.com* (blog), May 16, 2000. http://www.missiology.org/blog/GVR-MR-5-Missionaries-Pastors-or-Apostles-Part-2.

"Doing Missions without the Local Church." *Missiology.com* (blog), Jun 4, 2000. http://www.missiology.org/blog/MR-6-Doing-Missions-without-the-Local-Church.

Introduction

"The Church, A History-Making Force." *Missiology.com* (blog), Jul 10, 2000. http://www.missiology.org/blog/MR-7-The-Church-A-History-Making-Force.

"Missions: The Salvage Operation." *Missiology.com* (blog), Aug 15, 2000. http://www.missiology.org/blog/GVR-MR-8-Missions-The-Salvage-Operation.

"Can Local Churches Effectively Select and Care for Missionaries?" *Missiology.com* (blog), Sep 10, 2000. http://www.missiology.org/blog/GVR-MR-9-Can-Local-Churches-Effectively-Select-and-Care-for-Missionaries.

"Qualities of Effective Missionaries." *Missiology.com* (blog), Oct 11, 2000. http://www.missiology.org/blog/GVR-MR-10-Qualities-of-Effective-Missionaries.

"Maintaining Missionary Health." *Missiology.com* (blog), Nov 13, 2000. http://www.missiology.org/blog/GVR-MR-11-Maintaining-Missionary-Health.

"Church Planting Is More than Pioneering." *Missiology.com* (blog), Dec 5, 2000. http://www.missiology.org/blog/GVR-MR-12-Church-Planting-is-More-than-Pioneering.

"Money and Mi$$ion$ (Revisited): Combating Paternalism." *Missiology.com* (blog), Jan 12, 2001. http://www.missiology.org/blog/GVR-MR-13-Money-and-Miion-Revisited-Combating-Paternalism.

"The Rise of Folk Religion in the 21st Century." *Missiology.com* (blog), Feb 10, 2001. http://www.missiology.org/blog/GVR-MR-14-The-Rise-of-Folk-Religion-in-the-21st-Century.

"Using Money in Missions: Four Perspectives." *Missiology.com* (blog), Feb 14, 2002. http://www.missiology.org/blog/GVR-MR-15-Using-Money-in-Missions-Four-Perspectives.

"Ego: Impediment to Missions." *Missiology.com* (blog), Mar 16, 2002. http://www.missiology.org/blog/GVR-MR-16-Ego-Impediment-to-Missions.

"Transplanted and Contextualized Churches." *Missiology.com* (blog), Apr 11, 2002. http://www.missiology.org/blog/GVR-MR-17-Transplanted-and-Contextualized-Churches.

"The Missionary as a Listener." *Missiology.com* (blog), May 10, 2002. http://www.missiology.org/blog/GVR-MR-18-The-Missionary-as-a-Listener.

"Church Renewal: From Caterpillar to Butterfly." *Missiology.com* (blog), Jun 9, 2002. http://www.missiology.org/blog/GVR-MR-19-Church-Renewal-From-Caterpillar-to-Butterfly.

"The Theological Foundations of Missiology." *Missiology.com* (blog), Jul 11, 2002. http://www.missiology.org/blog/MR-20-The-Theological-Foundations-of-Missiology.

"The Missiological Foundations of Theology." *Missiology.com* (blog), Aug 12, 2002. http://www.missiology.org/blog/MR-21-The-Missiological-Foundations-of-Theology/.

"The Changing Cultural Ethos of Latin America." *Missiology.com* (blog), Sep 10, 2002. http://www.missiology.org/blog/GVR-MR-22-The-Changing-Cultural-Ethos-of-Latin-America.

"Evangelizing Folk Religionists." *Missiology.com* (blog), Oct 29, 2002. http://www.missiology.org/blog/GVR-MR-23-Evangelizing-Folk-Religionists.

"Cruciform Missionaries." *Missiology.com* (blog), Nov 14, 2002. http://www.missiology.org/blog/GVR-MR-24-Cruciform-Missionaries.

"From Theology to Practice: The Helix Metaphor." *Missiology.com* (blog), Dec 10, 2002. http://www.missiology.org/blog/GVR-MR-25-From-Theology-to-Practice-The-Helix-Metaphor.

Introduction

"The Missional Helix: Example of Church Planting." *Missiology.com* (blog), Jan 20, 2011. http://www.missiology.org/blog/GVR-MR-26-The-Missional-Helix-Example-of-Church-Planting.

"A Strange New Voice: Who Are Missional Leaders?" *Missiology.com* (blog), Jan 29, 2003. http://www.missiology.org/blog/GVR-MR-27-A-Strange-New-Voice-Who-are-Missional-Leaders.

"A Theology of Power." *Missiology.com* (blog), Feb 16, 2003. http://www.missiology.org/blog/GVR-MR-28-A-Theology-of-Power.

"Christian Prayer and Eastern Meditation." *Missiology.com* (blog), Mar 3, 2003. http://www.missiology.org/blog/GVR-MR-29-Christian-Prayer-and-Eastern-Meditation.

"Encountering Religious Pluralism." *Missiology.com* (blog), Apr 10, 2003. http://www.missiology.org/blog/GVR-MR-30-Encountering-Religious-Pluralism.

"A Change of Life." *Missiology.com* (blog), May 29, 2003. http://www.missiology.org/blog/GVR-MR-31-A-Change-of-Life.

"Modernity Sweeps Africa." *Missiology.com* (blog), Nov 15, 2004. http://www.missiology.org/blog/GVR-MR-32-Modernity-Sweeps-Africa.

"Imagining Christ's Church in the City." *Missiology.com* (blog), Jan 19, 2011. http://www.missiology.org/blog/GVR-MR-33-Imagining-Christs-Church-in-the-City.

"Contrasting Missional and Church Growth Perspectives." *Missiology.com* (blog), Jan 17, 2011. http://www.missiology.org/blog/GVR-MR-34-Contrasting-Missional-and-Church-Growth-Perspectives.

"Church as 'Place' or 'Service.'" *Missiology.com* (blog), Dec 13, 2004. http://www.missiology.org/blog/GVR-MR-35-Church-as-Place-or-Service.

"Dream the Dream . . . Again." *Missiology.com* (blog), Jan 21, 2011. http://www.missiology.org/blog/GVR-MR-36-Dream-the-dream----again.

"Unspeakable Pain." *Missiology.com* (blog), Mar 1, 2005. http://www.missiology.org/blog/GVR-MR-37-Unspeakable-Pain.

"Contextualization and Syncretism." *Missiology.com* (blog), Jan 7, 2011. http://www.missiology.org/blog/GVR-MR-38-Contextualization-and-Syncretism.

"Spiritual Formation in Church Planting." *Missiology.com* (blog), Jan 7, 2011. http://www.missiology.org/blog/MR-39-Spiritual-Formation-in-Church-Planting.

"Case Study: Translating God in Mongolia." *Missiology.com* (blog), Jan 7, 2011. http://www.missiology.org/blog/MR-40-Case-Study--Translating-God-in-Mongolia.

"'Christian' New Agers: A Growing Phenomenon." *Missiology.com* (blog), May 8, 2008. http://www.missiology.org/blog/GVR-MR-41-Christian-New-Agers--A-Growing-Phenomenon.

"What Is Missiology?" *Missiology.com* (blog), Mar 15, 2019. http://www.missiology.org/blog/What-Is-Missiology-Gailyn-Van-Rheenen.

1

Mission between Theory and Practice

Greg McKinzie

On the contemporary landscape of Christian mission, the rift between theory and practice poses a persistent problem for American churches. This rift is but one manifestation of cultural phenomena endemic to Western culture in general and American evangelical Christianity in particular. Nonetheless, the field on which missiological "scholarship" and mission "work" stand across from one another, separated by the theory-practice rift, represents a distinctive expression of the problem. In this chapter, I contextualize the theory-practice divide in relation to American Christian mission and advocate a mediation that relies on missional theology. These two movements, contextualization and mediation, place both sides of the divide under scrutiny for the sake of bridge-building. As the scare quotes around "work" and "scholarship" hint, such terms instantiate the problem, and both the medium of this reflection (a scholarly essay) and its recourse to theology risk privileging theory. Certainly, bridge-building from the other side of the rift is also necessary, but I leave that for another moment. In the present chapter, I contend that seeking a unified field is both possible and necessary for the life of the missional church. Theoreticians and practitioners—terms that once more inscribe the problem—must seek together to bridge the divide. Given our historical reality, theory for the sake of practice and practice for the sake of theory are necessary starting points. The union of theory and practice is a proximate goal that serves faithful, wise participation in God's mission.

Missional Life in Practice and Theory

CONTEXTUALIZING THE THEORY-PRACTICE RIFT

Four contextual factors contribute to the distinctive manifestation of the theory-practice rift in contemporary Christian mission: roots in Western philosophy, anti-intellectualism, consequentialism, and spiritual reductionism. After surveying these factors, I identify key manifestations of the dilemma on both sides of the rift.

Roots in Western Philosophy

Where theory and practice are concerned, the Western imagination is deeply rooted in Aristotelian philosophy. Aristotle conceived of theory and practice as distinctive activities aimed at different ends, developing a philosophical vocabulary that reflects the division of the two. But the picture is more complex. For Aristotle, *theoria* (knowing) stands apart from two kinds of practice: *praxis* (doing) and *poiesis* (making). Whereas *theoria* is an end in itself, *praxis* aims at action and *poiesis* at products. The Western rift between theory and practice assumes Aristotle's taxonomy, which conceives of knowing over against doing/making.[1]

Slavish adherence to Aristotle's distinctions is not the issue in the twenty-first century. Still, the Western tradition of theological education has roots in the retrieval of the philosopher's work, especially through Thomas Aquinas and the Protestant scholastics whose thought set the course of the European university system.[2] As a result, there continues to be a bifurcation of theory and practice in theological education that persists today.[3]

Among the philosophical currents that reified the theory-practice divide, two are of special importance. First, the theological academy's response to Cartesian rationalism produced a complementary rift between faith and reason. While the theological reaction to rationalism might be

---

1. For more detailed analysis of Aristotle's categories, see Adkins, "Theoria versus Praxis," 297–13; Balaban, "Aristotle's Theory of Πρᾶξις," 163–72; Bernasconi, "Fate of the Distinction between *Praxis* and *Poiesis*," 111–39; DeHart, "Convergence of Praxis and Theoria in Aristotle," 7–27; Squires, "Praxis: A Dissenting Note," 1–7.

2. See Reed and Prevost, *History of Christian Education*, chs. 13–14; González, *History of Theological Education*, 51. On the wider manifestation of the scholastic separation of theory and practice, see Roth et al., "Theory-Practice Gap," 521–36.

3. I concede the argument of Miller-McLemore, "Theory–Practice Distinction," that the distinction between the two is not the problem. But the gap between the two cannot be resolved by the affirmation of their distinctiveness.

placed on the theoretical side of the debate alongside Cartesian philosophy, the rationalist impulse that gave rise to the Enlightenment's subsequent empiricist turn stands in opposition to the church's largely abstract, theoretical response. Hence, both rationalist and empiricist philosophies generate *a kind of rationality* that is rightly characterized as practical in contrast to the essentially theoretical rationality of the theological academy.

Second, the Kantian division of the noumenal and the phenomenal solidified the division of theory and practice. Under Kant's influence, a "cognitive break between subjective experience and objective reality connotes a fundamental break between thought and action."[4] Modernity expressed this break through various social dichotomies, most prominently sacred versus secular, private versus public, and faith versus science. In these dichotomies, theory and practice do not strictly correspond to one side or the other: one might speak, for example, of both sacred and secular "practices." Indeed, the division of noumena and phenomena seems to generate complex cross-pressures where theory and practice are concerned.

On the one hand, the phenomenal becomes the proper concern of a public reason whose techno-scientific methods are interested in mastering the "real" world. In contrast with this practical pursuit, the noumenal (including private religious belief) is *impractical*—giving sense to the idea of "mere theory." On the other hand, the rise of the modern university was, to a considerable extent, the proliferation of the specialization necessary to make good on techno-scientific humanist ambitions regarding the phenomenal. To be sure, the story of the modern university is far more complex than this statement suggests. Nonetheless, it is noteworthy that, from much of the modern church's perspective, the theological academy is suspect not because of its connections to the wider university's secular empiricism but because it is *impractical* in relation to the life of faith. So, the phenomenal curiously becomes the domain of mere theory—the abstruse specialization of the ivory tower—whereas the noumenal (faith) becomes the realm of concrete ecclesial practices.

These philosophical influences exist in a symbiotic relationship with other developments in the cultures of Western Christianity. I will sketch some of these below, but others merit brief mention: for example, expressions of the ancient dichotomy of the contemplative life and the active life in church history; premodern iterations of educational elitism, especially late-medieval scholasticism's influence on the theological academy; and

4. Markey, "Praxis in Liberation Theology," 179–95.

pietistic reactions to intellectualism in the early modern era. In other words, surveying philosophical influences such as Aristotle, Descartes, and Kant cannot explain the theory-practice divide in abstraction from other historical movements. Still, the exercise orients us to major tectonic forces at work under the rift.

Anti-Intellectualism

Early American populism is the soil in which anti-intellectualism took root among American Christians. In the Stone-Campbell Movement, with which this book's authors are connected, that very populism was a defining mark.[5] But the anti-elitism and anticlericalism that the Restoration Movement took to an extreme was of one piece with the larger cultural movement that would carry all of conservative evangelicalism into what Mark Noll calls "the scandal of the evangelical mind." Noll characterizes the situation sharply: "To put it most simply, the evangelical ethos is activistic, populist, pragmatic, and utilitarian. It allows little space for broader or deeper intellectual effort because it is dominated by the urgencies of the moment."[6] These dispositions, however, are not yet anti-intellectualism, nor does it seem in retrospect that populism was destined to become anti-intellectualism. Many early American populists dedicated themselves to considerable intellectual endeavors. Their belief in "the rights, wisdom, or virtues of the common people"[7] entailed high expectations for the common person's intellectual capacity and responsibility, rather than a mere rejection of intellectual rigor in favor of common sense (even the Enlightened Scottish variety). For example, Alexander Campbell's erudition, the level at which he wrote for supposedly popular consumption, and the stated purpose for which he established Bethany College must nuance the story of Stone-Campbell churches. As critical as he was of denominational theological education and clerical specialization, Campbell's populism did not lower the educational bar but called the whole church to meet a high one.[8]

---

5. See Hughes and Allen, *Illusions of Innocence*; Hatch, *Democratization of American Christianity*; and esp. Hatch, "Christian Movement," 545–67.

6. Noll, *Scandal of the Evangelical Mind*, 12.

7. "Populist."

8. On this, see Olbricht, "Religious Scholarship and the Restoration Movement," 93–204, who echoes the sentiment; see also West, "Ministerial Education," 78–79.

Nonetheless, for the conservative heirs of the Stone-Campbell Movement, as for much of evangelicalism, the vicissitudes of history contributed to our populism's mutation into full-bore anti-intellectualism. First, the postbellum sectionalism that fueled the split between Disciples of Christ and Churches of Christ had consequences for the life of the Southern mind. Thomas Olbricht comments: "When the Disciples and Churches of Christ divided, officially in the census in 1906, few if any who remained in Churches of Christ had pursued graduate studies. Leaders such as James A. Harding and David Lipscomb certainly were not anti-education, but a number of Churches of Christ preachers, including Daniel Sommer, were suspicious of theological studies."[9] That suspicion became endemic as even Harding and Lipscomb disagreed about how best to facilitate ministerial training. This is noteworthy in relation to missions training because one of the surface-level disputes in the split was the missionary society, and the same reasoning that fueled that controversy was at issue in the dispute that delayed the development of theological education among Churches of Christ. Earl West notes, "While Harding believed in Christians teaching in schools, he differed with Lipscomb on the existence of a Board of Trustees to oversee the teaching of the Bible. As he saw it, if a human Board of Trustees could oversee the teaching of the Bible, this would make the school comparable to the missionary society."[10] What West elsewhere calls "a dichotomy on ministerial education"[11]—a dichotomy between the benefit of specialized training and the risk of the wrong kind of training leading back to denominational clericalism—was internalized by Churches of Christ just as the forerunners of our university theological education programs were founded. To borrow early Restorationist parlance, specialized theological education was placed in the dubious role of a mere *expedient*—cautiously permissible but certainly not necessary.

Second, in short order, this suspicion was given fuel by the liberal-fundamentalist controversy that wracked the early twentieth century. In regard to the broader phenomenon, Noll states that "because evangelicals, though often dissenting from specific features of fundamentalism, have largely retained the mentality of fundamentalism *when it comes to looking at the world*, there has been a similarly meager harvest of evangelical

---

9. Olbricht, "Coming of Ph.D.'s," 193–201.
10. West, "James A. Harding and Christian Education," 76.
11. West, "Ministerial Education," 79.

intellectual life."[12] The same anti-intellectual reaction affected Churches of Christ, particularly in regard to critical biblical scholarship.[13] The phenomenon had far-reaching effects, represented most notably in the failure of Jesse Sewell's "seminary" experiment at Abilene Christian College.[14] As Chris Flanders's articles on the beginnings of missionary training in Churches of Christ reveal, this episode bears directly on the development of the tradition's missiology.[15] Flanders rightly asks, "If it had been successful and endured, would this training program have pushed Churches of Christ much more quickly into the missionary-minded fellowship that it became after WWII? Might ACC have become a primary missionary center in the 1920s? In terms of missions education, had the vision succeeded, might ACC/ACU be included routinely among the premier conservative missions training institutions of today such as Fuller, Biola, Trinity, and Asbury?"[16] The point is not to dwell on what might have been but to reckon with what has, in fact, transpired: Churches of Christ missionary training was swept up in the powerful forces of American anti-intellectualism that have shaped conservative mission scholarship. These pressures not only stifled the progress of missionary training but now continue to exert a lingering influence on the relationship between the church and the academy in wake of subsequent developments. There is more to say about what has become of academic training in missiology since the maturation of mission studies as an academic discipline. For now, it is enough to observe the anti-intellectualism that has marred that relationship since its beginning.

If it seems that reference to "premier conservative missions training institutions of today" suggests that anti-intellectualism is a relic of the past where missiology is concerned, then it is necessary to consider the contemporary context with the sobriety that history commends. The present argument is not about the intellectual credibility of particular evangelical missiologists or programs, but rather the pressure that the cultural phenomenon of anti-intellectualism places on mission training. Without a doubt, anti-intellectualism is a force to be reckoned with as much today

12. Noll, *Scandal*, 137.

13. See, e.g., Boring, *Disciples and the Bible*, chs. 5–6, esp. 211–19, 234–40.

14. Casey, "First Graduate Theological Education in the Churches of Christ, Part 1," 73–92; Casey, "First Graduate Theological Education in the Churches of Christ, Part 2," 139–57.

15. Flanders, "Beginning of Missionary Training in Churches of Christ (Part 1)," 27–38; Flanders, "Beginning of Missionary Training in Churches of Christ (Part 2)," 65–76.

16. Flanders, "Beginning of Missionary Training in Churches of Christ (Part 2)," 76.

as ever, and among conservative Christians as much as anywhere else. As journalist Susan Jacoby puts it in an expanded edition of her book *The Age of American Unreason*, "America is now ill with a stream of intertwined ignorance, anti-rationalism, and anti-intellectualism that has mutated, as a result of technology, into something more dangerous than the cyclical strains of the past."[17] While many conservative Christian readers will experience Jacoby's cultural commentary as that of an aggressively snobbish secularist with an axe to grind, her presentation of the evidence remains disturbingly convincing. And she is not alone. Books like Tom Nichols's *The Death of Expertise: The Campaign against Established Knowledge and Why It Matters*, Greg Lukianoff and Jonathan Haidt's *The Coddling of the American Mind: How Good Intentions and Bad Ideas Are Setting Up a Generation for Failure*, and *The State of the American Mind: 16 Leading Critics on the New Anti-Intellectualism*, edited by Mark Bauerlein (senior editor of *First Things*) and Adam Bellow, register cultural tectonics that are no less significant for the relationship between church and academy than those that erupted in the Scopes Monkey Trial.[18] I see no reason to conclude that contemporary missiology is more resistant to such pressures than in the past.

American anti-intellectualism has nourished the philosophical roots of the divide between theory and practice. The popular suspicion of the academy as an intellectual preserve, wherein the impractical pursuit of mere theory dominates, thrives on the populism-*cum*-anti-intellectualism that the American culture wars continue to produce. The local church is lamentably prone to participate in this cultural melee by relegating "theory" to academics who work in the realm of scholarship and "practice" to those who are interested in the results of ministry efforts. This draws our attention to a third cultural force that separates theory and practice: consequentialism.

Consequentialism

The common term for a strong commitment to practical over against theoretical matters is *pragmatism*. In this essay, however, I avoid the use of *pragmatism* in the interest of distinguishing the popular use of the term

17. Jacoby, *Age of American Unreason*, xxviii.
18. Nichols, *Death of Expertise*; Lukianoff and Haidt, *Coddling of the American Mind*; Bauerlein and Bellow, *State of the American Mind*.

from its philosophical meaning. American pragmatism is a philosophical movement concerned with the relationship between human knowing and human doing.[19] This school of thought is relevant to the present discussion, not least because of its profoundly American character. The cultural predilections that give rise to pragmatism are part and parcel of the picture I am painting. Nonetheless, the epistemological interests of pragmatism as such do not contribute to the theory-practice divide.[20] Instead, I refer to the third cultural pressure separating theory and practice as consequentialism.

Consequentialism is also a technical term, referring to an ethical theory in which good action is judged to be that which produces good results.[21] Because "the good" is subject to specification, *consequentialism* is sufficiently broad to account for the tendency of Americans to judge many dimensions of life—not least business and politics—in terms of "results." Therefore, I refer to consequentialism in this essay as a cultural reflex according to which theory is unnecessary because the results of practice are what matter. *Consequentialism*, in other words, betokens a prior value judgment that short-circuits the interchange between theory, which may offer other evaluative criteria, and practice. Consequences are predetermined goods, and good practices are whichever serve those ends—whichever "work."

In recent years, the power of this cultural value system has been most evident among evangelicals (and here I subsume varieties of conservative Christianity whether they claim the label "evangelical" or not) in relation to Donald Trump. Robert Jones, whose interpretation of the Trump phenomenon among evangelicals has become a standard point of reference for pundits and journalists, states: "The Trump era has effectively turned white-evangelical political ethics on its head. Rather than standing on principle and letting the chips fall where they may, white evangelicals have now fully embraced a consequentialist ethics that works backward from predetermined political ends, refashioning or even discarding principles as needed to achieve a desired outcome."[22] This conclusion seems unavoidable, and

19. See Bernstein, *Pragmatic Turn*; Bacon, *Pragmatism*.

20. Indeed, they may be part of the solution. This is perhaps obvious in that pragmatism is a philosophical theory, a theoretical approach to practice. But more, pragmatism is specifically concerned with the relationship between practice and understanding, which echoes in the theological portrayal of *praxis* below.

21. See Sinnott-Armstrong, "Consequentialism."

22. Jones, "Donald Trump and the Transformation of White Evangelicals"; see also Jones, *End of White Christian America*, 248, and the findings of Jones's research institute,

some evangelicals have recognized the need to counter the tendency toward consequentialism.[23] Nonetheless, the national conversation has focused on the unprecedented shift in evangelical politics.[24] What seems to have gone largely unnoticed in the social commentary is the fact that this shift is toward conformity with the American cultural preference for consequentialist reasoning. Consequentialism is the state of the art in politics, and many Christians have opted to play the political game by consequentialist rules.[25]

I will expand on consequentialism in relation to mission below. Suffice it to observe at this point that the theory-practice divide is sustained in part by a powerful cultural predilection for "results" or "outcomes" that favors the practical over against the theoretical. Following the philosophical bifurcation of public and private, secular and sacred, the American church today struggles under the influence of a consequentialism that leaves aside theoretical questions of character, principle, and doctrine in order to ensure practical results. Ironically, the result of consequentialism in the popular sense I have highlighted is the church's loss of a theoretical evaluation of the results of such practice.

Spiritual Reductionism

The final contextual factor contributing to the theory-practice divide is spiritual reductionism. This is a uniquely Christian issue, and it is difficult to document because of the tendency of its proponents not to engage in (theoretical!) writing. Nonetheless, it seems important to note the influence of this factor. I rely on experience and anecdotal evidence to characterize the role of spiritual reductionism in separating theory from practice.

PRRI, "Backing Trump." Other findings corroborate the PRRI research: Jones, "Presidential Moral Leadership."

23. E.g., Doriani, "Why I Don't Think You Must Vote for the Lesser of Two Evils."

24. See Kim, "Born Again with Trump," 1–30.

25. Some, indeed, argue explicitly for a consequentialist politics. For example, Wolfe, "Consequentialist Theory of Voting," argues that "consequentialist voting theory does not necessarily assume or entail ethical consequentialism." The notion that ethics and politics could be separated is dubious, but, regardless, my point is precisely that many American Christians have come to accept the cultural norm of consequentialism in areas of life such as politics. This conformity implicates the church in a kind of reasoning that sidelines theory (despite Wolfe's claim to "voting theory") in favor of a straightforward interest in consequences.

By *spiritual reductionism* I refer to the idea that Christian spirituality will compensate for theoretical deficiency—indeed, that theory is unnecessary because the Spirit of God will empower and direct right practice regardless of theoretical understanding. In Protestant Christianity, this belief is an extension of the commitment to the "priesthood of all believers." In its most extreme versions, all believers are not only responsible for but capable of priestly functions *regardless* of education or training. In the American context, spiritual reductionism is bolstered by populism: anyone, as a human, has the rights, wisdom, and virtue necessary to obey the commands of God (say, the Great Commission). Theory is, therefore, unnecessary. Indeed, theory may be a problem, because it complicates and stifles "simple" obedience.

Though brief, this portrayal is not a caricature. It is, in my experience, a common construal of the relationship between spirituality and education (broadly conceived). The darling passage of spiritual reductionism is Acts 4:13, in which the Jerusalem elites marvel that Peter and John are "uneducated and ordinary men" nonetheless capable of speaking clearly in defense of their faith in Jesus. Interpreting this text in the context of anti-intellectualism and consequentialism tends to render a particular understanding of how Peter being "filled with the Spirit" (4:8) relates to his being "uneducated." This reading of the passage suggests why many Christians feel justified in dismissing "education" in favor of a notion of apostolic practice that needs only the Spirit. Given that "theory" typically maps onto "education" in the Western imagination, this perspective naturally contributes to the theory-practice divide.

Mission is the field in which spiritual reductionism comes to its most explicit expression. Therefore, I leave specific examples for the ensuing discussion. In the following subsections, I identify various expressions of the theory-practice rift in relation to Christian mission, first in the academy, then in the church.

EXPRESSIONS OF THE THEORY-PRACTICE RIFT IN CONTEMPORARY THOUGHT

The decade after Edinburgh 2010 and Cape Town 2010 was marked by a flurry of reflection on the definition and agenda of missiology.[26] One

---

26. E.g., Van Gelder, "Future of the Discipline," 39–56; Langmead, "What Is Missiology?," 67–79; Baker, "Missiology as an Interested Discipline," 17–20; Hanciles, "Future

high-water mark of the discourse was the annual meeting of the American Society of Missiology in 2013, which focused on the future of the field of study. The published report of that meeting summarizes a variety of concerns under four headings. First, under "Drawing together themes from the past," the report acknowledges that "a strong and perennial theme is the ongoing debate about missiology as a separate discipline or not."[27] Second, under "Capturing emerging themes," it notes that "the discipline struggles with the tension between its embrace of its own vulnerability and the struggle to find legitimacy within the theological and academic world."[28] Third, under "Identifying areas of growth and change," it states that "there is a need to develop a growing relationship with the social sciences and other theological disciplines. This trend requires imagining missiology not as a discipline but as itself multi-disciplinary."[29] Fourth, under "Imagining what is not yet on the horizon," the report observes that "there is a need to take the contemporary contexts more seriously, and to acknowledge and deal with the shift away from Western domination in mission."[30] Finally, under an additional heading, "Constructive comments," the report makes this vital observation: "There seems to be two distinct perspectives on ASM and the future of missiology—those who are members of an academic society and those who are practitioners or agency/board staff. Academics who are asking questions about teaching in the seminary and college appear concerned with graduate students in missiology and with further scholarship in the field. Practitioners and board/agency staff seem to be asking questions about pushing missiology out of the academy and more into the grassroots, where it can focus on the relationship between academy and church."[31] In summary, the theory-practice rift is internal to the definition and identity of modern missiology.

But in addition to the difference between the agendas of academics and practitioners, academic missiology itself is split between theoretical

---

of Missiology," 121–38; Roxborogh, "Missiology after 'Mission'?," 120–24; Verster, "Missiology: Rise, Demise and Future at the University," 879–93; Yip, "Contours of a Post-Postmodern Missiology," 399–411; Nehrbass, "Does Missiology Have a Leg to Stand On?," 50–65; Paas, "Discipline of Missiology in 2016," 37–54; Vassiliadis, "Mission and Theology," 51–58; Farrell, "Re-Membering Missiology," 37–49.

27. Fensham, "Group Discussion Conclusions," 81.
28. Fensham, "Group Discussion Conclusions," 82.
29. Fensham, "Group Discussion Conclusions," 83.
30. Fensham, "Group Discussion Conclusions," 84.
31. Fensham, "Group Discussion Conclusions," 86.

and practical approaches to study. Following the tradition's appropriation of Aristotle, I characterize these two types of missiology as *technē* and *theoria*.

Missiology as *Technē*

Missiology was originally organized in the modern theological encyclopedia as a component of "practical theology."[32] Since the field's inception, therefore, it has been embroiled in a debate about the legitimacy of distinguishing clerical preparation for ministerial and administrative duties from theoretical studies focused on philosophical and historical (dogmatic) concerns. Even for Friedrich Schleiermacher, the chief architect of this organizational schema, the point was not to separate theory and practice but to order them according to what Francis Schüssler Fiorenza identifies as "technical rationality."[33] Similarly, David Tracy argues that in this construal, "practice" is dominated by "instrumentalist notions of reason as purely technical and notions of practice as synonymous with technique and application."[34] The terms *technical* and *technique* echo the Aristotelian notion of *technē*, the kind of know-how that corresponds to *poiēsis* (production). Granting that *technē* is a kind of theory (thus, a kind of missiology), technical rationality is precisely the sort of knowing that one applies in the pursuit of productive ends. In the modern theological academy, this represents the culmination of a construal of the theory-practice relationship that orders practice as the application of theory and the results of practice as the primary criterion for evaluating theory. When missiology is conceived as *technē*, good theory produces "effectiveness" in mission work.

Movement Ideology

In contemporary missiology, technical rationality is most evident in the lineage of consequentialist thought that I refer to as *movement ideology*,[35] which runs from Donald McGavran's "people movements" to Ralph Winter's "unreached people groups" to David Garrison's "church planting

---

32. See Verkuyl, *Contemporary Missiology*, 6–7.

33. Fiorenza, "Theory and Practice," 113–41.

34. Tracy, "Theoria and Praxis," 167–74.

35. For my purposes, *ideology* refers to "the sense of any practical idea that motivates action, without prejudice to the theoretical ... or ethico-political ... quality of that idea." See Boff, *Theology and Praxis*, 254.

movements" (CPMs) to David Watson's "disciple-making movements" (DMMs). Animated by the idea of "completing" the Great Commission, movement ideology is committed to effectiveness and reproducibility.[36] Effectiveness is a criterion for assessing mission strategies aimed at producing "maximum growth."[37] This assessment is concerned with producing *more* disciples, churches, and evangelistic efforts. Reproducibility is a criterion for assessing mission strategies aimed at rapidly equipping new disciples to begin making more disciples. This assessment is concerned with *faster* production.[38] The core value of movement ideology can, therefore, be summarized as *rapid growth*.[39] Here, missiology is the know-how (*technē*) that corresponds to the production (*poiēsis*) of the predetermined good of rapid growth.

Since its beginnings, this ideology has been in tension and, often, conflict with traditional theological education. McGavran, eager to accelerate the epochal transition from mission stations to people movements, indicted schools and colleges alongside the rest of the "impressive institutions" of colonial missions that divert critical resources from people movements.[40] As his role at Fuller Theological Seminary indicates, McGavran

---

36. Key points of departure for movement ideology include (1) McGavran's pugnacious question, "Will Uppsala Betray the Two Billion?," in an essay of the same title in *Eye of the Storm*, 233–41; (2) Billy Graham's opening address at Lausanne, "Why Lausanne?," calling the church to "complete the task of world evangelization" (echoing, of course, the SVM/Edinburgh 1910 slogan "The Evangelisation of the World in This Generation") and (3) Ralph Winter's landmark Lausanne address "Highest Priority," which launched the strategic conception of unreached people groups.

37. McGavran, *Bridges of God*, 81.

38. The rise in prominence of this second dimension is symbolized in the shift in Winter's emphasis on the "task," from plans "to finish the task of world evangelization" to "completing the task by AD 2000." See Winter, "Momentum Is Building!," 67–78. Despite the passage of that date, the last two decades have seen no deceleration of evangelistic intentions. See the concern with rapid multiplication, e.g., in Trousdale, "Simple Churches"; Dent, "Decisive Discipleship"; Addison, "Rapid Mobilization."

39. Farah, "*Motus Dei*," aptly summarizes: "Movements are thus defined by healthy growth and rapid reproduction of discipleship groups and churches within a relatively short period." Notably, Watson and Watson, *Contagious Disciple-Making*, 7, claim that "nothing is quick. It only appears to be because more and more leaders are being produced in obedience to Christ's command.... So, in a DMM, rapid multiplication really isn't rapid. We go slowly, but appear to go fast. We invest extensively in one person to reach and train many.... As leaders multiply, churches grow and multiply." This means, of course, that their strategy of leadership multiplication possesses the *reproducibility* that effects rapid growth of the church, if not of leaders.

40. McGavran, *Bridges of God*, 92.

was not attacking education or ministerial preparation per se—indeed, he was pleading that educational resources be directed to chronically underprepared people-movement leaders.[41] Nonetheless, one of the implications of his argument for "the pattern which can be indefinitely reproduced" is the dichotomization of movement and the sort of education located on the theory side of the theory-practice rift. This dichotomy hardens as reproduction becomes *rapid* reproduction, and extensive or intensive training becomes a luxury and then an impediment to growth.

David and Paul Watson represent the tendency to appeal to "the priesthood of all believers" in order to justify a rejection of the bloated training models of the declining Western church: "By promoting and insisting on a professional clergy, the church has limited its ability and capacity to reach the world for Christ. We have made it impossible to *rapidly expand* the church because we cannot produce enough 'qualified' leaders to meet the expansion needs."[42] The rhetorical force of such an argument runs intuitively in their favor. Particularly among Believers' Church traditions grown in the soil of American populism (including Stone-Campbell churches), the notion that "professional clergy" is necessary for disciples to make disciples nears sacrilege. And, if movements of the sort that Garrison, the Watsons, and others describe are remotely close to reality, then they prove that the kind of ponderously theoretical theological education "the academy" represents is unnecessary and, indeed, detrimental to the continued rapid growth of disciple-making movements.[43]

To summarize from the perspective of missiology as *technē*, training that values effectiveness tends to focus on the strategies, techniques, and practical processes that produce desired results—typically, converts and congregations. Training that values reproducibility tends to prioritize methods and content that are (supposedly) accessible in any cultural, economic, and educational context. Accordingly, the kind of training that missionaries can use to make disciples in numerically effective ways and to train those disciples to continue reproducing rapidly delimits acceptable missiological education.

---

41. McGavran, *Bridges of God*, 79, 83.

42. Watson and Watson, *Contagious Disciple Making*, 52 (emphasis added); cf. Garrison, *Church Planting Movements*, 189.

43. See Arlund and Farah, "Discussing and Catalyzing Movements" for a representative critique of "'professional' standards formed in highly affluent and educated Western contexts." Unsurprisingly, the authors appeal to the "unlearned fishermen" of Acts 4:13.

Sustained critique of the "pragmatism" (what I am calling utilitarianism) of McGavran's church growth theory has raised serious doubts about the technical rationality at work in movement ideology.[44] Later iterations of movement ideology seem to have ignored the critique, however, and the literature that treats missiology as *technē* continues to grow.[45]

Short-Term Missions

The short-term missions movement—the recent, drastic increase in local-church and student involvement in "foreign" missions trips—is another area in which an understanding of missiology as *technē* manifests. Here as well, there is significant literature focused on "best practices" that function as *technē*-theory.[46] And once again, the driving interest of this literature is "effectiveness."[47] What counts as effectiveness varies, but the driving interest of the movement is the mobilization of participants regardless of the kind of preparation that characterizes missiology as *theoria*. It is, in other words, a populist movement that tends, as usual in the Western context, toward an anti-intellectual *modus operandi*. Short-term mission participants need not concern themselves with the kind of theoretical formation that long-term missionaries ideally undertake. Indeed, that sort of preparation obviously presents a barrier to the wide-scale participation that the movement represents.

The problems this sort of populism generates have given rise to a critical body of literature aimed at addressing the naïve good intentions of the Western church as well as the cultural ignorance that afflicts short-term efforts.[48] At its best, missiology-as-*technē* serves the short-term missions

---

44. See especially the scathing critique of "managerial missiology" by Escobar, "Movement Divided," 7–13. Notably, Escobar's presentation of this critique in a lecture at the Fuller Theological Seminary School of World Mission founded by McGavran had—at least in Fuller lore—a major impact on the direction of the school's missiology. In any case, while Fuller's large student body is extremely diverse, the SIS faculty no longer represent the lineage I am discussing. Its advocates are now mostly in nonacademic circles.

45. For further critique of the critique, which entails engagement with most of the key representatives of movement ideology, see Rhodes, *No Shortcut to Success*; Rhodes, "Advancing Conversations."

46. E.g., Peterson et al., *Maximum Impact Short-Term Mission*; see also S.O.E., "7 Standards of Excellence."

47. E.g., Priest, *Effective Engagement*.

48. E.g., Livermore, *Serving with Eyes Wide Open*; Corbett and Fikkert, *Helping without Hurting in Short-Term Missions*; and various chapters of Priest, *Effective Engagement*.

movement by directing participants toward a more conscientious, well-informed engagement through popular-level resources. The qualification of such resources as popular-level highlights one of the essential features of the theory-practice divide, namely, the difference between accessible and inaccessible theorizing about the practices of participation in God's mission (more on which below). The know-how that is apparently necessary for effective short-term mission is supposed to be easy to understand and implement.[49] It is notable that the average educational level of many congregations involved in short-term missions (larger, urban churches are the more common participants, for budgetary reasons if nothing else) is sufficient to engage such works. Anecdotally, however, it seems that even accessible resources are underutilized in local congregations involved in short-term missions. Critical theorizing about the difficulties of cross-cultural engagement, theological contextualization, interreligious dialogue, dependency, colonialism, partnership, and so on is commonly presumed unnecessary for the tasks of sharing the gospel, loving one's neighbor, or (most commonly) having a missions "experience."

For many North American churches, the theoretical challenges of short-term missions correspond to those of cross-cultural and interreligious engagement at home (see Jared Looney's chapter in the present volume). The conversation about what it means to be a missional church in globalizing local contexts increasingly corresponds to the dialogue surrounding the participation of local churches in short-term "foreign" missions in that both foreign and local missions highlight the key question of lay missiological formation. This reality calls the church to urgently address the assumptions sustaining the theory-practice rift. How might we bridge the divide? The answer requires an equally critical assessment of missiology as *theoria*.

---

49. Arguably, the critical edge of this literature represents the efforts of diligent popularizers to influence a readership uninterested in or unable to engage with more difficult works, or to provide church leaders with readily usable resources. In such cases, the assumption (sometimes explicitly stated) is that short-term missions are going to happen one way or another, so the best option is to offer easily digestible advice to offset the theoretical deficiencies of the movement. The realism of the perspective is commendable, though I wonder whether it concedes too much in many cases. Might it not also be possible to popularize an argument for missiology as *theoria*? Of course, such an argument would likely undermine the primary interest of the short-term missions movement: wide-scale mobilization.

Mission between Theory and Practice

MISSIOLOGY AS *THEORIA*

For those who approach missiology as the "study" or even the "science" of mission, preparation for participation in God's mission entails a certain depth and complexity often missing from treatments of missiology as *technē*. It is not obvious, however, that depth and complexity are the characteristics that distinguish *theoria* from *technē*. To the contrary, *technē*-theory can achieve considerable scholarly sophistication, and this is its ideal character in the context of the academy. Descriptors like depth and complexity are, instead, proxies for something else—something that makes missiology-as-*theoria* at home on the theory side of the rift. Aristotle's construal of *theoria* as knowledge for its own sake is a clue, but by framing the question in terms of preparation for participation in God's mission, I have already intimated that more is at issue for missiology as such. Knowledge for its own sake is, nonetheless, an accurate characterization of the problem with missiology-as-*theoria* at its worst. To speak anecdotally once more, missiology can become so mired in depth and complexity that it fails to serve anything but the accrual of greater depth and complexity. But if this is a worst-case scenario, not a defining trait, then what do depth and complexity signify? Why do the scholarly pursuits of academic missiology lead to an extreme at which *theoria* becomes separated from the needs and interests of practitioners?

The problem must be situated in the wider context of theological education, in which the quest for academic respectability among biblical, systematic, and historical theological disciplines has both validated methods divorced from the interests of practical theology and cast methodological suspicion on practical theology's ecclesial commitments. Inasmuch as academic missiology has sought to meet scholarly standards of legitimacy, methods that validate asking and answering questions for their own sake have come to characterize missiology-as-*theoria*. The literature of practical theology has, in recent decades, begun subversively to address this dimension of the problem, that is, in the academic mode that generated it. A significant body of scholarly work now advocates for practical theology to operate epistemologically on the basis of ecclesial commitments and interests.[50] Without defaulting to the consequentialist logic according to which good theory results in effective ministry, practical theology increasingly critiques the siloing of *theoria* and church practices.

---

50. Many of the essays in the following volumes are representative: Volf and Bass, *Practicing Theology*; Bass and Dykstra, *For Life Abundant*.

Still, a second dimension of the problem in academic theology, including missiology, requires attention. To put it simply, depth and complexity are commonly the requirements not of scholarly methods or academic credibility per se but of the difficulty that vital questions present. Missiologists are often called to theorize about questions to which superficial and simplistic answers are inadequate. In such cases, the result is scholarly analysis not obviously practical in any sense. Sometimes, this is the case because even theoreticians interested in practical appropriation leave it for another moment. For example, it seems perfectly reasonable to work on the history of mission in a particular geographical area without addressing contemporary practice. Such work may require archival research, interviews, historiographical and anthropological framing, and detailed analysis. This work may be thoroughly missiological without offering practical conclusions or contemporary applications. Indeed, further questions are often the primary result of such investigation. At other times, ignoring the practical is a result of the fact that the process of theorizing demands dedication to analytical work. In such cases, the point is that the church faces tremendously difficult missiological questions that merit the attention of devoted theoreticians. For example, the theology of mission often entails an exploration of biblical themes and theological concepts without consideration of what churches might do in their local contexts. Contextualization itself is a missiological contribution to theological reflection that, due to its complexity, can be developed theoretically without coming to concrete, productive applications.

Although the value of addressing theoretical questions without reference to practical matters seems indisputable in the abstract, such work almost inevitably contributes to the theory-practice rift. Especially in the context of a theological academy already given to methodological disregard for practical concerns, the work of missiological theoreticians can neglect the preparation of the church for participation in God's mission. Whether by deferring practical questions or by giving complex questions their theoretical due, academic missiology often disregards practice. This tendency has two primary manifestations: specialization and academic publishing.

Specialization

Specialization undoubtedly contributes to the theory-practice gap. The problem is well known: the typical narrowness of scholarly specialization produces work that appears irrelevant to most practitioners, to say nothing of the typical church member. Yet, it is not obvious that the problem is avoidable, nor what the solution might be. Specialization itself—or, to borrow another fraught term, expertise—is not in question, at least not in principle.[51] Across every field, specialization has engendered advances in understanding and, indeed, practice. As the old trope goes, even the most anti-elitist patient wants their physician to have extensive training and certified expertise. And while it may appear the physician proves the point that applied knowledge is what counts, the deeper truth is that we want our doctors, just like our lawyers and engineers, to be trained by and conversant with the work of scholars whose specialization is extremely limited and often highly abstract. Without the work of theoretical mathematicians, neither computers nor any technology that relies on them would have developed.[52] Without the laboratory research of chemists and microbiologists interested in abstruse questions, diagnosis and treatment of diseases cease to advance. Without legal theory, jurisprudence stagnates and fails in the face of new challenges.[53]

In each of these fields, as in *every* other, specialists have spent entire careers dedicated to questions and ideas that had no intended practical application. Their reasons for asking such questions are often purely theoretical: not knowing beforehand whether the answer to a question will be worth finding, the question is worth asking simply because the answer is unknown. Specialists' methods and jargon tend to be inscrutable to non-specialists, and this fact is not superficial but epistemological. Research methods and technical languages constitute ways of knowing; specialists are only able to ask and address certain questions because of them. This reality contributes to the theory-practice rift.

Theological scholarship, including missiology, is no exception. If specialized missiological knowledge is to be produced—if there are complex,

---

51. In practice, expertise is increasingly "dying" in American culture. For an outstanding defense of expertise, see Nichols, *Death of Expertise*.

52. See Kachapova, "On the Importance of Pure Mathematics," 421–22, for a brief but compelling portrayal of the fact that the gap between theory and practice is frequently temporal. That is, given enough time, many purely theoretical ideas have become the basis of revolutionary applications. A key question, then, is whether a given population has a sufficiently long-term vision to support theoreticians who develop ideas that might only become practical in another generation.

53. As in theology, the debate about the value of theory in relation to the practice of law is an ongoing, heated debate. See, e.g., Coleman, "Legal Theory and Practice," 2579–617; Vilaça, "Why Teach Legal Theory Today?," 781–819.

deep questions to address with the rigor that pertains to scholarly research and discourse—then missiology-as-*theoria* must necessarily operate in terms that are difficult for nonspecialists to understand, to say nothing of application. Examples abound. One classical dimension of mission work is biblical translation, which entails a staggering breadth of specialization: advanced abilities in biblical languages, textual criticism, linguistics, translation philosophy, and cultural anthropology. The translator must be able to navigate the methodologies and technical jargon of each of these fields. There is no such thing as a good contemporary translation that results from mere technique. The process is too complex, the problems too difficult, the resources too extensive. Still, readers entrenched on the practice side of the rift may suppose this example is an outlier. Perhaps most missionaries rely on finished translations (which fact begs the question!), but other aspects of mission still call for similar expertise. To speak in broad terms, anthropology, sociology, postcolonial studies, and religious studies—and, of course, history and theology—all contribute to academic missiology because the challenges that missionaries confront demand resources that exceed the capacities of the nonspecialist.

Certainly, the Christian who participates in God's mission need not become a specialist. That notion is beside the point. The question at hand is how missiology-as-*theoria* contributes to the theory-practice rift. The essential answer is that by bringing the resources of specialized study to bear on the challenges of mission, such missiology validates the development of and engagement with theory that cannot arise without specialization and does not necessarily concern itself with practical application. In other words, academic missiology functions, as a mode of equipping for participation in mission, to mediate the specialized knowledge of *theoria*. The result of this process is that missiological expertise of the academic variety is, for many, inexcusably difficult to acquire and use. It is, in a word, impractical.

Academic Publishing

The chief manifestation of missiology-as-*theoria* is technical writing. On the theory side of the rift, missiologists compose arguments that are incomprehensible to many practitioners. As I have already said, this is a function of engagement with scholarly jargon that pertains to a certain kind of knowledge. There is no other way to engage this knowledge on its own terms. Developing specialized missiological knowledge requires nothing less.

That so much of scholarly writing remains in need of "translation" to a more accessible idiom exacerbates the theory-practice rift.[54] The problem is twofold. On the one hand, there is a necessary division of labor according to which scholars leave the work of translation for another moment and, often, for other pens. This is necessary because scholarship is a process in which authors write in such a way that other scholars can critically engage the methods and language of advanced arguments. The scholarly author's concern is not whether a piece of work is understandable to popular audiences or usable for practical purposes but whether it holds up to rigorous, technical scrutiny. Knowledge advances uniquely through these means. On the other hand, the work of translation from scholarly jargon to popular representation is arduous. The assumptions, categories, and conceptual operations of a scholarly argument often cannot be simplified without significant loss. The demand for a bottom line or a basic idea frequently cannot be met without unusual gifts. (And, frankly, the demand itself reveals a populist assumption that every missiological concept should be accessible to anyone.) Successful popularizers are, therefore, a rare commodity.

The result is a division between academic and popular writing that mirrors and reinforces the theory-practice rift. Practitioners are commonly dismissive of technical publications, and scholars are commonly disdainful of reductionistic arguments. The former hold a commitment to the "simple" gospel and the participation of any disciple in the mission of God. The latter rest in the knowledge that history has proven the need for careful, critical engagement with the realities of mission. Given this state of affairs, the responsibility of theorists is to do the hard work of making their work understandable and compelling in terms that a wider audience can engage. This is a tall order, but it is hardly impossible. There is no escaping the need for many specialists to concentrate on the work of producing knowledge that is inconceivable without the apparatus of scholarship. The legitimacy

---

54. The idea of translating academic understanding for popular consumption is important for the "pastor theologian" model discussed below. See Hiestand and Wilson, *Pastor Theologian*, 83–85. Notably, where the pastor theologian is construed more specifically as a "public intellectual," she is "a particular kind of generalist who knows how to relate big truths to real people" (Vanhoozer and Strachan, *Pastor as Public Theologian*, 23). This comports with Nichols's criticism: "Where public intellectuals . . . once strove to make important issues understandable to laypeople, educated elites now increasingly speak only to each other" (Nichols, *Death of Expertise*, 11).

of such vocational concentration does not, however, answer the need for far more representation of missiological scholarship in winsome writing for the common reader.

So far, I have characterized the theory-practice rift in the context of American Christianity and examined some of its key expressions in missiology. Roots in Western philosophy, anti-intellectualism, consequentialism, and spiritual reductionism all widen the rift. Within missiology, movement ideology and short-term missions manifest the practice side of the rift, missiology as *technē*. Specialization and academic publishing manifest the theory side of the rift, missiology as *theoria*. In the final section, I advocate a theological appropriation of *praxis* in order to begin bridging the divide. Missional *praxis* entails a model of reflective action that calls for the church's embodiment of an integrative movement between theory and practice.

PRAXIS AS THEOLOGICAL MEDIATION OF THE THEORY-PRACTICE RIFT

All Things in Relation to God's Mission

Missiology comprehends the study of all things in relation to God's mission.[55] It is an interdisciplinary field of study that holds together reflection on the Triune God's multidimensional reconciling work and reflection on the church's participation in that work. Missiology is, therefore, both theoretical and practical in scope. This calls for a model of theological formation that integrates theory and practice and, ultimately, equips disciples—formally educated students and lay church members alike—to live in the continual movement between theory and practice.[56] Missional theology provides such a model and issues in the formation of missionary-theologians.

---

55. See McKinzie, "All Things in Relation to God's Mission."

56. One recent philosophical conception of such movement is Hammar, "Theoria, Praxis, and Poiesis," 107–24. I agree with the basic contention that "with a more differentiated concept of knowledge, one that takes more than epistemic claims and propositions into account, we can gain more insight into the transformation and circulation of knowledge" (120). Reckoning with the different kinds of knowledge is vital. Construing the nature of their relationship on the fraught terrain of the theory-practice divide calls for something more.

Missional Theology between Theory and Practice

Missional theology broke onto the scene at the turn of the twenty-first century, beckoning the church to a renewed understanding of both God's mission and the church's participation in it.[57] The essential claim of missional theology is that the mission belongs first to God, not the church. This assertion seeks to theologically correct ecclesiocentric, anthropocentric, colonialist, and secularist tendencies that variously marked both the "great century" of missions and the tumultuous twentieth century that followed it.[58] If the mission is God's, and the church is a mere participant in God's Triune work, then how should we think and what should we do? There is more to say in response to these questions than the present essay can address. Where the theory-practice rift is concerned, the upshot of missional theology is a critique of both missiology as *technē* and missiology as *theoria*. Balancing this, the missional theological critique encompasses a theoretical perspective on practice and a practical perspective on theory.

On the one hand, missional theory critiques missiology as *technē*. Mission cannot be reduced to techniques for achieving church growth, disciple-making, or social justice because God is at work in ways that do not conform to the ecclesial practices that serve these ends. Indeed, missional theology critiques these ends themselves. Any a priori affirmation of, say, social justice must reckon with the theological definitions of both community and justice. The question, missionally speaking, is what God is up to in the local context, and a wide-ranging theological discourse informs the missional church's answers and ends. Notions of mission that presume the ends toward which God is working, however noble they appear in humanist terms, may not withstand a theological evaluation that grants to God the primary agency of mission. Missional theology prioritizes discernment of the Spirit's work in the world before and beyond the church's presumptive interests and initiatives.[59] Discernment is a theoretical endeavor—a way of seeing. A missional church must, therefore, concern itself with theoretical questions. What information, frameworks, assumptions, and concepts

---

57. See Franke, *Missional Theology*.

58. For the designation "great century," see Latourette, *History of the Expansion of Christianity*; the titles of vols. 4 to 6 utilize the phrase, which has become a commonplace in missiology.

59. See, e.g., Van Gelder, *Ministry of the Missional Church*; Kim, *Holy Spirit in the World*; Yong, *Missiological Spirit*. Among Stone-Campbell authors, see the recent volume by Van Rheenen's former colleague, Allen, *Poured Out*.

inform participation? What interpretive methods shape discernment? And how might answers to such questions be articulated rightly in the theological idiom of the church's faith?

On the other hand, missional practice critiques missiology as *theoria*. Mission cannot be reduced to the concepts and arguments that theoreticians produce because the church's local participation is a *sine qua non* of Christian missiology. Stated differently, the church cannot speak faithfully apart from the reality of embodied participation in God's mission. The practices of participation are constitutive of missional theology.[60] *Theoria* is a visual metaphor at root: the church cannot *see* without missional participation. The view from the proverbial ivory tower is simply too limited. Theoretical notions of mission, however rigorous and scholarly their formulation, may not survive the experience of local, contextual engagement in the Spirit's work. Missional theology was born of such experiences in the twentieth-century world-mission movement, which compelled the ecumenical church to revise the theology of mission in Trinitarian, postcolonial, and holistic terms. This monumental sea change is paradigmatic, not final, and there is every reason to expect God's ongoing work in the world to continue giving the missional church eyes to see.

Missional theology lives in the tension between theory and practice. Indeed, the force that each exerts is necessary for the production of a theology that is properly missional. Without this tension, missionaries become mere practitioners and theologians become mere theoreticians. I have affirmed the value of specialization, and one might conclude that mere practitioners and mere theoreticians represent specialized roles that call for an integrative model of dialogue and collaboration. Certainly, dialogue and collaboration can fashion one sort of bridge across the theory-practice rift. May they increase! In my view, however, this bridge offers unsteady footing. Missional theology promises something more: a model for building a wide, stable pathway across which the whole church may constantly traverse the divide. The missionary-theologian, as an architect of such bridge-building, represents this promise.

The Missionary-Theologian

Difficult questions immediately arise at the mention of the missionary-theologian: who is a missionary, and who is a theologian? Do these titles

---

60. McKinzie, "Missional Hermeneutics," 160–69.

represent vocations or commitments that inevitably safeguard the theory-practice rift? And what of the church? What does the role of the missionary-theologian have to do with the average disciple? I propose that while the missionary-theologian is an architect, missional theology calls the church as a whole to the work of bridge-building. The missionary-theology plays a vital role, but the missional church must cross the divide.

With due regard for highly experienced, well-formed practitioners, a key assumption of missional ecclesiology is that "the church's missionary vocation" includes every disciple of Jesus.[61] "Missionary" is no longer a title reserved for those occupied with long-term cross-cultural ministry. The whole church is sent. Likewise, the label "theologian" has escaped the bounds of professional specialization. Everyone who speaks of God is engaged in theology, and the question is how well we speak.[62] These facts do not deny that those who have dedicated their lives to sentness or God-speak occupy a special place in the body of Christ.[63] Rather, the linguistic shift that contemporary uses of *missionary* and *theologian* bespeak is a commentary on the nature of the church. Every disciple is sent by the Spirit to participate in the Triune work of God. Every disciple's speech about God is liable to theological judgment. Moreover, these changes highlight the fact that the role of "professional" missionaries and theologians is to equip the church for faithful embodiment of the gospel in word and deed. More to the point, the missionary-theologian equips the church for the word-and-deed work of bridging the theory-practice rift.

I conceive of the missionary-theologian in conversation with the recent literature that seeks to retrieve the special role of the pastor-theologian.[64] From the perspective of missional theology, the pastor-theologian

---

61. Guder, *Missional Church*, 7.

62. Gutiérrez's discussion of theology as "talk about God" in *On Job: God-Talk*, xi–xix, representing the popularizing impetus of Latin American liberation theology, has been influential in this regard.

63. Working on one's car does not make one a mechanic. Doing one's taxes does not make one an accountant. Reserving terms for specialized functions is quite natural, and as the holder of hard-earned degrees in theology, I am not dismissing this simple truth. I am, however, acknowledging that language is fluid, and the indignation of specialists is beside the point. The whole church *is* sent. The whole church *does* speak of God. Highlighting these realities through linguistic innovation is perfectly understandable and appropriate. For missional theology, it is arguably necessary.

64. See Hiestand and Wilson, *Pastor Theologian*; Vanhoozer and Strachan, *Pastor as Public Theologian*; and Wilson and Hiestand, *Becoming a Pastor Theologian*.

just is a missionary-theologian. What, then, is a pastor-theologian? Three aspects of this vocation are vital.

First, the pastor-theologian operates in the space between the church and the academy. The pastor-theologian is not a mere translator of scholarly work, important though that work is. She is also a producer of theology from an ecclesial location.[65] That is, her primary habitus is the church, not the academy. From a missional perspective, this means conducting and articulating theological reflection from the communal experience of participation in God's mission. The missionary-theologian exemplifies the pursuit of practical theory and theoretical practice in the most robust terms.

Second, the pastor-theologian equips the whole church for ministry.[66] The responsibility for robust theological engagement does not fall on the pastor-theologian alone. Certainly, it may be that the gifts and predilections of the pastor-theologian result in a kind of theological production that is not the job of the whole church. Yet, the ecclesial commitments of this vocation entail a kind of work—writing (formally or informally), teaching, leading discussions and experiments, processing experiences, and so on—that both represents and serves the body of Christ. In this way, the missionary-theologian facilitates engagement in mission by equipping the church for discernment and action in a continual movement between the two.

Third, the pastor-theologian engages in public theology.[67] Public theology is the outward-facing articulation of the church's worldview. Much of Christian theology is inside ball because both the language of faith and the concerns of the church are frequently foreign to outsiders (not to mention the barriers to understanding that both complex Christian tradition and scholarly discourse entail). The pastor-theologian, therefore, concerns herself with the word-and-deed communication of Christian belief and practice in ways that are relevant to the wider public. This function is not

---

65. This is Hiestand and Wilson's primary contention in *Pastor Theologian*.

66. In my reading, the small body of literature on the pastor-theologian is, so far, anemic on this point. It is arguably implicit in much of the discussion, but rarely does it find expression. Vanhoozer, in *Pastor as Public Theologian*, comes close: "What are theologians for? What is the distinctive service of the pastor-theologian? We reply: for confessing, comprehending, celebrating, communicating, commending, and conforming themselves and others to what is in Christ. Theology serves the church to the extent that it helps disciples fulfill their vocation to put on Christ and to grow into the fullness of Christ" (125).

67. See esp. Vanhoozer and Strachan, *Pastor as Public Theologian*.

to be reduced to the typical outward-facing practices of evangelism and apologetics, nor to mere political discourse. Rather, public theology entails winsome, intelligible expressions of the church's perspective on "life, the universe, and everything" (to quote *The Hitchhiker's Guide to the Galaxy*). In missional terms, this work calls for thoughtful contextualization and empathetic engagement with the Spirit's work among the church's neighbors and friends. The missionary-theologian, then, seeks through modeling and equipping to bring the church into meaningful dialogue with the rest of the world for the sake of God's kingdom. The rest of the world is caught in the tension between theory and practice, requiring an approach that holds the two together. This is the burden of a public missiology.[68]

The role of the pastor-theologian, reconceived here as the missionary-theologian, represents the need for theological leadership in the American church. The whole church is sent to participate in God's mission, thus every disciple is a missionary, but discipleship is a process of formation. Disciples are de facto missionaries who need theological formation in order to engage their calling faithfully and wisely. The missionary-theologian equips the church through embodied teaching, modeling, and explaining the significance of the church's missionary practices. The purpose of theological leadership in this view assumes the movement between theory and practice, which validates both the critical dimension of theological reflection and the work of local engagement with contextual realities. Further, it assumes a missional theology, which centers the church's participation in God's mission. If the mission is God's, and the church is called to be collaborative agents of God's purposes in the world, the missionary-theologian must lead disciples to bridge the gap between theory and practice for the sake of participation. Neither theory nor practice alone will suffice. The missionary-theologian is, then, a paradigm of the missional church's witness, the word-and-deed ministry of disciples in community for the sake of the world.

---

68. The notion of a public missiology is a recent development. See Okesson, *Public Missiology*, for a robust account. Particularly relevant here are his characterization of the divide between private, academic theology and public, everyday theology (25–28); his discussion of the tendency to reach for technical problem-solving solutions (identified as *technē*) in the face of complexity (35–37); and his outline of the relationship between public theology and public missiology (ch. 4).

Missional Life in Practice and Theory

The Missional Helix as Praxis

The missionary-theologian mediates the theory-practice rift as a model and an equipper, but mediation also requires a paradigm for the integration of theory and practice. Gailyn Van Rheenen's missional helix offers one such vision of integration. It illustrates the key components of continual movement between theory and practice in the church's participation in God's mission. I suggest that the missional helix, implemented in relation to a theological definition of *praxis*, can serve as useful paradigm for missionary-theologians seeking to lead the church in bridging the theory-practice rift.

Van Rheenen's missional helix represents a spiraling movement in which "the missionary returns time and time again to reflect theologically, culturally, historically, and strategically under the guiding hand of God to develop ministry models appropriate to the local context. Theology, social understandings, history of missions, and strategy all work together and penetrate each other within this environment of spiritual formation. Thus praxis impacts theology, which in turn shapes the practice of ministry."[69] The mutual relationship between theology and practice suggests what Van Rheenen is after: "an integrative model of learning that brings together the strengths of studying in a seminary with those of ministering in a local church."[70] Here, then, is a model of missiological education that envisions the integration of theory and practice through a schematization of theoretical elements that are important for practitioners. Van Rheenen explains why each of the elements "within the internal structure of the spiral"[71] (spiritual formation is, by contrast, the external "environment" of the helix) is necessary for the development of "ministry models": without biblical theology, cultural forces dominate; without cultural analysis, grave contextual mistakes abound; without an understanding on the past, one's perspective on the present is blinkered; without strategic planning, the work of ministry remains haphazard at best.

Notably, Van Rheenen writes with "missionaries and ministers," "trained missionaries," "church planters," and "the Christian practitioner"

---

69. Van Rheenen, *Missions*, 311–12. Note that Van Rheenen, like many authors, uses *praxis* interchangeably with *practice*, in contrast with the technical definition I offer below.

70. Van Rheenen, *Missions*, 308.

71. Van Rheenen, *Missions*, 311.

in mind.⁷² That is, he presents the missional helix to the sort of student who would make use of a 514-page textbook on mission foundations and strategies. Adjectives such as *professional, full-time,* and *expert* come to mind. In other words, the missional helix represents "a model for theological education" in the traditional sense of seminary training, and the curriculum is recognizable. Van Rheenen has conflated biblical and dogmatic theology under "theological reflection," added cultural studies (appropriately for missiology), and designated the practical dimension as strategy formation, but the schema is still quite conventional. This is not to say that the model offers nothing constructive. It represents a commitment to an integrative movement aimed at local implementation often missing from the seminary experience. Nonetheless, the missional helix assumes the robust theoretical competence that traditional theological education values. Navigating the deep waters of historical study or utilizing the tools of anthropological analysis, for example, are requisite.

At the same time, Van Rheenen imagines "the community of faith collectively develop[ing] understandings and a vision of God's will within its cultural context."⁷³ He advocates a missional ecclesiology according to which "the church is *the distinctive people of God called by him through his mission and set aside for his mission.*"⁷⁴ Still, his focus remains on the role of the missionary, who "must appreciate all that is good about the church, be thankful for the heritage of faith she provides, and *help the church become an even more faithful agent of God's mission.*"⁷⁵ The reader may infer that this helping role, akin to that of the missionary-theologian advocated here, involves the use of the missional helix. The whole community, aided by "the missionary," should move through the spiraling integration of theological reflection, cultural analysis, historical study, and strategy formation. The missional helix is (at least incipiently) a paradigm for the integration of theory and practice that brings the dimensions of formal missiological education to bear in the equipping of the whole church for participation in God's mission. It is not obvious how the missionary-theologian might undertake this work, and the problems of specialization and academic form persist, but the paradigm provides a useful conception of the process that the missional church must engage.

72. Van Rheenen, *Missions*, 312, 314, 319.
73. Van Rheenen, *Missions*, 311.
74. Van Rheenen, *Missions*, 104 (emphasis original).
75. Van Rheenen, *Missions*, 105 (emphasis added).

What, then, does a theological definition of *praxis* add? We have seen that *praxis* in Aristotelian terms refers to action in contrast with knowing and production. Instead, I commend the definition of *praxis* operative in liberation theology: reflection on action that leads to action.[76] It is a kind of theological reflection that depends on prior action and serves further action; it is a holistic theological method. But which action? Liberation theology identifies solidarity with the poor and oppressed as uniquely theologically constitutive action. Missional theology, by contrast, includes solidarity with the poor and oppressed but expands practice to include a more comprehensive notion of witness. Without leaving behind the essential insight that *praxis* entails a continual movement between action and reflection, a broader vision of solidarity emerges.[77] Missional solidarity involves a robust word-and-deed engagement with the local context that addresses material, social, and spiritual poverty. But this is just one aspect of the praxis of the missional church.

Like Van Rheenen's missional helix, *praxis* also entails movement from practical engagement to theoretical reflection and back to practice. "Strategy" implementation is not merely a practical result of theory—a destination—but many waypoints on the church's journey of missional faithfulness. Therefore, theory is not to be judged by practical "results." Rather, theory is one dimension of a total way of life. The practical evaluation of theory happens alongside the theoretical evaluation of practice, and the two are mutually informative in the continual movement toward the church's faithful witness to the kingdom of God in dynamic historico-cultural situations. This movement is missional *praxis*.

---

76. *Praxis* does not have a single meaning among liberation theologians. See Markey, "Praxis in Liberation Theology." Further, it is necessary to note objections to the Marxist associations of *praxis* in liberation theology. See, e.g., Wolterstorff, "Theory and Praxis," 317–34; Thiemann, "Praxis," 544–49. For more appreciative analyses, see Loy, "Praxis," 7–14; Volf, "Doing and Interpreting," 11–19. I agree with Lamola, "Marx, the Praxis of Liberation Theology," 13, that liberationist *praxis*, because of its theological commitments, is not "is not praxis qua Marxian praxis." I argue, however, that Marxian *praxis* is ultimately appropriated in liberation theology so that "solidarity as praxis is now a *locus theologicus* in which action and reflection, practice and theory, are indivisible. In solidarity, the church can perceive the Word of God uniquely in order to act faithfully, which gives rise to new understanding" (McKinzie, "Hermeneutics of Participation," 220). Similarly, see Tracy, "Theoria and Praxis," 169; Schüssler Fiorenza, "Theory and Practice," 113–41; Kim, "Hermeneutical-Praxis Paradigm," 419–36.

77. See McKinzie, "Hermeneutics of Participation," ch. 5.

Adding a conception of *praxis* borrowed and expanded from liberation theology to the missional helix results in two necessary clarifications. First, whereas the missional helix, presented in a textbook on missions, is prone to relegation among students of mission who see themselves in the traditional "missionary" role, missional theology insists that the whole church is called to participate in God's mission. This assertion entails the translation of the missional helix into the local church's idiom and, therefore, the advocacy of missional *praxis* on the congregational level. Such advocacy is a primary function of the missionary-theologian. Second, whereas Van Rheenen contends that "theological reflection is the beginning point for ministry formation and the most significant element within the internal structure the spiral,"[78] the theological definition of *praxis* highlights the fact that theology is always already the product of reflection on practice (even the *absence* of missional practice). This fact is inherent in the structure of the missional helix, but a missional conception of *praxis* accepts the contingency of theological reflection and, thereby, challenges the linearity of the claim to a "beginning point." From these clarifications emerges a model of missional life in which *praxis* bridges the divide between theory and practice. In the conscientious, perpetual spiral from theology reflection, cultural analysis, historical study, and strategic action back to theology, the church embodies missional *praxis* as a way of perceiving and inhabiting the world.

CONCLUSION

This study has identified four influences that contribute to the separation of theory and practice in Western missiology—philosophical roots, anti-intellectualism, consequentialism, and spiritual reductionism—attending to key manifestations of the divide on both sides. In view of these contextual factors, I have argued that a liberationist definition of *praxis* appropriated through the framework of missional theology suggests the possibility of bridging the gap. Bridge-building requires both the architectural role of the missionary-theologian and the participation of the whole church in the continual movement between theory and practice. Van Rheenen's missional helix, critiqued according to the theological entailments of missional *praxis*, offers a paradigm for this constructive movement.

---

78. Van Rheenen, *Missions*, 311.

The upshot of my argument is twofold: (1) missional practice is theologically determined, and missional theology is practically embodied; and (2) participation in God's mission unfolds in the movement between theory and practice. These conclusions indicate that seeking a unified field is both possible and necessary. Wise, faithful participation in God's mission cannot capitulate to the forces that separate theory and practice. Ideology and expediency are powerful, akin to the tectonic forces that gradually, inexorably separate continents and give rise to different languages and forms of life. But Christian mission must envision and inhabit the whole world, and continental divides do not have the final word. The God and Father of all, whose kingdom encompasses and reconciles all things in Christ by the Spirit—even church and academy, faith and scholarship, practice and theory—is above all, through all, and in all. The praxis of Christian mission proceeds accordingly, and missiology finds its *raison d'être* in the continual movement between theory and practice.

2

The Conversion Process in the Stone-Campbell Movement Churches in Southern Africa (1914–1927)

An Historical Analysis

Paul S. Chimhungwe

Today's average Christian is a middle-aged indigenous (black) African woman in sub-Saharan Africa. Todd M. Johnson et al. found that "over the last 1,000 years, Europe had more Christians than any other continent. By 2018 Africa had the most Christians: 599 million, vs 597 million in Latin America and 550 million in Europe."[1] These statistics reflect the membership in the Stone-Campbell Movement (SCM) in sub-Saharan Africa, especially the Churches of Christ, a cappella, which equates baptisms to conversion.[2] These churches traditionally baptize candidates upon the confession of the lordship of Jesus Christ without prior catechesis. I identify these as instantaneous baptisms, ubiquitous in the Churches of Christ a cappella, especially in Southern Africa.[3] In this chapter, I argue

1. Johnson et al., "Christianity 2018," 1.
2. Huffard, "When Scholarship Goes South," 65–72.
3. Instantaneous baptisms are based on proof-texting, especially from Acts which is

that instantaneous baptisms inhibit spiritual and numerical growth in sub-Saharan Africa. Instructively, a critical historical study of SCM churches in Mashonaland, Zimbabwe's early years, 1914 to 1927, demonstrates that these instantaneous baptisms were the exception.[4] Indigenous preachers grounded their catechumens in sound biblical catechesis, worship, and lifestyle reminiscent of the first-century Christian communities, leading to the phenomenal growth of congregations in Mashonaland. For these uneducated early indigenous preachers and their partners—the unlettered missionaries—conversion was a gradual process, not an event. Baptism, an event, was the climax of conversion, a gradual process centered on catechesis, experience, and praxis.

The SCM saw the swift change of this methodology with the influx of supposedly trained missionaries after the Second World War. This study argues that the twenty-first-century SCM churches in sub-Saharan Africa can reappropriate this early model to reduce spiritual backsliding since the continent is now the epicenter of Christianity.[5] I divide this chapter into two sections. First, I summarize and contextualize the beginning of Churches of Christ in Mashonaland. Following this, I survey the conversion process in Mashonaland among these churches. In conclusion, I suggest some enduring lessons, emphasizing catechesis for the twenty-first century Churches of Christ in Mashonaland and Manicaland—where currently (2021) there are no Euro-American missionaries.

THE CONTEXT AND BEGINNING OF THE CHURCH OF CHRIST IN MASHONALAND, ZIMBABWE

Jack Mukaro Mzirwa (1885–1958) was born in Guyu, around the Macheke area in Southern Rhodesia. He was the SCM torchbearer to that region and one of John Sherriff's pioneer students at Forest Vale Mission. Sherriff's reports mention Mzirwa continuously, along with Peter Masiya, Elton Kundago, and George Khoza.[6] As a Shona, Mzirwa "grew up as a true traditional worshipper who believed in the creator," according to Tinaye,

---

read prescriptively. Texts like Acts 2:37–41, Acts 9:18, and Acts 10:47–48 are used to support instantaneous baptisms.

4. Olbricht, "Invitation," 6–16.

5. See Johnson et al., "Christianity 2018," 1.

6. See Williams et al., *Stone-Campbell Movement*, 135; Sherriff, "Forest Vale Mission," 13.

his only son.[7] This traditional religious posture would be typical, following Marthinus L. Daneel's description of the Shona religion:

> Of all the southern and eastern African tribes the Southern Shona have the most elaborate cult for worshipping and consulting the Supreme Being. For centuries they have believed in Mwari as the final authority behind their ancestors, a High God who was perhaps less directly involved in the affairs of individual lives than the ancestors, but one who could be consulted on matters of communal import. Far from being a remote deity, Mwari was believed to control the fertility of Shona occupied country, to give rain in times of drought and advice on the course of action in times of national crisis. Thus, the pre-Christian belief in a Supreme Being contributed considerably towards shaping the destiny of the Shona people.[8]

W. I. Brown, the founder of Nhowe Mission, described the indigenous peoples of Zimbabwe as "ignorant without God." Similarly, Henry M. Stanley depicted Africans as "debased specimens of humanity."[9] These unfortunate missionary caricatures profoundly misunderstood Shona religious beliefs. The indigenous people knew God as the source of existence but were uninformed about Jesus Christ. Hence Benézét Bujo's argument:

> Long before the arrival of Christianity in Africa, African religion recognized God as the source of all life . . . God is then the dispenser of life . . . Life is a participation in God, but it is always mediated by one standing above the recipient in the hierarchy of being. This hierarchy belongs both to the invisible and to the visible world. In the invisible world, the highest place is occupied by God, the source of life. Then come the founding fathers of clans, who participate most fully in the life of God.[10]

The gospel—the good news about Jesus Christ—was the missing link and part of the Euro-American enterprise, that is, converting the indigenous people to Jesus Christ. In the case of the SCM in Zimbabwe, Sherriff

---

7. Tinaye Mzirwa, interview by Paul S. Chimhungwe, Wuyuwuyu, October 31, 1991. According to Mzirwa's son Tinaye Mzirwa, his father spiritually transformed after coming back Bulawayo. Jack Mzirwa lost his father during the Ndebele and Shona uprising, according to Muganhi. Nyari Muganhi, interview by Paul S. Chimhungwe, Nhowe Mission, 3 October 1991. Mzirwa was from the Zezuru tribe, hence a Muzesuru.

8. Daneel, *God of the Matopo Hills*, 15.

9. Editor, "African Village," 41.

10. Bujo, *African Theology in Its Social Context*, 17, 20.

deposited the gospel into Mzirwa of Mashonaland from 1910 to 1914. Mzirwa established Siyankobe Mission near Livingstone, Northern Rhodesia, in 1914. It ceased operating in 1915 due to inadequate funding.[11] The closure of the Siyankobe Mission opened the doors for what would become the Mashonaland Mission.

Mzirwa arrived at Guyu, also known as Maryland, in Macheke, Southern Rhodesia, in 1915, when he got married. He also brought new farming technology to Guyu. While in Bulawayo, he learned from Sherriff the effectiveness and efficiency of the plow-based agricultural system, which "exchanged the hoe . . . and the rude garden work for the plough and spade. What had been done at Kuruman [Robert Moffat's Mission in South Africa] was imitated by natives elsewhere."[12] In the SCM, Mzirwa introduced ox-drawn-plow-based agriculture in Macheke and subsequently in Wuyuwuyu, which improved yields. Second, he started a school at Guyu and Wuyuwuyu after the colonial government forced them to relocate in 1919. These components of Western civilization—education and technology—made the gospel, the third component that Mzirwa brought to his people, attractive.[13] Through the gospel, Mzirwa, in the absence of Sherriff, was responsible for spiritually converting his kith and kin. At the end of 1927, Sherriff finally settled at Wuyuwuyu, where he found close to 300 faithful members.

WHAT IS CONVERSION?

Scholars define conversion in many ways, but Arthur Nock's classical definition resonates with my argument in this chapter, particularly his definition: "By conversion we mean the reorientation of the soul of an individual . . .

---

11. Sherriff, "South Africa, Seventh Annual Report," 12–13; Sherriff, "From South Africa," 4.

12. Leedy, "History with a Mission," 256–57. In the American Methodist Episcopal Church, the pioneer indigenous luminary was Abraham Kawadza, whom Jason Machiwenyika claimed "was the first African in Manyikaland to plough with European ploughs. . . . After him, the Christians became many in Manyikaland. Many Africans imitated Abraham Kawadza in handling church affairs as well as using European ploughs; he was a pioneer both for the church and for the fields" ("History with a Mission," 256).

13. Horton, "African Conversion," 86, suggests that at the beginning of "the twentieth century . . . Europeans came to be seen as symbols of power, and Christianity itself came to be seen as part of a larger order, comprising Western education, colonial administration, commerce and industry, with which everyone had henceforth to reckon. These changes created a much more favorable climate for conversion."

[the] deliberate turning from indifference or from an earlier form of piety to another, a turning which implies a consciousness that a great change is involved, that the old was wrong and the new is right."[14] For Nock, transformation happens through rigorous instruction. He quotes Augustine's treatise *On the Catechizing of Those Who Are Unversed*, pointing out that Augustine "explains how the Christian scheme of faith should be set forth. It is all done on the values of the thing in itself." Chapters 7 and 8 of Augustine's treatise emphasize what must be taught. Catechesis was part of the conversion process, a factor missing in the Churches of Christ a cappella in Mashonaland.

The Conversion Process in Mashonaland

The conversion process for Mzirwa exhibited two main features: first, prospective members were taught specific foundational doctrines resulting in the repentance of catechumens from their sins and unchristian beliefs. Repentance meant publicly confessing their sinful nature, usually at a church gathering, without naming the sins. Second, the catechumens were expected to show fruits of repentance before being buried in the waters of baptism. Turning from traditional religious practices was primarily what missionaries termed fruits of repentance. According to Karimanzira, catechumens were only baptized after proving that they were no longer appropriating or eschewing ungodly tenets of the African Traditional Religion (ATR).[15] These were replaced with the fundamentals of the gospel: the virgin birth, life of Christ, his death, burial, resurrection, ascension, and second coming. Ecclesiology was also central. In the following section, I explain specific doctrines that led to repentance and the activities that led to baptism.

Since the Shona knew and worshiped a Supreme Being—*Mwari*—their conversion was not accepting "an addition to the pantheon of lesser spirits. Rather . . . [they] accepted change and development in . . . [the] concept of the supreme being."[16] In the case of the Churches of Christ in Mashonaland, prospective members were taught for some years to appropriate the good news: the gospel of Jesus Christ. According to the table below, it took a catechumen in Mashonaland, colonial Zimbabwe, between

---

14. Nock, *Conversion*, 7. See also Masondo, "Indigenous Conceptions," 87–112.

15. Karimanzira, interview by Paul S. Chimhungwe, Chitowa African Purchased Area, October 1, 1991.

16. Horton, "African Conversion," 100.

1914 to 1927, an average of two years after their date of repentance before being baptized.

Catechumens' Records[17]

Name	Sex	Marital Status	Date of Repentance	Date of Baptism
Mirimi Makunde	M	M	?	27.05.1917
Mandiwawarira Makunde	?	?	26.01.1920	24.07.1921
Zwirimwe Makunde	F	S	6.06.1920	24.07.1921
Mwareweni	F	S	21.08.1920	11.06.1922
Masekeni Makunde	F	M	19.11.1922	26.11.1922
Matiyaya			10.06.1922	12.12.1926
Delay	?	?	19.11.1925	2.09.1928
Rosie Makunde	F	S	16.01.1938	10.04.1938
Hazwierekwi Makunde	F	?	11.09.1939	1.10.1939

Catechumens' Records (Interviews)

Name	Sex	Marital Status	Date of Repentance	Date of Baptism
Godi Karimanzira	M	S	1923	8.02.1925
Samson Mhlanga	M	S	1930	27.03.1931

Mirimi Makunde was one of the earliest Christians in Guyu who recorded family activities and events in a small notebook that his son Pindukai Elijah Makunde was willing to share. From this information, I argue the conversion process took a catechumen an average of about two years before baptism. The process agrees with Lewis Rambo, as quoted by Everett Ferguson, who identifies some "overlapping components or aspects of conversion. These are context, encounter, interaction, commitment, and consequences."[18] Why the delay, especially when considering the norm of instant baptisms in Mashonaland from 1946 onwards after the influx of Euro-American missionaries? I suggest the pioneer missionaries and their

17. Mirimi Makunde, personal notes, n.d.
18. Ferguson, *Early Church*, 19.

early converts spend time anchoring catechumens in Jesus of Nazareth after analyzing the indigenous Africans' *Weltanschauung*–their spiritual worldview.

I will consider Sherriff's teachings; he emphasized soteriology without demonizing other Christian movements. Sherriff taught catechumens the virgin birth of Jesus, his death, burial, resurrection, and ascension according to Nyari Muganhi, who was spiritually natured by Jack Mzirwa—Sherriff's earliest convert. Old Testament salvific stories like the Fall, the Exodus, and the Conquest were foundational to the spirituality of prospective converts. Teachers narrated these stories and prospective converts regurgitated. This teaching methodology produced enduring results in an oral community with a few literate people.

Interestingly, ecclesiology was secondary, the opposite of many missionaries in the Churches of Christ whose teaching about soteriology was based on ecclesiology.[19] Sherriff taught his early students the importance of instructing catechumen before baptism, and Jack Mzirwa reflects this in his evangelist career. Mzirwa was the leading teacher/preacher/evangelist at Guyu from 1915 and after 1919 at Wuyuwuyu and its environs. He followed Sherriff's teaching and practices by taking years indoctrinating his catechumens before baptism. According to Gladys Tandi (née Mpondi), "founders like Mzirwa did not easily baptize people. They took years teaching and training prospective church members before baptism because this is what Sherriff had taught them at Forest Vale Mission [Bulawayo]."[20] Mzirwa later got the moral and physical support of Choto, Mirimi Makunde, and Penny Mpondi after their conversions. The initial Church of Christ congregations founded at Macheke and Wuyuwuyu from 1914 to 1927 were the fruits of indigenous evangelists because Sherriff and Hadfield were confined in Matabeleland.[21] Samson Mhlanga succinctly portrayed the founding of congregations in Mashonaland during this period: "Sherriff, Mzirwa, [Zuma] Banza, Choto and people like Makunde, were interested in founding enduring work [congregations]; therefore, they made sure that prospective

---

19. Olbricht, "Hermeneutics in the Churches of Christ," 23. F. Hadfield joined Sherriff in 1906. He was also from New Zealand. W. N. Short, from the USA, joined the team in 1923 but he went to Northern Rhodesia. In this chapter, I am discussing conversion in Mashonaland, which was under the supervision of Sherriff.

20. Gladys Tandi, interview by Paul S. Chimhungwe, Tandi Village, Rusape, June 26, 2015.

21. F. L. Hadfield came to Southern Rhodesia in 1906. The missionaries visited Mashonaland three times during the period under discussion.

Christians were uprooted from the world and planted into Jesus and his church."[22] Here I wish to unpack the "world/worldview" that the catechumen was uprooted from—African Traditional Religion.

THE SPIRITUAL WORLDVIEW OF MASHONALAND

The SCM conversion narrative in colonial Zimbabwe is intimately tied to ATR because the indigenous people of Mashonaland worshiped *Mwari*—the Supreme Being. They approached him "in many and various ways" before the arrival of the missionaries who introduced Jesus Christ as the only mediator.[23] Ancestral spirits are the fulcrum of religion for the Shona. They revere the departed spirits of their ancestors—the living dead—through elaborate rituals and orgies. The living dead are intermediaries between the Shona and *Mwari*, pivotal in Shona life: success or failure in marriage, fecundity, land ownership, chieftainship, droughts, and death, to mention a few, all depend on one's relationship with the living dead—the ancestors.[24] *Kurowaguwa* was the defining ceremony that brought the dead spirit into the living space of the living.[25] Catechumens and Christians were not supposed to participate in this elaborate ceremony that involved the brewing of traditional beer and the consultation of witch-doctors.[26] This lack of participation was a significant challenge for catechumens since failure to attend such family ceremonies brought animosity between families. African Traditional Religion is a "communal phenomenon of which the individual is only a part."[27] Early Mashonaland Christians sacrificed family relations to accept the lordship of Jesus. This extreme social cost may have been one significant reason why it took them an average of two years before baptism because they were being catechized to the point they could accept what kind of social and familial sacrifice baptism would require.

---

22. Samson Mhlanga and Paddy Mhlanga, interview by Paul S. Chimhungwe, Wuyuwuyu, October 1, 1991.

23. Daneel, *God of the Matopo Hills*, 15.

24. See Bourdillon, *Shona Peoples*, 32, 69, 71, 86, 113.

25. *Kurowa guwa* or *kugadzira guwa* is an indigenous Shona traditional rite performed to enable the dead to attain ancestorship. The ceremony is held at least six months after burial. Daneel, "Review of Marshall W. Murphree."

26. Gelfand, *Genuine Shona*.

27. Dogbe, "Concept of Community and Community," 782.

Godi Karimanzira left Buhera in 1923 for Dziwarasekwa, where he got a job at a farm. While there, he met Zuma Banza and Chakanyuka Gonzo, Mzirwa's converts from Wuyuwuyu. These two taught Karimanzira for two years, and in February 1925, he came to Wuyuwuyu, where Mzirwa baptized him. Again, instead of an instant baptism, it took two years before he was baptized. He left for Buhera the following month, facing a difficult time with his family because he had accepted the gospel. Moreover, Karimanzira was of the Mwenye/Varembe totem.[28] Karimanzira finally left his village and settled in the Chitowa African Purchase Area close to Murewa after marrying a Makunde girl. The same happened to Samson Mhlanga. He was taught in 1930 by Goliath Nchena and S. D. Garrett at the now Mbare congregation before baptism at Wuyuwuyu from Mzirwa on March 27, 1931. Although he had been a member of what is now the United Baptist Church of Zimbabwe, it took him a year before immersion. These accounts show how conversion was a process, not an instantaneous event; even young girls went through an elaborate teaching process before baptism. Mandiwawarira Makunde repented on January 26, 1920, but was baptized on July 24, 1921, and her sister Zwirimwe, who had repented on June sixth of the previous year.[29] After repentance, catechumens were expected to show the fruits of repentance—which I will discuss in greater detail later in this chapter. I close this section with the conversion story of Mirimi Makunde, a polygamist who became a strong, influential member of the Church of Christ.

MAKUNDE'S CONVERSION TO JESUS CHRIST

Makunde had three wives when Mzirwa preached to him while the indigenous Africans were still at Guyu, Macheke, before the colonial government relocated them to Wuyuwuyu in 1919. Polygamy, that traditionally vexing subject for missionaries and African Christians, became an obstacle for some Africans to become Christians. Mzirwa, as the leader of the nascent

---

28. See Hove, "Muslims Court Varemba Community." The Mwenye/Varembe people shun meats that are not slaughtered by their own people. They use their own kitchenware, among other cultural norms. Godi Karimanzira, interview by Paul S. Chimhungwe, 1 October 1991.

29. Zwirimwe married Ndhlukula Nkomo, Alex Ndhlukula's father. Nkomo joined Sherriff in Salisbury when the latter was on his way to Wuyuwuyu Mission. Alex later became an outstanding leader in the Churches of Christ. Alex Ray Ndhlukula, interview by Paul S. Chimhungwe, Marondera, May 29, 2016.

church, assumed the traditional Western missionary policy on this thorny issue. This approach, as David Barrett describes, was that "polygamists with their families . . . could not be fully received into the Church. Many missions refused baptism of husbands, wives, and children; others accepted the two latter; while very few permitted the baptism of the polygamous husband and his family in the first generation only."[30] After hearing the gospel, in 1915, Makunde "had a mutual agreement with his wives, he separated from them and remained with the youngest, Masekeni Makunde."[31] After this repentance, Mzirwa baptized Makunde following the teachings he had received at FVM. This was a painful decision, but Makunde had given his life to serving God according to the teachings of the Church of Christ. This account of Makunde is reminiscent of Isaiah Shembe (1870–1935), the founder of Nazareth Baptist Church of South Africa in Sabbath. A polygamist with four wives, Shembe is reported to have received visions. In one of them, "it was revealed to him that he should leave his four wives, and though this was so hard that he almost committed suicide, yet he finally followed the divine command."[32] Whether Shembe had an epiphany as reported is insignificant; the fact is he divorced his wives, considered a sign of repentance, to become a follower of Jesus Christ. Similarly, this was the route followed by Makunde.[33]

Masekeni Makunde, the remaining wife, disclosed, "Mirimi Makunde told his two wives that he had decided to become a Christian, and this meant divorcing them since the new religion does not accept polygamy."[34] However, he was not going to let them go empty-handed. He gave his former wives cattle, easing their painful departure. For the Shona, cattle were a measure of wealth. Bourdillon writes,

> In the past, when there was no easy way of making a durable profit from a good harvest, cattle provided the main form of durable wealth, and the size of a man's herd of cattle remains a significant prestige rating. The Shonas are quick to point out that the rate of

---

30. Barrett, *Schism and Renewal in Africa*, 116–19.

31. Pindukai Elijah Makunde, interview by Paul S. Chimhungwe, Two Streams Farm, Virginia, Macheke, July 26, 2015.

32. Sundkler, *Bantu Prophets in South Africa*, 110.

33. Pindukai Elijah Makunde, interview.

34. Masekeni Makunde, interview by Paul S. Chimhungwe, Nhowe Mission, October 1, 1991, Nhowe Mission, Zimbabwe.

increase of their cattle herds provides a greater dividend than the interest rate of banks or savings accounts.[35]

The repentance and conversion story of Godi Karimanzira, Samson Mhlanga, Mirimi Makunde, and his daughters prove that Church of Christ missionaries to Southern Rhodesia—particularly Hadfield and Sherriff, who came out of New Zealand—and their indigenous students from 1914 to about 1927 took extended amounts of time in instruction teaching people before baptism. In particular, this also seems to have included a significant demand for catechumens to demonstrate evidence of real change.

Christian Life

After repentance, catechumens were taught Christian living and central Christian doctrines. According to Nyari Muganhi, "after repentance, one was taught baptism, sin, heaven and hell, the role of Jesus as the mediator, the evils of drinking [alcoholic beverages], smoking, marrying outside the church, polygamy, consulting witchdoctors, witchcraft . . . above all, why you should attend church every Sunday or whenever there is a church meeting."[36] Gladys Tandi added that giving was a major component of repentance. "According to my uncle, [Penny] Mpondi, prospective members were expected to give to the church. They could give agricultural products and domesticated animals since money was scarce."[37] The last lesson for catechumens was the Lord's Supper, which was taught for two hours every Sunday afternoon for three months. "The Lord's Supper was supposed to be taken by people who knew the significance of Christ's death on the cross, his burial, resurrection and second coming. Christians were encouraged to live a clean life. The Lord's Table was holy; it was only after understanding its significance that one was finally baptized," argued Karimanzira.[38]

---

35. Bourdillon, *Shona Peoples*, 76. In Northern Rhodesia, a similar incident occurred. Dow Merritt reported that "one young man worked for us as an ox-driver. He was baptized, learned to read and write in school, then went home and began teaching the girls and small boys to read and write and to sing. We finally started services there last year and now have a congregation of over 30. This man's father and mother have been baptized. He had to put away two wives and quit his beer and he also quit snuffing tobacco" (Merritt, *Dew Breakers*, 88).

36. Muganhi, interview by Paul S. Chimhungwe, Nhowe Mission, October 3, 1991.

37. Tandi, interview by Paul S. Chimhungwe, Tandi Village, Rusape, June 26, 2015.

38. Karimanzira, interview by Paul S. Chimhungwe, Chitowa African Purchased Area, October 1, 1991.

Missional Life in Practice and Theory

ANALYSIS

In this chapter, I argue for appropriating Mzirwa of Mashonaland's conversion methodology, anchored on rigorous catechesis before baptism. Mzirwa implements this conversion process between 1914 and 1927 in the absence of a resident Euro-American missionary in Mashonaland, Zimbabwe. However, the appropriation of Mzirwa's conversion methodology must consider the following points. First, this is not a call for introducing catechism, an anathema in the history of the Churches of Christ. Catechesis comprises doctrinal and moral instructions, the foundation of spiritual and numerical growth in Christianity. Everett Ferguson suggests that some parts of the New Testament, like 1 Thess 4:1–5:11 and Col 3:5–15, "reflect blocks of catechetical material."[39] In the absence of catechesis, the church will face perennial leadership, and financial and moral challenges directly resulting from instantaneous baptisms, as I argue in this chapter.

Second, the Church of Christ sometimes misinterprets baptismal texts in Acts to quench its thirst for restoring New Testament Christianity. The restoration principles are a noble goal, but descriptive passages like Acts 2:37–41, 8:36–39, and 10:49–48 became prescriptive in support of instantaneous baptisms, with proponents failing to appreciate the socio-religious context. Everett Ferguson argues that these "early converts came from Judaism or Gentiles already exposed to the teachings of the Old Testament. As the situation changed, more instruction was necessary; consequently, a longer preparation period for converts was considered helpful."[40] In hindsight, this is what Mzirwa and his coworkers practiced in Mashonaland between 1914 and 1927; conversion was a process that included thorough teaching, followed by fruits of repentance and immersion.

Third, Mzirwa's conversion methodology argues for prospective Christians to show the fruits of repentance before baptism. This might be labeled as making Christianity a religion of works. But catechesis rooted people in Christ and his church. When J. M. McCaleb visited Wuyuwuyu in 1929, he wrote,

> Brother Jack [Mzirwa] deserves more than a mere mention. He has been a Christian for about twenty years and in ten years' time at this place has baptized some two hundred people in his own and surrounding villages. He also has been teaching in the village

---

39. Ferguson, "Catechesis, Catechumenate," 223–24.
40. Ferguson, *Baptism in the Early Church*, 855.

> school, for which Brother Sherriff paid him $10 a month, but now he lives by farming and continues preaching. Two students are doing the teaching at present. So well has Brother Jack done his work that during the two years Brother Sherriff has been here, there has not been one to backslide.[41]

McCaleb's argument is anecdotal, but the apparent lower number of backsliders might be due to the practice of repentance and catechesis. People likely did not backslide because Mzirwa and his colleagues taught catechumens for one to four years before baptism. When catechumens were finally immersed, they would have been rooted in Jesus. Sadly, there are no extant records of those who dropped before and after baptism. Though it is possible that there were reversions, the evidence points clearly to a qualitative difference in results. Mzirwa's enduring work extended to other places in Mashonaland. "Many young men flocked to Mzirwa's church because there were disciplined young women worth marrying, and they were also taught and later became strong members of the Church of Christ," said Karimanzira.[42]

Fourth, Mzirwa's conversion methodology appears viable despite changes in the socio-religious and technological environment. While Mzirwa's agrarian twentieth-century society differs radically from the twenty-first-century context, my primary argument resonates with Jimmy Shewmaker's evaluation of the Church of Christ missionary enterprise in sub-Saharan Africa.

> I'll be glad when churches in the US quit pressuring missionaries to produce many converts. Many American churches measure results by the number of baptisms. We are told to baptize those who believe. One can have many baptisms in Africa, but many are not genuine. However, those statistics are impressive for sponsoring congregations in the USA. Missionaries have been known to be withdrawn from the field because they were low in baptisms.[43]

Shewmaker's assessment deserves the attention of every minister, preacher, evangelist, institution, or congregation involved in winning souls to Jesus in sub-Saharan Africa. Individual discipling, teaching, and mentoring are significant before and after baptism if the Church of Christ in sub-Saharan Africa will plant enduring congregations. Mzirwa, through Sherriff's

---

41. McCaleb, *On the Trail of the Missionaries*, 144.
42. Godi Karimanzira, interview.
43. Shewmaker, *Memoirs*, 21.

Missional Life in Practice and Theory

teachings, deserves credit; he implemented his mentor's teachings—grounding catechumens in the gospel before baptism, and conversions for him were not instantaneous.

Fifth, the conversion methodology emphasizes giving in kind rather than money. Mzirwa and his colleagues taught catechumens the significance of local produce resulting in abundant resources in the church. If that teaching had continued in the Church of Christ, this fellowship would not be struggling financially because many "gave goats, herds of cattle, maize, millet, to support church work."[44]

Although I am arguing for Mzirwa's conversion methodology, a caveat is appropriate at this point. There is no data to prove precisely when the practice of instantaneous baptism was begun. Catechesis and pre-baptismal instruction did not change even after Sherriff's visit to the USA and Canada in 1921, where it was practiced.[45] When Sherriff settled at Wuyuwuyu Mission in 1927, it was still the norm according to McCaleb's observation in 1929 when visiting the mission, "The custom of the brethren in Africa is to call for people to come forward and make the confession in the usual way, but to defer the baptism for more teaching unless there is good reason to believe they already understand."[46] Rigorous catechesis uprooted catechumens from evil ATR beliefs and practices and planted them into Jesus Christ, leading to spiritual and numerical growth during the infancy of the Churches of Christ in Mashonaland.

Jack Mukaro Mzirwa, through Sherriff's teachings, deserves credit; he implemented his mentor's teachings—grounding catechumens in the gospel before baptism, and conversions for him were not instantaneous.

CONCLUSION

Historically conversation was a process in the early Church of Christ congregations in Mashonaland—particularly in Guyu, Macheke, and Wuyuwuyu. It took an average of two years before catechumens were baptized. Baptism was the climax of the conversion process, resisting the practice of instantaneous baptism. The twenty-first century Churches of Christ in Zimbabwe can appropriate these lessons to reduce contemporary spiritual

---

44. Gladys Tandi, interview by Paul S. Chimhungwe, Tandi Village, Rusape, June 26, 2015.

45. Klingman, "John Sherriff in Toronto, Ontario, Canada."

46. McCaleb, *On the Trail of the Missionaries*, 143.

lethargy. The church should seriously consider taking time to teach prospective members Christ's mediatorship between human beings and God. This transforms the lives of indigenous Zimbabweans whose proclivity towards ancestral spirits (the living dead) cannot be ignored and denied. The doctrine that might be important for catechesis includes the divinity of Jesus, emphasizing the components of the gospel: the birth, life, death, burial, resurrection, ascension, and second coming. The doctrine of the Holy Spirit, which was ignored in the SCM for years but now receives currency because of the Pentecostal and charismatic movements, deserves emphasis. Especially critical for this type of catechesis is an emphasis on the dangers of the prosperity gospel. Mzirwa and his team taught the importance of in-kind contributions since money was still new for Zimbabweans. Although money is now the measure of wealth, many communal and urban dwellers can make in-kind contributions like domestic animals—cattle, goats, pigs, chicken—and agricultural products.

Sub-Saharan Africa possesses abundant natural resources, and Mashonaland's rich soils support church work; but in the absence of catechesis, the Church of Christ in Zimbabwe will forever depend on the generosity of the Euro-Americans. Ironically, the Zimbabwe Assemblies of God Africa, which started in colonial Zimbabwe in 1964 without external funding, has church buildings, hospitals, and the famous Zimbabwe Ezekiel Guti University, where professor C. J. Chetsanga, a biochemist and member of the Church of Christ, is the current (2021) vice-chancellor. It is catechesis, amongst other factors, that allows the Zimbabwe Assemblies of God Africa (ZAOGA) to fund its institutions in Mashonaland while the Church of Christ is struggling.[47]

The Church of Christ in Mashonaland, Zimbabwe, if not the whole of sub-Saharan Africa, will have a healthier future—spiritually, financially, numerically—if it minds the enduring lessons from Sherriff, Mzirwa, and his team in Mashonaland. Conversion was a process, and very few left the Church of Christ. On average, catechumens were instructed for two years with the fundamentals of the gospel before baptism. Instantaneous baptisms, where a person is immersed after an invitation without any teaching or after a day or two of studying, are not growing the church. Although we do not have statistical figures showing backsliders in Mashonaland, an area that requires further exploration, the church has been struggling for the

---

47. See David Maxwell's analysis of ZAOGA's membership drive and indoctrination. "'Delivered from the Spirit of Poverty?,'" 353.

past six years, according to Webster Kasava, one of Zimbabwe's outstanding preachers: "My brother, we are not sure if we are growing or not; the church requires revamping."[48] The church can be rejuvenated by revisiting what happened between 1914 and 1927; although the cultural, economic, spiritual, and political environments are different, some enduring lessons can be learned. Catechesis is part of the answer to the spiritual, financial, and numerical growth challenges in the Church of Christ in Mashonaland, Zimbabwe, if not the entire sub-Saharan Africa.

---

48. Webster Salowa (Kasava), phone interview by Paul S. Chimhungwe, Gaborone/Marondera, July 1, 2020.

3

Van Rheenen's Incarnational Model for Tribal Africa and Watson's Church Planting Movement Model

How Different Are They?

ANTHONY B. PARKER

> From every corner of the globe the reports are coming in. Only a few at first, but now more and more frequently, reinforcing one another with their startling accounts of hundreds, thousands, even tens of thousands coming to faith in Christ, forming into churches and spreading their new-found faith... Every region of the world now pulsates with some kind of Church Planting Movement.[1]

I FIRST READ THESE words in a booklet that I came across in Cotonou, Benin. As our team struggled to launch a movement of churches-planting-churches among the Fon people, I was eager to learn anything that might bring greater fruitfulness to our work.

Gailyn Van Rheenen and Richard Chowning, in their roles at Abilene Christian University, had deeply influenced our team. Their earlier work,

---

1. Garrison, *Church Planting Movements*, 3.

based out of Sotik, Kenya, among the Kipsigis people, had inspired other teams throughout the country.[2] We had in turn been shaped through internships with these teams. We believed that their methods would yield fruitful results in West Africa. In almost eight years of work among the Fon, however, we failed to experience the kind of movement we had expected.

As I perused the booklet, the principles I read seemed familiar. Was this material new or just a different presentation of the Kenyan strategies? I later learned that Garrison's booklet propagated methods that David Watson advocated. Some of my colleagues in West Africa attended Watson's trainings and felt that there were indeed new elements that we should introduce into our work.

Today, more than twenty years later, there is a shift from "traditional" church planting, represented by Van Rheenen, to "movement" methods, represented by Watson.[3] In this chapter I will compare the methods represented by Van Rheenen's and Watson's approaches.

PURPOSE AND METHOD

These two methods—"traditional" and "movement" church planting—have each furthered God's kingdom purposes immeasurably. Engaging in this critique feels like treading on holy ground. I enter this examination with the prayer that current and future mission practitioners will develop their own strategies with a fuller understanding of the history and presuppositions behind some of the models that they inherit.

Church planting strategies developed in Kenya in the 1970s and 1980s, as Van Rheenen describes them,[4] exerted a great influence on many missionaries from Churches of Christ, particularly those working in Africa in the 1990s and early 2000s. Today, however, training and sending organizations from this heritage speak of "Disciple Making Movements" and "Discovery Bible Studies" as the church planting methodology of choice. Pioneer Bible Translators, Team Expansion, Christian Missionary

---

2. Richard Trull Jr. divides the history of Church of Christ missions in Kenya into three periods: ground-breaking, vernacular, and phase-out. Trull notes, "The Sotik mission team set the foundation for the vernacular period of Churches of Christ in Kenya. Their work provided a foundational model which future teams adapted for their particular mission contexts" (Trull, *Fourth Self*, 60–61).

3. Coles and Little, "Church Planting Approaches in Tension."

4. Van Rheenen, "Introducing the Kenya Church Growth Philosophy," 5–10; Van Rheenen, *Biblically Anchored*; Van Rheenen, *Missions*, 347–62.

Fellowship International, and Mission Resource Network, among others, have embraced the language and methodology of the Disciple Making/Church Planting Movement approach. Although there is variety in the implementation of the strategy, this essay describes these movements based on the writings of their best known and their most public advocates.

The perspective of this chapter is strategic, historic, and somewhat formulaic. It is strategic in that it focuses on the "strategy formation" aspect of Van Rheenen's missional helix. Van Rheenen describes the movement from theological reflection to cultural analysis to historical perspective to strategy formation, which then prompts further theological reflection, and so the helical pattern continues.[5] This chapter focuses primarily on strategy and bends back toward theological reflection. The perspective here is historic because it focuses on Van Rheenen's influence at one particular stage of his ministry and also on a relatively narrow window of time in the development of movement methodologies. Van Rheenen's later writings, in particular, indicate that he broadened his appreciation of diverse approaches to mission.[6] Finally, it is formulaic because it cannot examine all the adaptations that Van Rheenen's and Watson's students have made to these strategies.

Van Rheenen's approach bears the "Incarnational Model" label, while Watson's methodology advocates "Church Planting Movements." These designations, drawn from the vocabulary of the advocates, are problematic. They do not highlight the distinctive features of each approach. Watson's followers may certainly embrace "incarnational" approaches, and the goal of Van Rheenen's approach is to produce a movement of churches that plant churches.

The "Incarnational" designation is based on Van Rheenen's revised *Missions* textbook.[7] The era of Van Rheenen's ministry that greatly influenced missionaries in Africa, however, is more fully presented in *Church Planting in Uganda*,[8] *Church Planting, Watering, and Increasing in Kenya*,[9] and *Biblically Anchored Missions*.[10] Richard Trull's volume *The Fourth Self*,[11]

---

5. Van Rheenen, *Missions*, 307–16.
6. Pocock et al., *Changing Face of World Missions*; Van Rheenen, *Missions*.
7. Van Rheenen, *Missions*, 347–62.
8. Van Rheenen, *Church Planting in Uganda*.
9. Kenya Mission Team, *Church Planting, Watering, and Increasing*.
10. Van Rheenen, *Biblically Anchored*.
11. Trull, *Fourth Self*.

supplemented by a personal interview,[12] provides insights into the methodology's influence across Kenya.

Garrison followed his initial booklet on *Church Planting Movements* with a larger volume of the same title.[13] In 2012, Jerry Trousdale told the story of such movements among Muslims in *Miraculous Movements*.[14] Trousdale, along with Glenn Sunshine, later framed the methodology with a theology of the kingdom of God.[15] David Watson and his son Paul explained their rationale and methodologies in *Contagious Disciple Making*.[16] Dr. M. Crowson[17] has spent over two decades working in four African countries and is influenced by both Van Rheenen's and Watson's models. An interview with Crowson helped identify where the methods converge and how they diverge.[18]

I have a long-standing relationship with Van Rheenen, dating from my years as his graduate assistant (1988–1991). Our relationship includes collaboration on *Communicating Christ in Animistic Contexts*[19] and the second edition of *Missions*.[20] My interaction with David Watson is limited to a one-day event during the course of my doctoral studies. My experiences on the field in Africa and with Pioneer Bible Translators, as well as exposure to a broader range of literature on cross-cultural church planting, have given me additional perspectives.

VAN RHEENEN'S INCARNATIONAL MODEL FOR TRIBAL AFRICA

Incarnation is one of four theological themes through which Van Rheenen expresses the foundations of Christian mission.[21] Van Rheenen's description of his model as "incarnational" is not unique, nor is it without

---

12. Richard E. Trull Jr., Zoom interview by Anthony B. Parker, April 2021.
13. Garrison, *Church Planting Movements*.
14. Trousdale, *Miraculous Movements*.
15. Trousdale et al., *Kingdom Unleashed*.
16. Watson and Watson, *Contagious Disciple Making*.
17. Full name unpublished to honor security request.
18. Dr. M. Crowson, Zoom interview by Anthony B. Parker, March 3, 2021.
19. Van Rheenen, *Communicating Christ in Animistic Contexts*.
20. Van Rheenen, *Missions*.
21. Van Rheenen, *Missions*, 63–90.

objectors.[22] Van Rheenen, however, adopts the incarnation as a model for the work of ministry, particularly that of cross-cultural missions. He writes, "The sending of Christ becomes the pattern as to how evangelists should go into the field. The ministry of Jesus Christ becomes the ideal pattern for Christian ministry."[23] What God did in Jesus was foreshadowed by the complete story of God's interactions with humanity beginning in the garden and continuing through his work in his people, the body of Christ.[24]

Earlier writings by Van Rheenen emphasize an "identificational" approach,[25] but the idea of incarnation is present. Van Rheenen insists: "Despite human fallibilities, the Christian evangelist must struggle to preach the same message and live with a similar world view as 'the Word that became flesh.' . . . For if the message is not incarnated into life, the message is incongruent to the life and from the standpoint of the audience, lacks *ethos*."[26] Van Rheenen contends that incarnation is "redemptive identification," adapting to local cultures for the purpose of extending God's redemptive purposes.[27]

No single passage from Van Rheenen's writings summarizes everything that he practiced, modeled, and taught about mission methodology. This passage from *Biblically Anchored Missions*, however, provides the framework through which this essay will describe Van Rheenen's Incarnational model: "These guidelines show evangelists (1) going to the people, (2) seeking a harvest, (3) making the message of the gospel comprehensible to an indigenous people, (4) becoming 'all things to all men' as a way of life, (5) training leaders in action, and (6) receiving material aid as a reciprocal response to spiritual ministry."[28]

---

22. Cheong, "Reassessing John Stott's, David Hesselgrave's, and Andreas Köstenberger's Views," 39–60.

23. Van Rheenen, *Biblically Anchored*, 123.

24. Van Rheenen, *Missions*, 83–88.

25. Van Rheenen, "Kenya Church Growth," 7; Van Rheenen, *Biblically Anchored*, 118–19.

26. Van Rheenen, *Biblically Anchored*, 124.

27. Van Rheenen, *Missions*, 217–18.

28. Van Rheenen, *Biblically Anchored*, 21.

Going to the People

Van Rheenen's Incarnational approach requires that church planters live among or in geographic proximity to those to whom they minister. The reasons for this will become evident in the discussion of the fourth guideline. Functionally, "going to the people" requires that one identify *which* people one should go to. Most of the Kenya mission teams worked among single ethno-linguistic groups. The Sotik team worked among the Kipsigis, one of nine subgroups of the Kalenjin people in Western Kenya.[29]

Van Rheenen's earlier ministry and influence demonstrated a preference toward going to receptive, rural peoples. Reflecting Donald McGavran's influence, Van Rheenen writes,

> No field of the world should be neglected. Nevertheless, fields that are not bearing fruit should be held lightly until signs of a possible harvest are evident. When such signs are evident, workers should be called into the harvest in concentrated numbers . . . . This orientation demands that missiological leaders be sensitive to historical, cultural, and psychological trends of a wide variety of ethnic groups in order to determine varying receptivity.[30]

Van Rheenen believed that, in Africa, people derived their identity from their ancestral homelands even if they lived temporarily in cities.[31] He held that "effective church growth in Africa begins in rural areas and spreads to urban centers by transfer growth," and that "the most receptive locations for missionary endeavors were usually in areas of least Christianization."[32] Van Rheenen would eventually conclude: "While looking for receptive areas in Africa the author has typically looked for *largely animistic areas where newly settled populations have been only lightly evangelized by denominational groups and where there is a political climate conducive to church growth.*"[33] Van Rheenen influenced many to believe that "going to the people" involved selecting a specific people group and, in Africa at least, a rural, receptive people.

---

29. Hallet and Hallet, "Kipsigis Kalenjin in Kenya."

30. Van Rheenen, *Biblically Anchored*, 101, cites McGavran, *Understanding Church Growth*, 230.

31. Van Rheenen, *Church Planting*, 116.

32. Van Rheenen, *Church Planting*, 117.

33. Van Rheenen, *Biblically Anchored*, 114–15 (emphasis original).

Seeking a Harvest

Van Rheenen emphasizes that church growth is the goal. "God wants harvest," he writes. "Workers must be sent in to take advantage of the plentiful harvest (Matthew 9:36–38)."[34] The goal of the harvest "is not the baptism of scattered individuals," but "the planting of fellowships that follow Christ."[35]

Van Rheenen holds a high view of the church. The Kipsigis team nurtured new churches by teaching ecclesiology from the book of Ephesians.[36] In *Missions*, he demonstrates that the church is the product of the *missio Dei*. It manifests the kingdom of God. As the body of Christ, it is the continuing incarnation of the presence of God in the world. It embodies the suffering of the cross and the hope of the resurrection.[37] Van Rheenen is clear, however, that the church is the result of the proclamation of Jesus Christ.[38] "Called into existence by urgent proclamation of the death, burial, and resurrection of Jesus, [the church] is 'a cross-formed yet hopeful community.'"[39]

Church planting is "*initiating reproducing fellowships that reflect the kingdom of God in the world.*"[40] Van Rheenen's strategy aims to establish fellowships that (a) reproduce and (b) reflect the kingdom. While Van Rheenen is wary of social concerns overtaking evangelistic endeavors,[41] he came to recognize that social engagement may play a role in developing churches that reflect the kingdom.[42]

Making the Message Comprehensible

If the message is to result in the initiation of reproducing fellowships, then those who hear must accurately understand the message that it taught. "The first step in making the Christian message coherent cross-culturally is for evangelists to become fluent in the language of the people. It is almost

---

34. Van Rheenen, *Biblically Anchored*, 22.
35. Van Rheenen, *Biblically Anchored*, 71.
36. Van Rheenen, *Missions*, 350–52; Van Rheenen, *Biblically Anchored*, 73–79.
37. Van Rheenen, *Missions*, 93–106.
38. Van Rheenen, *Biblically Anchored*, 11–12.
39. Van Rheenen, *Missions*, 101.
40. Van Rheenen, *Missions*, 324 (emphasis original).
41. Van Rheenen, *Biblically Anchored*, 24.
42. Van Rheenen, *Missions*, 343.

impossible for a translated message to be culturally relevant."[43] The evangelist must resist the temptation to "deculturalize the people and remake them in a Western image."[44]

The evangelist must also understand the cultural context well enough to present the message so that it is comprehensible. In the New Testament, "the verbal forms and illustrations used to proclaim Jesus were diverse. . . . The preaching of Jesus was formulated to fit a local contextualized situation."[45] Some level of contextualization is necessary even in the most basic presentation of the gospel. Van Rheenen speaks of communicating within "the plausibility structures of the culture."[46] As they walk alongside believers, "church planters must guide new converts to visualize what God's church should look like within their culture and to implement this vision."[47]

Becoming "All Things to All Men" as a Way of Life

The Kenyan missionary goes out to identify with local peoples. He eats their food, sleeps frequently in their homes, speaks their language, learns local problems, attempts to preach the eternal gospel message in understandable terms and learns to love people vastly different than himself.[48]

"Identification is a heart condition," Van Rheenen writes. It comes from an affectionate longing for fellowship with the local people, and results in "active social participation" in the people's lives.[49] Learning the local language is the means of entering into "reciprocal dialogue with those of another cultural background."[50] By becoming "sensitive to the native understanding of reality," the evangelist "learns to feel the struggles and glory in the successes of his audience."[51]

---

43. Van Rheenen, *Biblically Anchored*, 27. Van Rheenen is referring to missionaries who preach in a foreign language that is then interpreted by a local person. He is not referring to Scripture that has been faithfully translated into the local vernacular.

44. Van Rheenen, *Biblically Anchored*, 29.

45. Van Rheenen, *Biblically Anchored*, 25.

46. Van Rheenen, *Missions*, 229.

47. Van Rheenen, *Missions*, 329.

48. Van Rheenen, "Kenya Church Growth," 7.

49. Van Rheenen, *Biblically Anchored*, 118–19.

50. Van Rheenen, *Church Planting*, 118.

51. Van Rheenen, *Biblically Anchored*, 118.

Identification, like "incarnation," is "an inter-personal experience. It takes place between people and is not easily transmitted through organization structures."[52] Van Rheenen's early observations in Uganda led him to conclude that reliance on institutions undermined personalized identification.[53] Many of the institutional trappings stood in stark contrast to "the personalized orientation of mission being *among the people*."[54]

Training Leaders in Action

Against institutional methods of leadership training, Van Rheenen favors the "personalized training in action" that he sees in the early church. This approach requires close relationships between teachers and trainees.[55] Van Rheenen's approach calls first for nurturing the whole church. Local assemblies would, in turn, recognize and formally select their leaders.[56] Trull observes,

> The Sotik mission team focused primarily on evangelism with "one of the premier aims" being "to involve as many nationals as possible in evangelism" . . . . This reflects what Van Rheenen calls "personalized training" where leaders are "trained in action" much like Jesus' training of the twelve. This is in contrast to the "institutional classroom setting" where the teacher cannot demonstrate or model the concepts being taught and the students are so "busy studying the message that they have little opportunity to apply the message."[57]

Van Rheenen's approach to leadership development coincides with the stages of church growth and development outlined both earlier and later in his career.[58] In the Initial church stage, leadership development occurs as believers from other villages accompany the church planters as they visit, pray for, and teach in the new setting. As people come to faith, evangelists and coworkers teach and train in the context of the emerging Christian

---

52. Van Rheenen, *Church Planting*, 117.
53. Van Rheenen, *Church Planting*, 115–19.
54. Van Rheenen, *Biblically Anchored*, 22 (emphasis original).
55. Van Rheenen, *Biblically Anchored*, 31.
56. Van Rheenen, *Missions*, 334; Van Rheenen, *Church Planting*, 118.
57. Trull, *Fourth Self*, 61, references Allison, "God's Work among the Kipsigis."
58. Van Rheenen, *Biblically Anchored*, 79–86; Van Rheenen, *Missions*, 353–61.

community.[59] In the Developing church stage, church planters, along with "Timothys and Tituses" who accompany them from other villages, model Christian life and teaching through house-to-house visitation, along with collective teaching. Church planters are careful *not* to elevate individuals as leaders, but to nurture the body collectively.[60] In the Independent church stage, leadership training formally begins, preferably through "localized courses" and Theological Education by Extension. It is not until the end of this stage, as assemblies enter the Mature church stage, that churches formally recognize their leaders. The church planter no longer plays a direct leadership role in the newly planted church.[61]

Other works in Kenya, and eventually the work among the Kipsigis, embraced more structured approaches to leadership development. This was a response to rising educational standards in Kenya, the desire of local leaders for "real education," and government pressure for churches to have trained, ordained preachers.[62] Trull explains that various missionary teams in Kenya developed extension training centers, while the Nairobi Great Commission School acted "as a central training center by which curriculums and graduation requirements could be coordinated."[63]

Reciprocity of Material Aid and Spiritual Ministry

According to Van Rheenen, "The principle undergirding the use of financial aid in the early church was reciprocity"[64]—that those who benefit from spiritual teaching should supply the material needs of their teachers. He suggests that observing this principle would overcome many of the challenges faced in missions in the developing world.[65] Expatriate or foreign support of local evangelists or churches risks exposure to the accusation of "raising up Christians who are after the loaves and the fishes rather than the living Bread of Life."[66]

---

59. Van Rheenen, *Missions*, 353–54.
60. Van Rheenen, *Missions*, 354–56.
61. Van Rheenen, *Missions*, 356–61.
62. Trull, interview.
63. Trull, *Fourth Self*, 59.
64. Van Rheenen, *Biblically Anchored*, 37.
65. Van Rheenen, *Biblically Anchored*, 39.
66. Van Rheenen, *Biblically Anchored*, 37.

Van Rheenen's early distinction between "material aid" and "spiritual ministry" left little room for physical relief and economic development in church planting. Van Rheenen believed that works that began by offering social services were in danger of displacing "harvest as the goal of missions." He preferred to see "social services following redemption and being directed toward a saved community." Even local churches that invested in such services could allow them to "absorb so much of a church's resources that very little is left for evangelistic endeavors."[67]

I recall that Van Rheenen encouraged missionaries to give physical assistance in direct, personal ways, as opposed to working through institutions. In this way, Van Rheenen's approach to both leadership training and material aid were similar. He advocated highly personal, non-institutional methods. In Van Rheenen's later writings, he makes room for financial partnerships with agencies and mature churches, while rejecting direct foreign support of individual national leaders.[68]

WATSON'S CHURCH PLANTING MOVEMENT MODEL

In 1994, Garrison began investigating Watson's claims concerning rapid church multiplication in India, and similar reports from East and Southeast Asia.[69] Garrison's initial booklet[70] was translated into about thirty languages.[71] Garrison saw his work as descriptive rather than prescriptive.[72] He identified ten universal elements found in Church Planting Movements, and ten additional elements that frequently appeared.[73] Citing specifically the situation in Kenya, Garrison insisted that the growth resulting from these movements went beyond what other methods produced.[74]

---

67. Van Rheenen, *Biblically Anchored*, 24.
68. Pocock et al., *Changing Face*, 279–97; Van Rheenen, *Missions*, 421–28.
69. Garrison, *Church Planting Movements*, 15–17.
70. Garrison, *Church Planting Movements*, booklet.
71. Garrison, *Church Planting Movements*, 18.
72. Garrison, *Church Planting Movements*, 21.
73. Garrison, *Church Planting Movements*, booklet, 33–41.
74. Garrison, *Church Planting Movements*, 87.

Definitions

Garrison defines a Church Planting Movement (CPM) as *"a rapid multiplication of indigenous churches planting churches that sweeps through a people group or a population segment."*[75] Later, David Watson and his son Paul write, "We defined a Church-Planting Movement as an indigenously led Gospel-planting and obedience-based discipleship process that resulted in a minimum of one hundred new locally initiated and led churches, four generations deep, within three years."[76]

Jerry Trousdale and Glenn Sunshine used identical criteria in defining a Disciple Making Movement (DMM).[77] According to the Watsons, DMM is the strategy by which God produces a CPM.[78] In practice, advocates often use CPM and DMM interchangeably.

Garrison differentiated between CPMs and other approaches to mission. Distinctive features include an emphasis on the unreached, multiplication, the cross-cultural validity of the approach, and the potential to reach multiple ethnic groups.[79]

The DMM/CPM Process

The Watsons describe a methodical process for initiating Disciple Making/Church Planting Movements. Movements always begin and continue with prayer. Once disciple-makers enter communities, they look for ways to address the felt needs of the people through service, education, or business. In this process, they develop relationships and share about the kingdom of God in the context of these relationships. They look for a Person of Peace. Once they discover this Person of Peace, disciple-makers begin a Discovery Group with the Person of Peace and their family. When the family comes to Christ, the disciple-maker helps them become a church. Disciple-makers identify and train a leader that both leads this group and initiates more groups through this family's network of relationships. "We define success," the Watsons acknowledge, "by reproduction."[80]

---

75. Garrison, *Church Planting Movements*, 21 (emphasis original).
76. Watson and Watson, *Contagious Disciple Making*, 4.
77. Trousdale and Sunshine, *Kingdom Unleashed*, 121.
78. Watson and Watson, *Contagious Disciple Making*, 7.
79. Garrison, *Church Planting Movements*, 23–27.
80. Watson and Watson, *Contagious Disciple Making*, 36.

For the Watsons, the Person of Peace strategy is what sets this method apart from "traditional disciple-making." "The disciple-maker has one job—find the Person of Peace."[81] As the disciple-maker lives among the people and shares relationally about the kingdom of God, those who want to discover Christ will, they say, make themselves known. Disciple-makers focus their attention on this person and their household as they "make disciples of this family, who then takes on the responsibility for reaching their community for Christ."[82]

The Discovery Group is the method by which the evangelist makes disciples. A Discovery Group is "an inductive group Bible study process designed to take people from not knowing Christ to falling in love with Him."[83] According to the Watsons, cross-cultural disciple-makers using this method only present the Bible without introducing elements of their own culture. "If I am honest with Scripture and critical in my thinking and planning, I can present Jesus in a near acultural way that can be assimilated and transformed into a cultural model by the ones God has chosen and prepared."[84] "The role of the cross-cultural worker is to *deculturalize* the Gospel," while "the role of the cultural worker is also to *contextualize* the Gospel."[85] Discovery Groups always seek to identify how learners can obey the commands of Christ in Scripture.[86]

Outside and Inside Leaders

Watson's approach differentiates between the roles of cultural outsiders and insiders. Outsiders are less visible, interacting primarily with leaders who they personally disciple. The outsider leader's role is to "Model, Equip, Watch, Leave." Modeling, however, is limited to modeling Christian life, personal discipleship, and use of the Discovery method of Bible study.[87] According to Watson, outsiders cannot model interpretation of Scripture without fear of hindering reproducibility.

---

81. Watson and Watson, *Contagious Disciple Making*, 126.
82. Watson and Watson, *Contagious Disciple Making*, 128.
83. Watson and Watson, *Contagious Disciple Making*, 5.
84. Watson and Watson, *Contagious Disciple Making*, 13.
85. Watson and Watson, *Contagious Disciple Making*, 17 (emphasis original).
86. Watson and Watson, *Contagious Disciple Making*, 17.
87. Watson and Watson, *Contagious Disciple Making*, 130.

> When working with lost people, we have to avoid falling into the role of explaining Scripture. If we do, we become the authority rather than allowing Scripture to be the authority. If we are the authority, replication is limited by our leadership capacity and the time we have to teach every group. . . . [I]f we want to disciple people who look to Scripture and the Holy Spirit for answers to their questions, we can't be the answer-people. We have to help them discover what God says to them in His Word.[88]

Outside leaders train, coach, and mentor inside leaders, who play a similar role among their own people.[89] Some of these inside leaders are capable of leading and influencing larger or multiple groups. They move into the role of outside leaders as movements spread beyond the original contexts.[90]

Ecclesiology in Church Planting Movements

Because CPMs are the result of DMMs,[91] adherents focus on disciple-making rather than church planting. Disciples, they assume, will form churches. In this process, church is no longer defined as a group meeting on Sundays.[92] According to the Watson's definition,

> The church is a group of baptized believers in the Lord Jesus Christ who meet regularly to worship, nurture one another (feed and grow one another), and fellowship (practice the "one another" statements of the Bible), and depart these gatherings endeavoring to obey all the commands of Christ in order to transform individuals, families, and communities.[93]

Although Watson emphasizes the importance of training leaders, this definition of a church lacks any reference to denominational or local church leadership but highlights mutual edification. Crowson insists, "In DMM, there is no branding and no ownership. We are connected relationally and through networks, but there is no branding."[94] Much church "branding" re-

---

88. Watson and Watson, *Contagious Disciple Making*, 149–50.
89. Watson and Watson, *Contagious Disciple Making*, 129.
90. Watson and Watson, *Contagious Disciple Making*, 175–77.
91. Watson and Watson, *Contagious Disciple Making*, 7.
92. Crowson, interview.
93. Watson and Watson, *Contagious Disciple Making*, 160.
94. Crowson, interview.

flects extra-biblical Christian culture, denominations, and doctrines, which CPM adherents strive to not introduce into their new work.[95] Making a restorationist claim, Watson writes, "The DMM is about doing what was done in the first century."[96]

To DMM/CPM advocates, institutions are suspicious because "when the institutional functions begin to take over, movements can die."[97] Although leadership is essential, adherents believe that the professionalization of church leadership undermines multiplication. The doctrine of the Priesthood of Believers "opens the door and fuels the passion for any believer to be an apostle, prophet, evangelist . . . , and pastor/teacher. . . . By promoting and insisting on professional clergy, the church has limited its ability and capacity to reach the world for Christ."[98]

HOW DIFFERENT ARE THESE STRATEGIES?

Similarities

Van Rheenen's and Watson's models contain multiple similarities. Van Rheenen's own review of Garrison's booklet was highly favorable.[99] Both are influenced by Donald McGavran and the Church Growth Movement.[100] Both view evangelism that produces disciples as the highest priority of missions. Both seek reproduction without a perpetual influx of outside resources. Both are highly relational. Teaching, leadership development, and evangelism happen in face-to-face contexts. Churches and Discovery Groups spread through relational networks. Both methods have been most fruitful in rural contexts. Both favor allowing new believers to grow and leaders to develop within their own contexts. Both approaches favor less formal training and lay leadership.

---

95. Watson and Watson, *Contagious Disciple Making*, 20.
96. Watson and Watson, *Contagious Disciple Making*, 26.
97. Trousdale and Sunshine, *Kingdom Unleashed*, 129.
98. Watson and Watson, *Contagious Disciple Making*, 51–52.
99. Van Rheenen, "Review of 'Church Planting Movements,'" 128.
100. Van Rheenen, "Kenya Church Growth," 5; Van Rheenen, *Biblically Anchored Missions*, 71; Trousdale and Sunshine, *Kingdom Unleashed*, 34–35.

Differences

Conversely, the scholars also demonstrate key deviations. First, in Van Rheenen's model, the outside church planter plays a highly visible role. In the DMM model, outsiders may lead small groups, but as these multiply, outsiders seldom interact with the larger movement. Instead, they focus on developing a small group of leaders.

Second, cultural outsiders play contrasting roles in contextualization. In Van Rheenen's approach, outsiders present the gospel to the local people within "the plausibility structures of the culture."[101] Some contextualization takes place in early evangelism. The evangelist then works with believers to biblically contextualize the message and the forms of the church. In Watson's model, outsiders "present Jesus in a near-acultural way."[102] Watson's seeks to present a culture-free gospel which local believers can contextualize without the involvement of outsiders.

A third, related difference is the attitude toward learning vernacular languages. Crowson reports that Watson discouraged him from investing the time to learn the local vernacular in his current context because Crowson is already fluent in two Western languages used in the country. Because outside leaders do not contextualize, they do not need vernacular language. Persons of Peace in that context, Watson believed, would speak a Western language. Calling himself "a hybrid," Crowson says that the values instilled in him by Van Rheenen's model compel him to learn the local vernacular.[103]

Fourth, the two models differ as to the stage of ministry in which church planters identify and train leaders. DMM strategy begins with "Persons of Peace," who become the key leaders based on their standing in their household. In Van Rheenen's model, church planters develop the whole fellowship toward maturity in confidence that leaders will emerge and be recognized by the church. Some of the mission teams in Kenya, however, saw a need to begin formal training of leaders at an earlier stage than the Sotik team had done.[104]

Fifth, the two approaches vary concerning priority groups for evangelism. Van Rheenen's earlier writings value going to *receptive* people groups, whereas the CPM/DMM approach favors going to *unreached* people

---

101. Van Rheenen, *Missions*, 229.
102. Watson and Watson, *Contagious Disciple Making*, 13.
103. Crowson, interview.
104. Trull, interview.

groups.[105] In practice, these different emphases may not be consequential. Initially, Van Rheenen observed that "areas of least Christianization" were generally more receptive.[106] In his later work, Van Rheenen balances different criteria for field selection.[107] Van Rheenen's approach has been most used among African folk religionists, whereas many stories of Disciple Making Movements are drawn from Islamic contexts.[108]

A sixth distinction between the two approaches is the attention given to ecclesiology. Though both methods aim at multiplying churches, Watson's approach views churches as the by-product of multiplying disciples. Discovery Groups become churches of "baptized believers who gather together for fellowship, worship, nurture, and discipleship, and who leave the gathering to obey all that God has commanded."[109] Advocates point out, anecdotally, "If you plant a church, you won't necessarily get disciples. But if you make disciples, you will always get a church." Devotion to and imitation of the Lord Jesus should take priority over institutional advancement.

While DMM advocates emphasize personal discipleship, Van Rheenen places greater emphasis on the church as a corporate body in fulfilling the divine purposes of God. In *Biblically Anchored Missions*, he writes, "The church, already pictured as the result of mission and God's distinct people in the world, must also be conceived of as God's receptacle carrying the Living Water to the world. God, the Eternal Spring of Living Water, sends forth his Water to be carried by the church, God's receptacle of mission."[110]

A seventh distinction between the approaches is their view of access and physical development ministries. In Van Rheenen's work in Kenya, the outside workers publicly identified as missionaries. Their role was to plant and mature a network of churches. Other activities in which they might become involved would be distractions from their primary purpose.

Crowson speaks with admiration of Van Rheenen's "good missiology that sticks with me to this day."[111] The one area where he departs today is by shifting away from a "spiritual only" approach to missions. The message he understood from Kenya was, "We are here to save their souls and the

---

105. Garrison, *Church Planting Movements*, 23.
106. Van Rheenen, *Church Planting*, 117.
107. Van Rheenen, *Missions*, 455–74.
108. Trousdale, *Miraculous Movements*.
109. Trousdale and Sunshine, *Kingdom Unleashed*, 323.
110. Van Rheenen, *Biblically Anchored Missions*, 17.
111. Crowson, interview.

Holy Spirit will help them to endure to the next life. If you step into the development world, it will suck up all your time and energy." Crowson says that, with his adoption of DMM/CPM principles, his mission mandate has shifted to a more holistic approach.

DMM/CPM workers usually develop access ministries which constitute their primary public identity. These ministries provide access to the physical territory of the people. They allow outsiders to receive permission to remain in the country. These ministries also provide relational access to the people. They form contexts in which ordinary interactions take place. Local people may find it less threatening to relate to an outsider who authentically uses an access platform.

CONSIDERATIONS FOR FIELD WORKERS

Learning from a methodology or missiologist need not imply that practitioners adhere to all aspects of one particular approach. There are no doubt many "hybrids." Such hybridization—incorporating the strengths of both approaches, adapted to the context—will be the healthiest approach in most contexts. Successful hybridization requires that cross-cultural workers develop the tools that will enable them to approach their ministries in ways that are biblically and culturally informed.

In restricted access contexts, the DMM/CPM approach has much to commend it. Cross-cultural workers need access to restricted territories. They need ways to build relationships with local people. They need to remain in the background to allow for sustainable multiplication and to protect themselves and their local friends. Access ministries provide viable public identities, allow for more natural relationship development, and may better serve the incarnational purpose as local people see believers living out their faith in roles they can identify with.

There are other reasons for outsiders to play a less visible role. Even if they follow the lead of their national coworkers, their high visibility is often interpreted in counterproductive ways. Local people assign ownership of the mission to highly visible outsiders. They often believe that the outsiders are really in control and that national coworkers are benefiting economically from their association with the outsiders. Cross-cultural workers whose methods resemble Van Rheenen's methods should anticipate these challenges.

There are reasons, however, to be wary of uncritical adoption of the DMM/CPM methodology. Many strategists succumb to the temptation to claim that *their* way of doing things is *the* biblical way something must be done. When this happens, Scripture is interpreted so that it not only justifies but actually commands a certain methodology. Advocates of DMM/CPM approaches are not immune to this danger. One example is the centrality of finding a "Person of Peace." As noted, Watson sees this strategy as the key distinctive in his approach.[112] He believes that it is biblically rooted in Jesus' teachings in Matt 10 and Luke 9–10.[113] A. Matthews and others, however, have questioned whether DMM advocates have correctly interpreted and applied Jesus' instructions.[114] Looking for receptive people who can lead others may well be a fruitful strategy. To claim that it is *the* biblical approach or that it is unique to Watson's methodology is an overstatement.

Field workers must evaluate these conflicting approaches to contextualization. Is Watson's encouragement to present a "near-acultural Jesus"[115] desirable, or even possible? Certainly, disciple-makers should make every effort to prevent their own culture from distorting the picture of Jesus that they present. The historical Jesus, however, *is* cultural. An acultural Jesus is someone other than the Jesus of Scripture. All of God's self-revelation unfolds in the context of culture. Van Rheenen's strategy of entering the culture, learning the language, and walking alongside new believers as they contextualize both the message and forms of the faith is more likely to result in faithful contextualization. Any attempt to communicate the gospel without considering the biblical or receptor contexts will result in *mis*communication of the message.

The Discovery approach, as practiced by some, seeks to interpret Scripture without any reference to the biblical, historical, or cultural context. Emphasis on obedience to the commands of Scripture without regard for their contexts risks degrading into legalism. In practice, proponents of the Discovery method often introduce contextual perspectives not found in the specific biblical text. New disciple-makers will benefit from training that allows them to move beyond an intuitive hermeneutic so that they

---

112. Watson and Watson, *Contagious Disciple Making*, 127.

113. Watson and Watson, *Contagious Disciple Making*, 125–27.

114. Matthews, "Person of Peace Methodology," 187–99; Coles and Little, *Movements vs. Traditional*.

115. Watson and Watson, *Contagious Disciple Making*, 13.

and those they disciple can understand Scripture in its historic and cultural context.

Those who wish to initiate transformational, kingdom communities should develop an ecclesiology informed by Scripture. Reproduction is indeed a priority, but only insofar as the reproducing communities actively make known God's divine wisdom and reflect the kingdom of God.

Neither Van Rheenen's nor Watsons's strategies provide a perfect pathway for new disciples to enter into dialogue with historic and global Christianity. The teams in Kenya recognized this challenge in Van Rheenen's initial strategy and developed a network of training centers throughout the country. Such centers, however, are not always sustainable without outside resources—a situation that presents its own set of challenges.

CONCLUSION

There is great value in learning from others. At the same time, new cross-cultural workers must avoid searching for a silver bullet that will remove all of the challenges or clarify all of the ambiguities of ministry. Silver bullets rarely exist. When cross-cultural workers think they have found one, they easily become frustrated, disappointed, and full of self-doubt when the desired outcomes do not result. Cross-cultural church planting is complicated. No strategy is faultless. God, however, honors faithful, humble obedience by using less-than-perfect methods to call people to himself. The observations in this chapter are offered in hope that new cross-cultural and cultural workers, sparked by God's creative impulse, will develop even more effective and appropriate approaches to mission that reflect and anticipate the fullness of God's kingdom in the world.

4

They Call Him Father

The Metaphorical Image of God as Father among Modern Shona in Zimbabwe

Linda F. Whitmer

Among the Shona people in Zimbabwe, one of the most historically prominent roles within the family structure is that of "father." The sacredness with which this role is treated belongs not only to the biological father, but also the father *figure*: the missionary, pastor, and even government official who actively or passively take on the identity, status, and character of the Shona father. In negative manifestations associated with the father role, issues of dependency and identification may arise in connection to issues of honor and respect. Today with cultural, economic, and medical crises bearing down on all sides, the Shona people can offer a helpful model of what it means to be God the Father.

Everyone has a concept of "father," whether that comes from a relationship with their biological or adopted father or from interactions with other male figures in daily life. We often do not think about it; it is just there. I wanted to know who God the Father was and is to these dear people. When they hear Jesus' words, "Our Father," "my Father," and "your Father," what image do they see? How does that relate to us and to our work? How does that speak to pastors, missionaries, and development workers as we all strive to serve the same God, our Father?

After decades of working among the Korekore people in Zimbabwe, learning the language, and living life in their presence, I gradually became aware that my conception of fathers and their conception did not always match. Curious about the differences and similarities between my culture and theirs, I worked to understand the wider family structure, and the father personage in particular, from the Korekore's perspective. I set out to explore why these cultural differences often resulted in misunderstandings between the Korekore, pastors, missionaries, and development workers.

Everything in the Korekore culture revolves back to the father of the family. Pastors and politicians alike, along with many others, are called fathers. After many conversations and intentional interviews, the question became, "What am I missing about the Korekore father?" The father stands as a central figure in the community, but it was more than that. Father seemed to be a primary metaphor in the culture. Understanding the father in its metaphoric imagery became essential in order to better conceive of the way other roles, expectations, respect levels, and relationships are pieced together.

BACKGROUND

The 2020 census estimated the total population of Zimbabwe to be 16.3 million people.[1] Of that population, approximately 80 percent of the people are Shona. Included in the Shona grouping are five major dialects scattered throughout the country. The Korekore,[2] a people group located mainly in the northern and northwestern sections of Zimbabwe, comprises approximately 1.7 million people who live in conditions ranging from rural subsistence farming to urban wealthy living. This is the people group with whom my husband and I spent over twenty years and who are the focus of my research.

---

1. World Population Review, "Zimbabwe 2022."

2. This study deals exclusively with the Korekore of Mashonaland West and does not address the same issues with those people of other dialects or heritage within Zimbabwe. Though there is considerable conceptual overlap, and my conclusions can be broadly applied to other Shona and Bantu speakers throughout eastern and southern Africa, I have focused my research on the Shona.

In searching to understand God as Father to the Shona, it is first necessary to comprehend the nature of the Shona father as a kinship unit. The role of the Shona father is extremely complicated. We must start by learning who the father is known to be to the Shona themselves. After over twenty years in Zimbabwe, living and working among the Shona people, I still know myself to be looking at the Shona kinship structure from an *etic* (outside) perspective, even though I also endeavor to approach the *emic* (inside) view.[3] What I have determined from my research is that no single man is father in himself to the Shona family. Rather, there exists a vast network of fathers who work at various levels and at various times to keep the family operating in an acceptable Shona manner. This is why developing a detailed kinship analysis of the Shona Korekore people is so critical as my research shows the concept of father among the Shona to be especially complex.

UNDERSTANDING THE FATHER AS A KINSHIP UNIT

A. R. Radcliffe-Brown rightly stated, "For the understanding of any aspect of the social life of an African people—economic, political, or religious—it is essential to have a thorough knowledge of their system of kinship and marriage."[4] Anthropologists have studied the kinship aspect of cultures all over the world in an attempt to become knowledgeably aware of a people's social behavior in a way that illumines other aspects of their lives. Through the study of kinship we can observe regular and repetitive behavior in cultural groups. These repetitive phenomena catch the anthropologist's attention and allow the researcher to begin making generalizations which can then be tested.[5] Kinship is a window into a people's world.

Over the past century, many anthropologists have made a concerted effort to develop methods of analyzing kinship groups. Edward Tylor,[6] Lewis Henry Morgan,[7] W. H. R. Rivers,[8] Meyer Fortes,[9] Radcliffe-Brown,[10]

---

3. Pike, *Language in Relation to a Unified Theory*, 37–41.
4. Radcliffe-Brown and Forde, *African Systems of Kinship and Marriage*.
5. Schusky, *Manual for Kinship Analysis*, 1.
6. Tylor, "On a Method of Investigating," 245–72.
7. Morgan, *Ancient Society*.
8. Rivers, "Genealogical Method," 1–12.
9. Fortes, *Kinship*.
10. Radcliffe-Brown, "Mother's Brother in South Africa," 542–55.

Bronislaw Malinowski,[11] E. E. Evans-Pritchard,[12] David Schneider,[13] and Ernest L. Schusky all made major ethnographic, theoretical, and anthropological contributions. While these researchers rarely agreed on steps to be taken in the development of kinship analysis, they did succeed in building upon each other's work, and in so doing, brought us to the robust ability to examine the family structure. Likely, none of them envisioned their work contributing to our venture into the metaphoric image of God as Father. However, based upon the work of these and other anthropologists, I have been able to delve into the Korekore Shona reality, which leads to a broader vantage point of who God is and how we may be on mission with him among the Shona.

Metaphoric Father in the Shona

Who is the father to the Korekore Shona person? Anthropologists typically understand kinship father/child relationships as either blood relations (consanguineal) or marriage relationships (affinal), with rarely a fictive relationship coming to the foreground. The relationship between the father and the family is deeper than anthropologists have traditionally recognized. The worldview theme of father is so deep and widespread that a metaphorical understanding of fatherhood is necessary. The following conversation from my research in 1998 illustrates the depth and breadth of the theme:

> Linda: What about people like Steve,[14] you call him *Baba*. Why?
>
> Temba: Because who takes care of you is your father. Look what he has done for us and our country! He is our father! Not born, but he took the job. Even the government will say so, when you are taking care of someone, you *are* their father. Just because a man is a biological father doesn't mean father to us. My sisters call me father because I took care of them. They call my older brothers "brother."[15]

---

11. Malinowski, *Sex and Repression*.
12. Evans-Pritchard, "Study of Kinship," 190–93.
13. Schneider, "Introduction"; and *American Kinship*.
14. This is a direct quote from my field notes. Steve, referred to here, is my husband, Dr. Steve Whitmer, who speaks Shona and has worked among the Shona for many years. This conversation was in English.
15. Chikonye, interview by Linda F. Whitmer, Gweru, Zimbabwe, March 31 and April 7, 1998.

Linda: When people call Steve *Baba* and come to him for help, they expect him to do it. Why?

Temba: He is *Baba*. If he has it, he will do it. They don't expect a big thing. They expect your love. You don't go straight to the father and ask. You go to the older brother first. People do that here. They go to Temba (me), or Roy, or Isaac, and so on, and talk to them and ask their advice before they come to Steve.

Linda: So, by coming here to Zimbabwe, and taking on the roles and responsibilities that he did, he actually made himself a father?

Temba: Yes! He gave himself to the children as a father.

Linda: When someone comes to Steve and asks for help, they expect it?

Temba: He will give it [pause] if he has it. He may have money, but it may be for another child. That's OK. He will give it if he has it. When Steve says No, they think it is because he doesn't have it.[16]

As this conversation illustrates, the Korekore do not describe the father relationship using consanguineal or affinal kinship terms. To those on the outside looking in, the kinship structure may seem somewhat illusive. As with all cultural inquiries, an outsider must cast aside assumptions and observe and listen with new eyes and ears. Assumptions and comparisons to our own way of life are easily made and often lead to misunderstandings which may make well-meaning church workers feel frustrated or confused in their ministry activity. Oftentimes, people use words that are not understood the same in each mind, even though each thinks they are assuming the same definition. For example, an outside church-worker may be expecting funds to be used in a particular way, but the insider perceives that culturally the money will have to be used differently. Conflict and discouragement can easily result. Goodenough saw that the identity, status, and role of people within a culture is critical for comprehending the social system, but the actual expectations assumed by those within the Shona culture determines who is father among the Shona.[17] *Identity* solidifies a position in both the kinship and the social group. *Status* communicates the rights and duties of the identity, which are the behavioral expectations of the people with respect to the concept of "father." *Role* is the actual performance of rights and duties, the actual behavior of individuals as they live out being a father. The identity of a father to the Shona is established not

16. Temba, interview.
17. Goodenough, "Rethinking 'Status' and 'Role,'" 1–24.

only by the verbal linguistic label but by the status and role established by a person acting out the expectations prescribed by the usage of the term.

Identifying those raised to the father status within the culture by the performance of certain rights and duties and held in place by expectations within those around them is essential in the social structure of the community. By unintentionally taking on the roles and responsibilities of a family father in the Shona context, the missionary I mentioned above had become a father to the people with whom he interacted daily. He was not a biological father but seen as a father nonetheless. A fictive father relationship had developed. Metaphor seems to be necessary to fully describe the Korekore father. Metaphor is a comparison in which two unlike items are equated to point out one point of resemblance.[18] The metaphor of father above, then, demonstrates a fictive kinship relationship. The use of the primary metaphor of father allows the Shona to put words to aspects of metaphorically conceptualized subjective experience, cataloging them into the primary or root metaphor "father," each Shona automatically knowing what that means.

Ultimately, when a person takes on the roles and responsibilities of a father, they are assigned the identity and status of the father, whether they know it or not. This has caused no end of conflict and disappointment among missionaries who did not know their true identity. Outside missionaries are often fathers to people as well. They may wonder why they are approached again and again with simple problems that could be solved by the church leaders. The fact of the matter is, however, that by taking on the roles and responsibilities of the Shona father, even unknowingly, they have become a real father to their children. A father loves, protects, provides, gives advice, and more. These are all things a missionary does because of a godly love for the people with whom they work. To the missionaries, they are simply doing the work of the Lord in this place. To the people, the male missionary is the Ultimate Father's representative and has become a father in his own right. As such, the people take their problems to the "father" because that is what a child does. They tell their father about their problems. The father cannot always do something about the problem, but he does care and must be told. A deeper understanding and appreciation of their real and actual role in the culture would enable the male missionary to show greater love and respect for the people who continually address him

---

18. Clinton, *Interpreting the Scriptures*, 21.

as father. It would also enable him to more accurately represent the Father God to the people.

Father-Son: The Dominant Dyad

Hsu proposes that one relationship is dominant over all others in any given kinship system, and the attributes of that relationship dominate the attributes of the other relationships.[19] The father-son relationship within the Shona kinship system is the dominant dyad within the society and family. In the Shona family, where the father-son relationship is in the foreground, the father-son dyad determines the understanding of all other dyads. All other relationships are built upon this father-son relationship. This is similar to the Chinese father-son dyad that Hsu describes: "In the Chinese family, where the father-son relationship sets the tone, the son comes into close and continuous contact with his father and other adult males fairly soon; he early gains a good measure of the realities of life."[20] Awareness of the father-son relationship as a dominant dyad tends to determine the behavior, attitudes, and action patterns of people toward other dyads within the system.[21] In the Shona culture, the dominant dyad of Shona fathers and sons must follow closely set roles and responsibilities in order to maintain the social organizational structure.

EXAMPLES OF THE FATHER

To better encapsulate the various forms of the father image among the Shona, it is helpful to have a short examination of relevant kinship identities. Although there are numerous identities in place, I have chosen a few significant father roles.

The Father *Baba*

Beyond the dominant dyad of the father-son relationship is the role of the father within the entire Shona family. The father is seen as the most foundational person in the family. He is the protector, provider, organizer, and

---

19. Hsu, "Effect of Dominant Kinship Relationships," 640–41.
20. Hsu, *Clan, Caste, and Club*, 52.
21. Hsu, *Kinship and Culture*, v.

disciplinarian. Building upon Malinowski's field descriptions that provided an understanding of relationships between such phenomena as economics, inheritance, and the behavior between kin statuses,[22] I determined what the father's roles and responsibilities are within the culture in order to identify the significance of the father for the Shona.

Repeatedly, when I asked what the jobs of the father are, the response was that he is the family protector. Being the protector does not mean just protection from violent trouble but a guardianship of the family from all manner of problems. Contrasting the real and ideal, and demonstrating the status of the father in the role of family protector, the actual behavior demonstrated by the father is tangible. There was a time in the very recent past when the father of the family would walk along with his wife and children trailing behind. His hands would normally be empty except for tools he might be using while the wife and mother of the family was carrying the baby on her back and other possessions on her head. Informants suggested that, in this case, *Baba* is freed up to protect the family from any danger, such as wild animals or enemies. Although danger from wild animals is less imminent, usually the man still walks with little to encumber him while the wife carries the baby and all other possessions. When the women commented about this custom, they were shocked that I would even question the fact that they carried heavy loads while the husband was walking empty-handed. "His is the big job. What would happen if we needed his protection from a snake or something worse?" they asked. The role of protector remains paramount.

Protection from danger in the physical sense is not the only protection the father is to provide. It is the responsibility of the father to teach the children the ways of the family. In doing so, he protects them from the dangers of the outside world and the spirit world. The father must be strong and in control of the family so that things from outside the family village do not come in and harm the family.

He faces enemies, and if there is an argument with another person or family in the village he will stand for his family. It is the father to whom anyone who has a problem with one of the members of his family will go. He is responsible for all those within his family: the children, his wife or wives, and even his extended family if he is the senior father in the family—the *baba mukuru* (big father), extending out even to those who are of the same totem. Therefore, one of the dominant attributes of the Shona

---

22. Malinowski, *Argonauts of the Western Pacific*.

father-son relationship is protection.[23] With this realization, the deduction can be drawn that fathers, from Father God to the consanguineal nuclear father, should be protectors to their children. This further defines the metaphor of father among the Shona.

It is the father's responsibility to love the children and teach them how to be Shona. In showing love to the children of the family, the father will interact and teach both boys and girls while they are very young. This connection changes as the child grows, however. A father is not supposed to physically discipline a child after they reach early maturity. For boys, the delineation seems to be whether or not the child is still living at home. With the daughter, this connection changes to an avoidance relationship. The daughter cannot approach her father directly but must access her father through the mother or another brother. When there is trouble with a son, *baba mukuru* (big father) or possibly the father's father (*sekuru*) would provide discipline. It is not customarily the job of the father to physically discipline a son. Daughters are disciplined by their brothers, or by an aunt when they are older. Words are seen as a serious punishment, and it is only after three verbal punishments that physical punishment is considered appropriate.

It is interesting that although all of my informants spoke of "beating" a child, they said that a child is not forced to obey, especially when they were older. All assumed the lack of physical force. A child should want to obey and make the father happy in doing so. On the odd occasion that a child (especially a grown son, as the daughter would be married and be the responsibility of her husband) would disobey a father, he would be sent away from the father's presence as punishment. This is seen as harsh punishment indeed and is not a desirable outcome of a problem between the father and son, so it normally does not take long for the son to seek forgiveness. "Fathers always forgive" is another important factor in the development of the father metaphor of the Shona of the father/child relationship.

Exoneration does not come easily. All of my informants told me that a father will *always* forgive his children their wrongs in time, but the son cannot come directly to the father to ask for forgiveness. The son must go to a mediator. Various persons can be this go-between. The most common is the mother when the children are still young, but this quickly moves to the father's mother (*ambuya*) or father's father (*sekuru*). The identity, status, and role of the Christian minister as father to the Shona family is a relatively

---

23. Hsu, *Kinship and Culture*, 8.

new development in the Shona culture. The growth of Christianity in Zimbabwe and the increasing respect for ministers as fathers communicating with Father God has brought this role, including the actual performance of rights and duties of the father,[24] to the foreground in recent years: "Pastors are considered fathers and are still looked at as such today."[25] "It has not changed. Pastors are looked to as fathers and are expected to give wisdom and guidance and help the children of the churches."[26] This is a pivotal part of grasping God as Father and the development of the father metaphor as it expands in the Shona worldview.

The father's role within the family is the hinge upon which the entire family turns. His relationship with his sons is seen as the most important because those sons are the ones who will rise up to lead the family in the future.

Baba Mukuru

The *baba mukuru* (big father) is the most important father of the family. *Baba Mukuru* is not necessarily the oldest brother in the family. Instead, he is someone who is chosen by the family as someone who can best carry out the responsibilities of the highest-ranking member of the family. Financial capabilities, education, employment, and age are all factors that are considered. Thus, a younger brother may become the father of the older brother at times. The father-son relationship and the multiple fathers and their relationship to the family within the culture are the most important relationships to the Shona. Each identified father has roles and responsibilities within the kinship structure, and the metaphoric understanding of father is apparent to the Shona, arising unquestioned by them in their worldview having been learned and practiced at an early age.

The *baba mukuru*'s job is to organize and even rule over the extended consanguineal family with their affinal ties. He disciplines people within the family when it is needed. He will even discipline the other fathers if necessary. He is also responsible for talking to the ancestral spirits on behalf of the family at large and his personal nuclear family. In doing so, he is responsible for appeasing and pleasing the spirits in ritual and ceremony. If beer is to be brewed for the rituals, it is his job to take care of the brewing.

24. Shaw, *Transculturation*, 73.
25. Fanny Nyamutora, interview by Linda F. Whitmer, May 24, 2021.
26. Simba Nyamutora, interview by Linda F. Whitmer, May 23, 2021.

He may assign jobs to others, but the responsibility is ultimately his. When there is death or illness within the family, he is responsible for consulting the *nyangas* (spiritual healer/diviner) and leading any funerals. If a family member is sick, he determines what must be done and speaks to the family members about it, ensuring that the proper procedure is carried out. This may include a trip to the *nyanga* or to the hospital, but the responsibility is his. At funerals, before the burial of the body, he must go into the house with the body and speak to the ancestors, saying, "Here is this one; take and keep him (or her)."

As the elder father of the family, the *baba mukuru* holds the *lobola* (bride price) book. When a marriage is to take place, he has the biggest say in setting the *lobola* amounts and parameters. If the in-laws fall behind in payment of the *lobola* after the marriage, he sends the *munyai/dombo* (intermediary) to sort out the problem. As the ultimate organizer and architect, the *baba mukuru* is therefore at the heart of the Shona family.

Baba Mudiki

The baba mudiki (little father) is valuable to the family as well. Though he is not the highest father in status within the family, he carries the same roles and responsibilities as *the baba mukuru*, deferring only to the *baba mukuru* in times of hierarchical need. The roles and responsibilities of a Korekore father include the following:

1. Prepares Males for Marriage
2. Organizes the Family
3. Gives Advice
4. Acts as Intermediary
5. Organizes All Families
6. Loves His Children
7. Does Not Force Obedience of Adult Children
8. Always Forgives His Children
9. Acts Human
10. Collects *Lobola* (Bride Price)
11. Provides "Life Insurance" for the Family

12. Teaches Togetherness

13. Provides for the Family

14. Protects

15. Cares for the Younger

16. Cares for Girls and Arranges Their Marriages

17. Chooses Sister to Teach His Sons

THE METAPHORIC FATHER

Terminology in kinship studies has long been assessed as both limited and distinct. Ideally, kinship terminology covers all biologically and non-biologically conceived relationships. The ideal is, however, stretched to its limit with the Shona culture. The typical kinship definition of the fictive relationship is "pseudo-kin" and denotes a relationship as unreal.[27] The Korekore array of fathers is, in some cases, neither affinal nor consanguineal; it is fictive. This relationship is real. The person who is grafted into the family as a fictive father is from outside but is seen as a full member of the family with all the identity, status, and roles connected with it. In this case, the person is outside the consanguineal or affinal family relationship structure but is given, and expected to be, the father in a true sense. Each person knows the difference between the fictive relationship and the use of the term father as a term of politeness. The deep-level fictive father of the family becomes so by taking on the roles and responsibilities of a family father.

Family connection determines how the father is connected to the family, whether by blood, marriage, or fictive relationship. Wisdom leader aspects, such as giving advice and solving family problems, provide the identity of the father by means of his intelligence and good judgment role within the family. Aspects of character also surfaced as critical in the identification of the father among the Shona. The functionality of the one identified as father holds additional weight: to the Shona, the one who functions as a father in all his roles and responsibilities is a father. Issues of power—to whom it is given and who receives power from bigger fathers—are also critical in identifying a father. Lastly, location is important in identifying a father, highlighting questions of totem identification and origin.

---

27. Schusky, *Manual for Kinship Analysis*, 8.

GOD THE FATHER

Jesus used the term *father* well over one hundred times in his parables and prayers. In the first-century Jewish context, his manner of using the term was a new insight—one we take for granted today. There are relatively few instances of reference to God as Father in the Old Testament, but the references are there. With the coming of Jesus, the depth of understanding of God as Father grew and flourished. Jesus referred to God as "Father" no less than 170 times in the Gospels. The picture of God as Father appears most clearly in the parable known as the "Prodigal Son" (Luke 15:11–32). This parable is one of the most decisive in Jesus' use of story to vindicate the proclamation of the gospel to the despised and outcast of the world and to proclaim the boundless love of God for those who return to him as a wayward child.

There were times, especially in the parables, when Jesus used the Greek term *oikodespotes* parabolically to refer to God, which referenced the authoritarian nature and ability of the householder. The father was literally the master of his household and everyone in it. At other times in the New Testament, we find that Jesus used the Greek term *abba*, occurring only three times in the New Testament (Mark 14:36, Rom 8:15, and Gal 4:6), which by this time had developed into a familiar term one might use for a warm father relationship. When Jesus used the term *abba*, he was using a term that was familiar with his hearers as that of father and child. An *abba* is someone who cares and is concerned for the elements of his child's life. The combination of these ideas is similar to the picture we see in the Shona culture regarding fathers. The *baba* is someone, like the *oikodespotes*, who has ultimate authority over the household. But, like an *abba*, he cares so deeply for the household that he is trusted in that position. These are ideals. No human can fully attain the ideal, but God can and has. Would it not be wonderful if the Shona could embrace God as the ultimate father and then teach us how to love and be loved by their *Baba*?

The goal of mission within the Shona Church, then—keeping the father image in mind within the culture—is to gather in family members who are lost, to make contact with potential family members, and to introduce them to their father whom they have forgotten. The goal of the Zimbabwean Shona Church up to now has been inward-facing. Only the missionaries were facing outward, and not very fruitfully. With the renewed awareness of the sacredness of fatherhood coming into light, the whole goal of the Church should shift from inward to outward. Yes, Shona people care for their family, those in their midst and those within reach, but they should also have concern for those who are not in their "family"; since all have the child/Father relationship, all can be considered family. The broadening of acceptable and expected family then becomes a sodality in structure; to some extent, a church within a church, or a family within a family. The goal of mission is still to reach the unreached. For the Shona, this goal should likely be met by family groups, much as we see in the New Testament. Yet, the ability to see their family as part of the larger family, and the mission of the church being to honor and praise the Father by bringing more of his children to him and to live as a proper child should in deference to his/her father, is a new insight that fits contextually within their cultural framework. It remains, however, for the Shona Christians themselves to address the concept of mission, look to the Scriptures, tell and retell their story, and continually come up with new theologies of mission.

IMPLICATIONS FOR TODAY

Because of the way the Shona culture conceptualizes God as Father and fatherliness in general, we as a community of believers around the world can grasp a deeper appreciation of God as our Father. We understand God on a deeper level than ever before. God, our Father, loves his children and cares for them at all costs, always looking to the greater good of the family. Human fathers are not always comparable to the ideal, but our Heavenly Father is.

The father theme among the Shona is a major metaphorical root image, much as Nishioka's rice metaphor is to the Japanese.[28] The Shona father is the axis upon which the Shona culture turns. By highlighting the weightiness of the father in the Shona culture, we can begin to look at mission in a clearer manner.

As we look at the Shona father in context, the motivation for mission should be reassessed. The mission of the church among the Christians in Zimbabwe is no longer simply preaching and the making of new converts (which the missionaries had mistakenly determined it to be) but is rather an effort on the part of the church as the family of God to develop stronger and deeper relationships with God as their father and, from there, reaching out to others who are not yet a part of the family of God. Yes, new converts are desired and sought out, but that is no longer the only mission

28. Nishioka, "Rice and Bread."

motivation. For the motivation for mission, the Shona must look beyond their own family to the families of those who are outside of Christ.

In looking at the significance of the father in the Shona context, it may well be that the fathers, those who are recognized as fathers in the community,—whether pastors, biological fathers, or missionaries and development workers who have taken on the role—should be the ones who are seen as specially called to share the gospel. The entire family of God is responsible to share the gospel, but among the Shona it may be that the fathers can most successfully carry out the mission of God. If that were the case, the impact on the mission of the church would be tremendous. Church members would then approach, convert, and bring converts to the church fathers who, in turn, would teach and advise, just as the culture requires. My personal cultural understanding of individualism fights against this, but in order for the church to be culturally relevant, this is biblically acceptable and appropriate. In spiraling from culture to Scripture and back again, telling and retelling the story, the church must be allowed to find a culturally appropriate and biblically sound approach to worship and mission.

IMPLICATIONS FOR MISSIONARIES AND DEVELOPMENT AGENCIES

Missionaries have long held that they are simply on the field to work themselves out of a job, to become redundant and irrelevant. They have often bemoaned the fact that people are constantly coming to them with their problems, needing help of some sort or asking for money.

In this case, it may be that the Korekore are simply behaving as good children and going to a father with their problems. Culturally, it would be horrible for a child to have a problem or a need and not go to the father. Shona interviewees reiterated again and again that they understood a given father might not be able to help or have the answers to their problems, but they absolutely had to be respectful and go. It would be rude and even unthinkable not to tell their father of their problems. Missionaries, on the other hand, commonly see such requests as people coming for handouts instead of standing on their own two feet. The Shona people do not see it that way. Instead, they are showing love. If the missionary can help, that is great. If not, the missionary should sit and listen and present a caring fatherly attitude. If that is the case, then instead of being frustrated with what the missionaries and development workers see as dependency, possibly the answer is to share tea and talk, always showing the love of a father. This would change how missionaries operate among cultures like the Shona's on a daily basis.

An outsider who becomes aware of the reality of the father in the Shona culture can gradually accept these cultural customs and learn to adapt their thinking. The one difference that stands out for the Shona is the fact that non-biological persons can be adopted into the father structure and become fathers in their own right, commonly without their knowledge or realization. Male missionaries often fall into this family custom without knowing what they are doing. Goodenough's taxonomy of identity, status, and role was the key to navigating this cultural kinship structure. When a man takes on the role and responsibilities of a father—loving, caring, protecting, advising, and so on—he becomes a father to those he is serving. He takes on this identity, often without realizing it.

Missionaries to the Shona often think that when the community keeps coming to them with problems and needs, they are simply demonstrating dependency, and that such dependency must be dealt with appropriately. However, dependency is not the issue here. The real issue is one of respect and honor. Such missionaries have become a father by caring for their children (possibly through development assistance, theological teachings, or much-needed advice and assistance). All Shona know that one must take their problems to their father, not necessarily for assistance, but for advice and because a father loves his children and wants to know what is happening in their lives. The assumption is: "I know he (the missionary) cannot help with this problem, but he is my father and I must tell my father my problems." Missionaries and other development workers must recognize and appreciate the father role within the culture of the Shona people.

IMPORTANT TAKEAWAYS

Not everything about the metaphorical imagery of the Korekore father is ideally relatable to God. As with all cultures, so too in Shona culture. There are both positive and negative aspects of the Korekore father. In the case of viewing God as father, the Korekore have problematic elements. "Fathers always forgive." "*Vana* is *vana*" (Children are children)." "Fathers teach." "Fathers discipline." "Fathers provide." "Fathers always protect." "Fathers always love." These are all characteristics of a true father among the Shona.

Applied to family fathers, those with biological connections easily see the correlation to their lives and their way of seeing the world; to the biological and totem family, the way forward is clear. When applied to the Father God, all of the quotes above are clearly relevant. However, in the cultural understanding of the Shona, there are times when application is more of a challenge. For example, "Fathers always forgive." On the surface, that sounds perfectly natural to apply to God the Father. Surprisingly, over 70 percent of my informants said this saying means that, upon their death and judgment day, if they were deemed in sin and sent from the presence of God the Father, they only had to be patient in hell for a time because "fathers always forgive." God would call them back and forgive them for their errant ways. Further work is needed in this area.

CONCLUSION

Charles Van Engen states that, as people probe into the deep-level meanings of a culture, they will encounter certain themes and motifs that are central to that culture's worldview: "These worldview themes provide the connecting links whereby the self-definition of the people of God at a particular time in biblical history can be associated with the self-definition of the mission of God's people in that new context."[29] Van Engen's statement is clearly true regarding the metaphorical father theme in the Shona context. Because of the way the Shona culture conceptualizes God as Father and fatherness in general, we, the community of believers around the world, can grasp a deeper appreciation of God as our Father. We can conceptualize the nature of God on a deeper level than ever before. God, our Father, loves his children and cares for them at all costs, always looking to the greater good of the family. Human fathers are not always comparable to the ideal, but our Heavenly Father is. As God's workers, examining the larger implications of the reality of who we really are among the people we work with must become a high priority. The actual role of dependency in the fields where we work, especially beyond the Korekore, likely needs to be re-examined.

---

29. Van Engen, *Mission on the Way*, 42.

5

From Missions to Missional

Preparing a Royal Priesthood

EARL LAVENDER

IT IS ALWAYS INTERESTING to note changes made when an author chooses to revise a book, especially if the first version was well received. Gailyn Van Rheenen, a well-known and deeply respected missiologist blessed many preparing for the mission field with his book *Missions: Biblical Foundations and Contemporary Strategies*.[1] I used his book in several mission-related courses I taught at Lipscomb University in the late 1990s and early 2000s. When I heard of its revision, I was immediately interested because I knew of his passion for church planting and his developing understanding of missional theology. I have found his second edition to be all I expected and more.[2] It is not just an updated edition—it is a significant rewriting of the text. Though much information from the first edition is included in the second, Van Rheenen's basic theology of mission manifests a significant development. The new edition presents an approach to missions that is much more participatory and, in my view, compelling. It reveals a move

---

1. Van Rheenen, *Missions*.
2. Van Rheenen, *Missions*, 2nd ed.

from missions to missional, from mission as *proclamation* to mission as *participation* in God's mission to redeem all of creation (*missio Dei*).

In both editions, Van Rheenen provides two varying scenarios with "Jim and Julie." One represents the default missions approach many assume, but one which ultimately proves inadequate. The second scenario for each issue presents a better-informed approach. In the second edition, they are a missionary couple heading to Haiti, in the first to Eastern Europe.[3] Van Rheenen identifies the purpose of his writing in both editions of the book. That purpose is to bring into stark relief important issues the Jim and Julie scenarios demonstrate, which depicts them as willing to dedicate themselves to careful preparation through training and study. The other scenario ("pattern" in the first edition) presents the couple going into the mission field with great hearts and enthusiasm but no training. "This book guides missionaries" is the beginning phrase in both editions, after which Van Rheenen identifies the objectives he hopes the reader will come to realize through this study. In the original work, Van Rheenen states his first objective as helping the missionary readers to "understand purposes of God that empower mission."[4] In the newer edition, he hopes missionaries will "attune their hearts to the missionary narrative of mission in the Bible—to live out the missional stories of *missio Dei*, kingdom of God, incarnation, crucifixion, and resurrection."[5] The second objective of the book in the first edition is "to discern personal motives for carrying the mission of God."[6] This objective is included in his second edition, but he lists it third, after "to spiritually transform their lives into God's likeness."[7] The emphasis of the newer edition is on those training for intercultural missions to actively participate through an ongoing missional narrative that by its nature is spiritually transformative. This goal of missional and spiritual transformation actively embodies God's mission in the world (*missio Dei*) by pursuing God's image as seen in Christ Jesus (*imago Dei*).

Van Rheenen invites readers to participate in the missio Dei through the biblical narrative, a significant development in his paradigm of missions.

---

3. Eastern Europe was the mission trend after the fall of the Berlin Wall and would have been of particular interest in the 1990s. During the writing of the second edition, Haiti would be the more likely mission interest.

4. Van Rheenen, *Missions*, 10.

5. Van Rheenen, *Missions*, 2nd ed., 10.

6. Van Rheenen, *Missions*, 10.

7. Van Rheenen *Missions*, 2nd ed., 10.

This change in understanding coincides with the rapid development of the missional church movement.[8] Responding to the apparent decline of Christian churches in the West, this missional movement attempts to redefine the purpose of the church as an active expression of God's desire to redeem all creation (*missio Dei*). Thus, missions should be at the core of all activities of the church, requiring full engagement of every member in every aspect of their lives in demonstrating God's concern for the lost.

The influence of the missional church movement on Van Rheenen's theology of mission is evident in the content, footnotes, and bibliography of the second edition of *Missions*. In particular, chapter 4, "The Church: God's Embodiment of Mission," demonstrates Van Rheenen's embrace of the foundational principles of the missional church movement. The church as the result of *missio Dei*, the church as the visible manifestation of the kingdom of God, and the church as the continuing incarnation are all characterizations of a community of faith participating in God's mission to redeem creation. These all mirror major themes among prominent proponents of the missional church movement. Missions is no longer treated as a specific activity the church should engage as supporters and senders but rather as the very purpose for which the church exists. That is, the church exists for mission. This same understanding of the church is evident as well in the first chapter, "The Biblical Narrative of Mission: Entering God's Story."[9] Van Rheenen's invitation to missions is a call to participate in the biblical narrative—a way of life rather than a specific vocation. It is no longer the work of the chosen few but the life purpose for every follower of Jesus.

This idea of the "missional calling of God" to all believers permeates the second edition. While the first edition immediately dives into the theological foundation for missions, the second begins with an invitation to join Jim and Julie in "looking at the world through God's eyes."[10] The first edition presents God as "the source of mission."[11] In the second, Van Rheenen recounts the "missionary story of God" into which we are invited.[12] Van

---

8. The beginning or at least the rapid expansion of this movement is often traced back to the publication of Darrell Guder's *Missional Church*.

9. Van Rheenen, *Missions*, 21.

10. Van Rheenen, *Missions*, 2nd ed., 22.

11. Van Rheenen, *Missions*, 14.

12. Van Rheenen, *Missions*, 2nd ed., 22.

Rheenen encourages his readers to "claim the story" by embracing the mission of God (*missio Dei*) as their reason for living.[13]

Chapter 2 is entitled "Spiritual Awakenings for Mission: Reflecting God's Glory."[14] Van Rheenen references the compelling children's book entitled *Hope for the Flowers*, in which a caterpillar learns the true purpose of life. It is a call to "develop wings" by being transformed into the nature of God and embracing God's mission as the purpose for life. Van Rheenen calls his readers to "dream the dream" of walking personally, intimately, and faithfully with God.[15] This new conception of missions calls for a flourishing, intimate relationship with God rather than an obedient response to a call from a distant God to pursue a particular mission. Such a motivation is consistent with this broad shift in missional theology and represents a stark change from Van Rheenen's first edition.

Later in the text, Van Rheenen includes another new chapter entitled "Becoming Incarnational." His treatment of moving beyond identification to incarnation is another helpful construct to encourage the movement towards embodiment of God's missional heart rather than attempting culturally appropriate mission strategies.[16] His exploration of incarnational ministry as redemptive identification by considering Jesus's approach to encountering others is extremely helpful. I cannot help but think how different the history of missions would have been, especially among Churches of Christ, if we had heard this message several generations ago.

MY MOVE FROM MISSIONS TO MISSIONAL

The view of mission as the dynamic expression of God's missional heart has influenced deeply the approach to the undergraduate general Bible requirement at Lipscomb University. It has also affected the curriculum for training students interested in a life of ministry and missions. I am presently the director of missional studies at Lipscomb University. I have been serving in this specific role since 2011. Before that, my title was "director of missions" (1999–2011). When originally asked to consider accepting the role of director of missions (summer of 1999), I agreed to do so—but only under the condition that I could dismantle our missions program as it was then

---

13. Van Rheenen, *Missions*, 2nd ed., 43.
14. Van Rheenen, *Missions*, 2nd ed., 47.
15. Van Rheenen, *Missions*, 2nd ed., 53.
16. See Van Rheenen, *Missions*, 2nd ed., 218–19.

organized. My vision was to take missions from a special concentration in our degree of ministry in the college of Bible and Ministry and instead present missions as the heartbeat of the university—inviting every student to consider their role in God's mission to redeem the brokenness in the world. Even though I did not have the specific language (at that time), my desire at Lipscomb has always been to facilitate a move from missions (as a specific activity) to missional (as a way of life for every follower of Jesus). Rather than preparing a small group of specialized missionaries to be sent, I wanted Lipscomb to prepare and equip a royal priesthood—working to help form a view of life that would bring glory to God for every student in all programs of study offered by the university.[17]

A Brief Autobiographical Journey

I can best explain my arrival at this understanding of mission through a brief autobiographical journey. I was born in Trieste, Italy, to missionary parents. Soon after our family returned to the United States, my parents began taking college students to Italy for the entire summer to support the Italian churches in any way possible. This involved forming a chorus and singing in the town squares, as well as distributing offers for a free Bible correspondence course. This work began in the summer of 1966 and continued for over twenty years. It involved students recruited from Lipscomb, Harding, and Ohio Valley (colleges at that time). For a good portion of my life, I had spent more time in Italy than in the United States.

In my youth, I had no interest in continuing my family's efforts in missions. When we returned from full-time work in Italy, I was in grade school. I threw myself into sports, trying to establish my identity in our new neighborhood in something valued by my new friends. Though I participated in the summer mission efforts to Italy with my family, it was more out of obligation than passion.[18] I wanted to stay home and finish what was an always-shortened baseball season.

---

17. I had already been deeply influenced by significant missional writings such as Newbigin's *Open Secret* and *Gospel in a Pluralist Society*, Bosch's *Transforming Mission*, and Guder's *Missional Church*. Texts like Eph 4:11–16 and 1 Peter chapters 1 and 2, together with the negatives and positives of my experience in missions, were also formative.

18. "Project Italy" was the name of what was then called a "summer campaign." Short-term missions did not yet exist, as least in name.

From Missions to Missional

When I reached college age, I was certain I wanted to coach baseball or basketball. I chose to major in physical education so that I could teach and coach. My mission experiences in the summers were not without blessings. During the summer of my freshman year in college, I met Rebecca Nance (I was attending Ohio Valley College, and Rebecca was a student at David Lipscomb College). We married the summer before my senior year (I was also studying at Lipscomb). My student teaching experience was very positive and turned into a job offer to coach and teach physical education upon graduation. Life was set—or so it seemed.

The summer we were married a devastating earthquake struck northeastern Italy, the region in which I was born and raised. The Project Italy summer campaign group saw some of the devastation. One of the couples who participated (we did not go because of our wedding and the need to work) came back convinced we should start a relief effort for those who had lost their homes and were living in tents. I agreed to help raise money. We found a church willing to collect and forward the funds *if* we would commit to two years following up on the benevolent work by planting a church in that area. Another couple was enthusiastic about the idea. We would go as a team. Rebecca and I initially had no interest. But, through prayer and persuasion, we agreed to go. I would serve on the church staff of the supporting church for a year and do my best to prepare for work I had never anticipated doing. At the last moment, the other couple chose to pursue other opportunities, but Rebecca and I set sail from New York with our nine-month-old daughter, a vehicle, and all our worldly possessions to this new adventure. We were the "Jim and Julie" scenario with enthusiasm but almost no training.[19]

On our arrival, I encountered a unique opportunity. Italy was encouraging the founding of baseball clubs because it would soon be an Olympic sport. I had played baseball through high school and studied coaching baseball in college. The city to which we were moving had a newly founded team. When I inquired if I could be involved, the team owners and players were excited about my participation as a player/coach (manager). This gave me an identity within the community that validated our presence. As we planted and helped grow a small church, I came to realize the importance

---

19. I was the proud owner of the notebook provided by Harding College's 13 in 1 Mission Workshop—but that was the extent of my missions library and training, with the exception of a few poorly written tracts!

of equipping other believers to lead the journey. I never considered myself a missionary or preacher. I could only be what I was (and am)—a coach.

When the time came for our return to the United States almost seven years later, I was not sure what to do during re-entry. David Lipscomb College invited me to be a resident missionary for a two-year appointment. This consisted of teaching a full-time undergraduate course load. I had never taught, at least not in a formal setting. To be honest, we had no other options. David Lipscomb College had just started a new master's program in Bible, and they invited me to consider enrolling since I had no formal biblical training. Once again, I had no interest, but tuition was free, and I did not see a reason to turn down furthering my (woefully inadequate) Bible knowledge. Two weeks into my first formal teaching experience, I found something that gave me more satisfaction than anything I had ever experienced. Helping shape minds around the truth of the gospel—helping college-age students reconsider the secular direction of their lives was thrilling!

After that two-year experience and a master's degree in biblical studies, I knew I wanted to pursue a terminal theological degree so that I could continue to teach. The church that had supported us in Italy asked that we consider planting another church, but this time within driving distance of central Tennessee so they could be actively involved. After a long and sometimes discouraging search (another story for another time), that community was Highland, Illinois. Arriving there just before school began for our children, we set out to plant another church. While I had finished my master's degree in biblical studies, I still had no formal training in missions or church planting. Saint Louis University graciously (and provisionally, with much leveling work required) accepted me into their PhD program in historical theology.

We knew from the beginning that our role in this new church would be that of equipping. We took very seriously the teachings of Eph 4:11–16. I was convinced each person God led into our community of faith had gifts entrusted to them, and it was the responsibility of the church not only to help them develop those gifts but to give them opportunities to utilize them to God's glory. It was the responsibility of the leaders of that community to equip a "priesthood of believers." That community grew quickly and flourished. We were practicing missional principles without yet knowing the missionally coded language.

A Missional University?

After completing my PhD work, a church in Nashville invited me to join their staff as the "minister of community outreach." A significant element of the invitation was the opportunity to teach as an adjunct at Lipscomb. After eight years of a divided life of church ministry and university teaching, Lipscomb invited me to consider a full-time teaching position as "director of missions." Because of my experience in church planting both in Italy and Illinois, I was particularly intrigued by the possibilities of reshaping the curriculum around all vocations being a part of the mission of God. The *Missional Church*, edited by Darrell Guder and George Hunsberger, had just been published. I had encountered Dallas Willard's *Divine Conspiracy* and Lesslie Newbigin's *The Gospel in a Pluralist Society*, as well as *The Open Secret*. In short, my worldview had been transformed into the wonder of participating in *missio Dei*. I was now focused on how I could bring a missional perspective to all my work.

This, perhaps, is where I begin a journey slightly different than that of Van Rheenen. Though I know from my personal discussions with Van Rheenen that he fundamentally agrees with my approach (he has been a great encouragement and conversation partner with me in this), my ultimate dream was that missions would be removed from the Bible department and become instead the heartbeat of the university. I did not want to train just "Jim and Julie" to plant churches by living missional lives—I wanted every student at Lipscomb to discover or at least consider the possibility of living missionally through every conceivable major and vocation as the continuing creative work of God in the world. This would necessitate a significant change to our Bible curriculum, especially in our general education requirements. As Lipscomb continued to grow and our student body became more diverse, this change became critical to our survival as a college within the university. Survey courses which assumed a certain amount of Bible literacy were ineffective and even counter-productive. Through the courageous leadership of Dr. Terry Briley, then the dean, we retitled our core required Bible courses as "The Story of Jesus," "The Story of the Church," and "The Story of Israel." The idea was to invite our students to consider the narrative of the Bible. As the great missiologist Lesslie Newbigin insists, it is in fact the true story of the world into which we are invited to participate.

During that same time, missions at Lipscomb was taking on a very different role. There are so many heroes to list in this development that I fear leaving out someone. But to avoid the misperception that any of this is due to my brilliance, know the move from missions to missional at Lipscomb could not have occurred without the Spirit providing amazing participants along the way.

As I continued to develop my understanding and teaching on missions and evangelism, students who caught the vision became major players. Matt Rehbein, a future missionary to Brazil, then an undergraduate student, helped me develop a student-led interest group in missions. Jeff Fincher, after graduating, came to me and asked if he could help me develop the missional vision further. He knew I had no budget, so he offered to raise his own salary if I would allow him to join the effort. And so he did! Mark Jent made the same offer a year later. We began to build on former short-term mission efforts by students based on their vocational interests. Steve Sherman, a former missionary to Nicaragua joined our faculty as a missionary in residence. The entire mission program was largely led by non-paid faculty being trained by our volunteer staff. The unifying vision was giving every student the opportunity to taste a life focused on this mission of God, preferably through their future vocational interests.

Lipscomb's budding school of engineering jumped on board with the missional vision early in the game. With the help of Steve Sherman, they began carefully planning engineering projects in Nicaragua. Then student Kris Hatchell became instrumental in organizing and participating in this effort. Ultimately, this led to the founding of the Peugeot Center for Engineering Service in Developing Communities.[20] The incredible number of projects done over the years by our engineering students is a study within itself. I personally experienced students in my Bible courses coming to faith in Jesus because of these missional engineering projects.

Other colleges and co-curricular entities were catching this missional vision. Our athletic teams began going on mission trips under the guidance of Chris Klotz and Shannon O'Brien, directors of spiritual formation for men's and women's athletics. This is another story that deserves a major study because of its amazing results. Many athletes come to Lipscomb with little or no religious interest but quickly find the story of God through a compelling mission experience. I receive almost weekly emails of another athlete being baptized because of Chris and Shannon's dedication to missional principles.

---

20. https://www.lipscomb.edu/peugeot

Rob Touchstone helped develop and now leads a business as missions (BAM) program unlike any other. His class on entrepreneurship is one of Lipscomb's most popular courses. His founding of the coffee shop The Well[21] is a wonderful example of creative thinking in the business arena that has led many to embrace the mission of God. Our School of Pharmacy and School of Nursing, as well as other colleges, have also embraced the missional vision.

We have much work yet to do. But the missional vision at Lipscomb University is spreading. In one of the courses I have been blessed to create, Faith and Culture, I directly challenge students (general education students) to consider their navigation of culture through the lens of the kingdom of God. It is one of the courses in the six-course general education Bible requirement. Generally, students take this course following the narrative courses (The Story of Israel, Jesus, and the Church). The question in this course is, "Now that you know the biblical narrative, what would it look like to engage culture as a follower of Jesus?" I use Andy Crouch's excellent book *Culture Making: Discovering Our Creative Calling*.[22] After defining culture and reviewing the compelling missional narrative of the Bible, I lead the students through assessment exercises that lead to a final personal life valuation. We compare contemporary cultural artifacts and values to those Jesus invites us to produce and embody. I recognize the power differential—I know students tend to produce the work they believe their professor will endorse. But I have designed the course so that students are allowed anonymity in their final evaluations of the process.

I have found the outcomes of this course to be compelling. I do not have the time here to expound on the many stories of transformative conversion experiences. Here are the basic presuppositions and objectives of the study:

1. Every person is handcrafted by God, entrusted with gifts/abilities that need to be discovered and developed. This is their "God-image" that will ultimately bless the world when accomplished.

2. Each student should find "the best possible version of themselves"— and the accompanying life of *shalom* (meaningful and flourishing relationship with God, humankind, and creation).

---

21. https://wellcoffeehouse.com.
22. Crouch, *Culture Making*.

3. We each choose a narrative in which to live (a validating narrative, language house, probability structure, social imaginary, faith—all these are functional equivalents).

4. The trajectory of our lives and the artifacts we produce will be determined by the story we choose to pursue.

5. There is no greater story for humankind than that which Jesus came to inaugurate—finding our created purpose through learning kenotic living as we walk daily and purposefully with Jesus.

Their final exercise is to identify the vocation they are considering and then determine:

1. The potential of that vocation for being a part of God's continuing creative work (its creational *telos*).

2. Ways in which this vocation has been distorted and twisted by sin and idolatry.

3. Meaningful ways to be a healing influence within that vocation (taking into consideration what I call the spiritual Hippocratic oath "to do no harm"—or Paul's admonition to speak only that which is for the "building up" [Eph 4:29]).

My last question on their life valuation is to complete this thought: "If I embrace the narrative that I am created to continue the creative activity of God (created in God's image), I perceive my gift of creativity activity through my vocation to . . . ."

I am deeply encouraged by the responses. Almost all students want to live out the mission of God through their vocations. They want to make the world a better place. They want to bring *shalom* to the world. Whether they understand the language, they intuitively want to be "ministers of reconciliation" and "a royal priesthood."

A CONCLUDING CHALLENGE

Herein lies the problem. Once students catch a vision of what they could be in God's narrative and are immersed into this new life of Spirit-led missional living, where do they go to church? Once the newly baptized athlete returns from their mission experience to campus, what church will invite them to similar activities of ministry? As in many congregations throughout the

Nashville area, the idea of a good college ministry is to have a gifted teacher offer a compelling study to students during the Bible study hour. We need to rethink this approach. Students are not generally looking for *another* class to attend and in which to simply passively listen, no matter how gifted the teacher. They want to make a difference in the world for God's glory.

My experience with undergraduate students fuels my conviction that the gospel is a powerful and transformative force. But it is so much more than an offer for life after death in heaven—it is an offer for life after one's death to the self-centered narratives of this world through baptism. It is an offer for meaningful life lived pursuing the missional purposes of God. Shouldn't this be the work of the church?

This is the sense I get from reading Van Rheenen's description of missional communities.[23] The church is to be both sent and sending. It should be the community where people discover their contributive purpose to the mission of God.

The practices of contemporary Christianity and the general organization of churches will likely not produce the church described in Eph 4:11–16. For the most part, in my observation, leaders are not equippers for missional living. They are more focused on Sunday activities than equipping each part of the body for their unique purpose in Christ's active body. God's mission will never be accomplished through the specialized few. We need all to be equipped to embrace our unique God-imaged giftedness. Ephesians 4:16 indicates this as the natural path to growth.

Moving from missions to missional calls us to seriously consider what a "priesthood of believers" could and should be. The most underutilized resource in the world is the God-imager who "comes to worship" to passively receive rather than coming to be equipped to live a life of worship—embracing *missio Dei*.

---

23. Van Rheenen, *Missions*, 2nd ed., 373–417.

6

Let My People Go!

Diaspora Mission in the North American Context

DANIEL A. RODRIGUEZ

FOR THE PAST TWO decades, colleagues in the Lausanne Movement, the Evangelical Missiological Society, and elsewhere have been contributing to a growing body of literature in the relatively new field of "diaspora missiology." In 2009, "The Seoul Declaration on Diaspora Missiology" affirmed that this discipline "has emerged as a biblical and strategic field of missiology, defined as a missiological framework for understanding and participating in God's redemptive mission among people living outside their place of origin."[1] My goal here is to advance the diaspora discourse among members of the Stone-Campbell Movement in the United States by drawing attention to the evangelistic opportunities and theological insights presented by the growing and diverse diaspora communities originating in Latin America and the Caribbean.

Concerning the field of diaspora missiology, Enoch Wan observes that "the tasks of missiologist and missions leaders are to realize the scale, frequency and intensity of people moving both internally and internationally. They are, not only demographically to describe and analyze such

---

1. Hartwell, "Seoul Declaration."

phenomenon [sic], but to also responsibly conduct missiological research and wisely describe mission strategy accordingly."[2] Therefore, I will first describe and analyze the relevant demographic phenomena among Latinos[3] in the US then describe mission strategies that inform holistic mission and ministry *to* and *through* diaspora communities today. In the words of our esteemed colleague Gailyn Van Rheenen, my ultimate desire and goal is to "equip leaders to plant and renew hundreds of churches, thereby catalyzing movements of discipleship and mission."[4]

RELEVANT DEMOGRAPHIC PHENOMENA

In *The Changing Face of World Missions*, Michael Pocock, Gailyn Van Rheenen, and Douglas McConnell explain the impact of globalization and changing demographics on Christian ministry worldwide.[5] One result of globalization[6] in the twenty-first century is the unprecedented human migration occurring in our world. In 2020, worldwide, the number of people residing in a country other than their country of birth reached a historic high of more than 280.6 million. However, over the past decades, the share of the world's population that consists of international immigrants has remained stable at 3 percent.[7] Closer to home, the United States leads the world with the largest foreign-born population. The Pew Research Center reports that in 2018 a record 44.8 million immigrants were living in the

---

2. Wan, "Diaspora Missiology," 6.

3. *Hispanic, Latino/a/x*: These terms are used interchangeably to refer to all individuals of Latin American ancestry or with ties to the Spanish-speaking world who reside either legally or illegally within the borders of the United States of America. While about 25 percent of Latinos are aware of the term Latinx, just 3 percent say they use it to describe themselves, a share that is similar across all major demographic subgroups (Lopez et al., "Who is Hispanic?"). In this paper, I will use *Latino* as a noun (e.g., native-born Latinos/as) and *Hispanic* as an adjective (e.g., Hispanic churches). Any prolonged debate over which terms should be used is self-defeating because all three terms ultimately fail to deal with the complexity of the Hispanic experience in the United States.

4. Van Rheenen, *Missions*, 17.

5. Pocock et al., *Changing Face of World Missions*, chs. 1–2.

6. "Taken as a whole, globalization is a trend, compressed interaction between peoples, cultures, governments and transnational companies. It is a heightened multi-directional flow of ideas, material goods, symbols and power facilitated by the Internet and other communication, technologies, and travel" (Pocock et al., *Changing Face of World Missions*, 23).

7. Global Migration Data Analysis Center.

US, representing 13.7 percent of the total population. This means that the foreign-born[8] population has more than quadrupled since 1960 when only 9.7 million immigrants lived in the US, accounting for only 5.4 percent of the total US population.[9] While growth in the number of immigrants living in the United States has begun to slow in recent years, the US Census Bureau projects that number will double by 2065.[10]

In 2018, the largest share of immigrants in the US were Asians (28 percent) followed by Mexicans (25 percent) and other Latin Americans (25 percent), while Europeans, Canadians, and other North American immigrants accounted for just 13 percent of the immigrant population. Of the 44.8 million immigrants living in the US in 2018, only 25 percent (12.2 million) were undocumented.[11] Mexicans accounted for 52 percent (4.9 million) of all undocumented immigrants, while another 3.2 million undocumented immigrants were from Central America, South America, and the Caribbean.[12] However, it would be a mistake to assume that the majority of Latinos in the US are undocumented immigrants or immigrants at all. In 2017, there were nearly 60 million Latinos in the United States, representing approximately 18 percent of the total US population. However, only 33 percent of the US Hispanic population was foreign-born.[13] The remainder of this chapter will focus on diaspora missions among the 33 percent of the Hispanic population in the US that is foreign born, including 8.1 million undocumented immigrants from Mexico, Central America, South America, and the Caribbean.

Missiologists associated with the Lausanne Movement insist, "The current global phenomenon of diaspora is a God-initiated and God-orchestrated missional moment in contemporary history."[14] This perspective on diaspora missions is validated by many examples found in the New

---

8. The US Census Bureau uses the term *foreign-born* to refer to anyone who is not a US citizen at birth. This includes naturalized US citizens, lawful permanent residents (immigrants), temporary migrants (such as foreign students), humanitarian migrants (such as refugees and asylees), and unauthorized migrants (United States Census Bureau, "About the Foreign-Born Population").

9. Budiman et al., "Facts on U.S. Immigrants, 2018."

10. Brown and Stepler, "Statistical Portrait."

11. Pew Research Center, "Facts on U.S. Immigrants, 2018."

12. Lopez et al., "Key Facts about the Changing U.S. Unauthorized Immigrant Population."

13. Pew Research Center, "Facts on Latinos in the U.S."

14. Tira, "Diasporas from Cape Town."

Testament, especially in the book of Acts. In fact, it is impossible to overestimate the value of diaspora mission in the spreading of the gospel as recounted in Acts. For example, the primary audience of Peter and the apostles on the day of Pentecost (Acts 2:5–11) consisted of diaspora Jews from throughout the Greco-Roman world. Furthermore, diaspora Jews including Steven, Philip, Barnabas, Paul, Timothy, Lydia, Aquila, Priscilla, and Apollos were instrumental in reaching fellow Jews in the region.

Informed by the example of the early church and contemporary diaspora missions, Enoch Wan identifies three types of diaspora missions. The first two are readily evident in mission and ministry among Hispanic diaspora communities in the US.

1. Mission *to* the diaspora (e.g., foreign-born Latinos reaching other foreign-born Latinos in the US)

2. Mission *through* the diaspora (e.g., diaspora Latinos reaching their *paisanos* [relatives] wherever they are in the world, especially in their country of origin)

3. Mission *by* and *beyond* the diaspora (e.g., motivating and mobilizing diaspora Latinos for cross-cultural mission)[15]

Due to limited space and reliable data, I will focus my attention on mission *to* and *through* the Latin-American diaspora in the US.

MISSION TO THE LATIN-AMERICAN DIASPORA IN THE US

During the past two decades, Protestant and evangelical scholars have focused considerable attention on mission *to* the Latin American diaspora in the US.[16] Research indicates churches that target foreign-born Spanish-dominant Latinos continue to multiply and grow in the United States. Like diaspora communities elsewhere in the world, when migrants from Latin America come to the US, they typically look for and gather with compatriots for mutual support and companionship. The need for community in a strange and often hostile environment facilitates evangelism

---

15. See Wan et al., *Diaspora Missiology*, 6.

16. See Ortiz, *Hispanic Challenge*; Espinosa, *Latino Pentecostals in America*; Martinez, *Walk with the People*; Mulder et al., *Latino Protestants in America*; Martinez, *Story of Latino Protestants in the United States*.

and the formation of new churches that cater to members of specific ethnic groups (e.g., Mexicans, Guatemalans, Cubans, Puerto Ricans, etc.). Familiar language, values, cultural idiosyncrasies, and worship styles from the country of origin also enhance the appeal of diaspora churches among the unchurched.[17]

In 2019, a LifeWay study sponsored by the Send Institute at Wheaton College's Billy Graham Center surveyed more than 200 Hispanic church plants from fourteen Protestant denominations. Researchers discovered that 94 percent of the founding or lead pastors were Hispanic, and 80 percent were foreign-born. Pastors surveyed estimated that 89 percent of their congregation was Hispanic, and that two-thirds (66 percent) were born outside of the US, while 22 percent were native-born (i.e., second- and third-generation Latinos). Clearly, this is an example of mission *to* the diaspora (e.g., foreign-born Latinos reaching other foreign-born Latinos in the US). The LifeWay study also revealed that these underfunded church plants were more effective than well-funded church plants among the dominant group when measured by the average number of first-time professions of faith among previously unchurched Latinos.[18]

Notwithstanding the success of ministry to the Latin-American diaspora, demographic changes in the Hispanic population of the United States are forcing church leaders to reconsider historic paradigms in Hispanic ministry. My research during the past decade has focused on Hispanic evangelical churches that are responding in creative and contextually appropriate ways to the demographic and linguistic changes taking place in some of the oldest and largest Hispanic communities in the United States, including Los Angeles, New York, Houston, Chicago, Dallas/Fort Worth, Miami, Phoenix, and San Antonio. I have observed that when considering Hispanic ministry in the United States, many denominational and local church leaders continue to equate Hispanic ministry with ministry conducted almost exclusively in Spanish. While this approach continues to be very effective for reaching and nurturing the faith of first-generation Latinos, it is generally not successful when targeting the growing number of native-born English-dominant Latinos in the United States.[19]

---

17. Downes, "Mission by and Beyond," 79.

18. See LifeWay Research, "New Hispanic Churches"; McNeel, "Latino Immigrants Are Evangelizing America."

19. See Rodriguez, "Multigenerational Hispanic Ministry," 11–35; Rodriguez, "Hispanic Youth Ministry in the USA."

The dilemma I discovered is that conventional Spanish-speaking ministry models are unintentionally designed to preserve the language and cultural preferences of foreign-born Latinos. Sadly, this is usually done at the expense of their native-born English-dominant children and grandchildren. Though they represent more than 65 percent of all Latinos in this country, native-born Latinos, especially those who are English-dominant, have been largely ignored by denominational and local church leaders who uncritically equate "Hispanic ministry" with "Spanish-language ministry." Like the Greek-speaking Jews described in Acts 6:1–4, "Hellenistic Latinos" (i.e., English-dominant Latinos) are often overlooked, at least insofar as most Hispanic Protestant, evangelical, and Pentecostal churches are concerned.

My research has identified a rapidly growing number of Hispanic evangelical congregations that strategically moved beyond "Spanish-speaking ministry models" toward different "multigenerational and multilingual models." The new models seek to address the needs of two or even three different generations of Latinos under the same roof where the linguistic and cultural preferences of each generation are accommodated in an effort to become "all things to all Latinos," where language is not a barrier.[20]

MISSION THROUGH THE LATIN-AMERICAN DIASPORA IN THE UNITED STATES

More recently, Latinos in the US have recognized the opportunities to do mission *through* the diaspora. Hispanic church leaders observe that continued immigration from Latin America and the Caribbean reinforces the cultural values, traditions, and language preferences of immigrants living as "foreigners and aliens" in the United States. This is particularly evident in communities throughout California and the Southwest with large immigrant populations from Mexico. The same is true in south Florida where many immigrants from Cuba reside. Similar observations are made by pastors in Orlando, the Southside of Chicago, and the Bronx, New York, where continued migration from Puerto Rico reinforces the values, language, and practices of the immigrant generation.

The cultural values, traditions, and language of immigrants from Latin America and the Caribbean are also reinforced by improvements in international transportation and by advances in telecommunications,

---

20. See Rodriguez, *Future for the Latino Church*.

especially the smartphone. Thanks to smarter phones and inexpensive data and cell phone plans, immigrants can instantly communicate via text, voice calls, and emails with the touch of a button. Video chat applications including Skype, Facebook Messenger, FaceTime, and Google Hangouts allow Hispanic immigrants and many of their second-generation children to maintain close relationships with family and friends in their countries of origin, thereby creating and nurturing transnational identities. Smartphone applications and social media help immigrants to cross the border into the United States and still preserve the values, traditions, and language of their countries of origin while simultaneously creating new hyphenated identities *en el extranjero* (abroad in a foreign land).[21]

A growing number of Hispanic church leaders recognize the transnational character of the Latin American diaspora as a blessing in disguise. They are now considering creative ways to leverage the transnational character of many first-generation Latinos. These congregational leaders recognize what Enoch Wan refers to as "the immense potential of 'diaspora missions' in ministering to diaspora and ministering through diaspora." Not only is it true that "people on the move are receptive to the Gospel"; but now, thanks to the proliferation of smartphones and the worldwide popularity of social media, the Latin American diaspora in the US is spreading the gospel throughout Latin America and the rest of the world, particularly among millennials.[22]

For instance, thanks to video chat applications and social media sites including Facebook and Twitter, Sixto Rivera encourages members of his church in Dallas to share their new-found faith under the lordship of Jesus Christ with family and friends back in El Salvador. Ongoing relationships between expatriates living in Dallas and their homelands have led to fruitful mission trips to Central America that have resulted in many conversions and the planting of missional communities where holistic spiritual formation is promoted, modeled, and nurtured with strong and mutually-beneficial ties to the Salvadoran diaspora in Dallas.[23] The availability of ever-improving video-conferencing applications like Zoom and GoTo-Meeting helps Rivera and his team to facilitate discovery Bible studies and even recruit, train, and coach church planters in Central America from his desk in Dallas. Similarly, leaders at the Sunset Church of Christ in Miami

---

21. Castor, "Mapping the Diaspora with Facebook©," 21.
22. Wan, "Global People and Diaspora Missiology," 95, 99.
23. Sixto Rivera, interview by Daniel A. Rodriguez, October 15, 2016.

encourage members of the Latin American diaspora to use social media strategically to stay connected to friends and family back home. They then make annual mission trips to Latin America planned and led by Christians who are members of the Central and South American diaspora communities in south Florida.[24] Another Hispanic church near Fort Lauderdale, Florida, encourages members of the Latin American diaspora to utilize their smartphone video chat apps, as well as Twitter and Facebook, to introduce people back home to their new church in South Florida, directing interested family members and friends to websites where they find links to helpful resources, including contact information for missional churches in the countries of origin.[25]

Enoch Wan reminds us that diaspora mission challenges "the traditional missiological distinction between 'foreign mission' and local missions," replacing it with "a 'multi-directional' conceptualization of 'world missions.'"[26] This is also evident in mission efforts initiated in Latin America by Christians putting family and friends living in the United States in contact with Christians who are members of churches among the Latin American diaspora. Once again, it is impossible to overstate how invaluable smartphone app usage has been in efforts to reach immigrants with the gospel, especially those who have recently arrived in the United States.

DIASPORA MISSION IS A BIBLICAL PARADIGM

It should come as no surprise that mission *to* and *through* diaspora believers has proven effective particularly among first-generation Latino Christians in the US. Recall that diaspora believers were critical in the expansion of the early church as it is recorded in Acts. For example, Stephen attempted to reach Greek-speaking diaspora Jews residing in Jerusalem (Acts 6). Additionally, note how after his conversion on the road to Damascus, Saul of Tarsus immediately began mission *to* the Jewish diaspora in Damascus (Acts 9:19–21). Later, Luke tells us that during the first missionary journey, Barnabas and Saul would first target Jews living in the diaspora (Acts 13:13–15; 14:1). During his second missionary journey, targeting diaspora Jews became a custom (Acts 17:1–4, 10–12, 17; 18:4; 19:9). And the book

---

24. See Sunset Church of Christ, Miami, Florida, at https://www.sunsetmiami.org/ministries.

25. Sixto Rivera, interview.

26. Wan, "Phenomenon of Diaspora."

of Acts concludes with Paul meeting in Rome with local Jewish leaders (28:17).

Similarly, mission *by* and *beyond* the diaspora also has precedents in the early church. Most notably, it was in Antioch of Syria where Greek-speaking Jewish refugees for the first time targeted Greek-speaking Gentiles (Acts 11:19–21). Shortly thereafter, Paul and Barnabas were sent from Antioch to participate in mission *to* and *through* the Jewish diaspora (Acts 13:1–3). Church-planting among diaspora Jews led to mission *beyond* the Jewish diaspora to include God-fearing Greeks (Acts 13:26, 43–48; 14:1; 16:14; 17:4, 12, 17; 18:4, etc.) and ultimately to unbelieving and pagan Greeks (Acts 13:6–12; 14:8–18; 16:25–35; 17:25–34).

MISSION BY AND BEYOND THE LATIN-AMERICAN DIASPORA IN THE UNITED STATES

The biblical precedent for mission *by* and *beyond* the diaspora as well as the growing and urgent need for cross-cultural mission draws attention to the tremendous potential of diaspora believers and churches for reaching other immigrant communities in the US and abroad. Missiologists like Jessica Udall insist that "believing immigrants may be the American church's greatest asset in effectively reaching the world on their doorstep."[27]

Unfortunately, globally and domestically, very few diaspora churches are effectively reaching people from other cultures with the gospel. While one might look at Central American diaspora churches reaching the Ethiopian diaspora in Los Angeles as an exemplary manifestation of this outreach, finding similar examples poses a challenge. Language barriers and cultural bias are among the most formidable barriers to mission *by* and *beyond* the diaspora.[28]

CONCLUSION

In honor of our colleague Gailyn Van Rheenen, this chapter seeks to advance the conversation and research in the area of the diaspora mission in the North American context, especially among members of the Stone-Campbell Movement in the United States. In response to the unprecedented

27. Udall, "Ethiopian Diaspora," 183.
28. Downes, "Mission by and Beyond," 78–81.

human migration occurring in our world, especially to the United States, I have drawn attention to the evangelistic opportunities and theological challenges presented by the growing and diverse diaspora communities originating in Latin America and the Caribbean. I have also drawn attention to biblical paradigms of mission that find analogous situations among diaspora communities in the United States today. Each suggests that rather than consider the growing numbers of foreign-born residents as a threat to our national identity and security, disciples of Jesus must consider the possibility that we are witnessing a "God-initiated and God-orchestrated missional moment in contemporary history"[29] designed to mobilize diaspora Christians to participate in creative and unprecedented ways in the mission of God to "gather up all things in [Christ], things in heaven and things in earth" (Eph 1:10 NRSV).

Notwithstanding the socioeconomic, cultural, and linguistic barriers preventing diaspora Christian communities from engaging in cross-cultural mission, such communities still represent the best hope of reaching unreached peoples in the US as well as in restricted-access countries.

In order to facilitate mission *by* and *beyond* the diaspora, Hispanic church leaders need to understand the incredible potential their congregations have to participate in the mission of God. Like the unnamed refugees in Acts 11:19–21, many foreign-born Latinos come to the US as disciples or soon become disciples through the efforts of their *paisanos*. Their biological and cultural *mestizaje*, as well as their bilingualism, uniquely positions them to reach immigrant groups feared and marginalized by many dominant-group Christians in the US. Like the early church, believers in the Latin-American diaspora must continue to participate in mission *to* and *through* the diaspora. But like first-century Jews living in the diaspora, the Latin-American diaspora must also embrace the challenge and opportunity to engage in mission *by* and *beyond* the diaspora, reaching other immigrants as well as those of their own culture.

---

29. Tira, "Diasporas from Cape Town 2010 to Manila 2015 and Beyond."

7

Understanding by Movement

Seeking Sensible Interdependence for Latino and Hispanic Missionaries

J. OMAR PALAFOX

IN LATIN AMERICA, MISSIONARIES tend to be traditionally trained in Anglo-American-based biblical institutes with a slight preference for framing a contextual missional understanding. This education, however, often falls short, leaving them lacking a deeper understanding of the contexts they serve. This traditional training practice to missiology has engaged contexts through people, primarily Anglo-Americans, who take the gospel to Latin American contexts and invest in learning the culture, language, and historical backgrounds. These missionaries then transplant doctrine already established as truth to them, expecting it to be replicated. Although expatriate cross-cultural servants demonstrated goodwill and noble intentions, they have often wrought tension and created frustration with the residents in these contexts.

Worsening this dynamic, the emerging generation of Latino and Hispanic (LATHIS) missionaries, the result of the efforts of these Anglo-Americans, cross borders in their own countries only to intensify tensions and frustrations because these local missionaries lack an understanding of LATHIS theology.[1] Such Latino missionaries are often stressed and frustrated since they are not Anglo-American. They are expected to keep traditional Anglo-American practices and doctrinal positions without adequately considering their contexts. For example, this context in Latin America (and recently the US) is characterized by tensions and frustrations between the Catholic theology known as *Teología de Liberación* (Liberation) and the evangelical theology *Misión Integral* (Integral), respectively. Exacerbating these intercultural problems presents a missiological situation in the Americas that reminisces a history characterized by opposing viewpoints, dissonance, rising discouragement, and, in many cases, the end of churches. Globalization and social engagement have recently expanded communication between LATHIS missionaries, facilitating more extensive engagement among themselves. There is a vast wealth of 500 years of LATHIS perspectives for training others to be missional. This includes at least the considerable impact of theologians such as Ignatius of Loyola, Sor Juana Inés de la Cruz, John of the Cross, Bartolome de las Casas, and others. The spiritual capital from these LATHIS sources serves a crucial role in the church for improved contextualization. To remedy these traditional, historical, and contextual stresses and strains, a new implementation of movement to these theological capitals must commence. I argue that *understanding* formed by sensible, interdependent movement can foster a healthy and stable spirit while continually serving God's mission. To develop this notion of *understanding by movement*, I present these fast-growing connections between growing LATHIS theological tensions, and the movement between these considerations using Gailyn Van Rheenen's missional helix.

Physical exercise improves and strengthens a person with stability, balance, and coordination. The performance of action for our purposes is not a physical motion that is required. Instead, it is an *epistemological* interaction with these tensions and frustrations with an attitude of dependence on others with empathy or *sensible interdependence* (SI).[2] In other words, it is to understand all the related theories of knowledge, especially regarding their methods, validity, and scope, as well as a distinction between justified

---

1. With this term, I am combining all practical theology found within 500 years of Latin and Hispanic traditions. This topic covers a wide range of traditions and teachings that deserve more attention, but that is for another context.

2. The concept of sensible interdependence (SI) is a reflection I have taken from my dissertation at Fuller Theological Seminary. See Palafox, "Seeking Sensible Interdependency."

belief and opinion. These are people, priorities, practices, and proficiencies found already present in the 500-year history of LATHIS theology.

In the context of missiology, Gailyn Van Rheenen has created the missional helix (MH), which has similar benefits to its helical movement. Using the MH to frame a missional understanding of Latino SI with perspicacity intentionally and continuously, LATHIS missionaries can gain proficiency in establishing a balanced spiritual experience in a context-appropriate manner while participating in God's mission.

Sensibility speaks to a stance of empathy that brings out real emotions and attitudes from a unique LATHIS experience. What SI does is incorporates physical and spiritual stability with everyday engagements and communal conditions. Without this capacity for *sensible interdependence*, the missionary misses valuable missional pieces located in their exclusive context. Seeking to understand this type of SI blesses the missionary, their family, and the church. One should ask: What are the causes and effects of importing a theology that ignores context? How does it relate to the training models used in the Restoration Movement? What benefits does LATHIS theology offer in terms of capital wealth to the field of missiology? What can cultural capital do to help bridge the gap in church growth today? And more importantly, how can it address the present concerns among LATHIS missionaries?

THE MISSIONAL HELIX

According to Van Rheenen, all missionaries must listen to God and discern his voice through the MH.[3] Van Rheenen's MH provides a missional priority in the learning model that progressively forms the Christian servant contextually.

All this learning happens transformatively while having a covenant with God and Jesus.[4] The MH is an integrative learning model that emphasizes incarnational theology, requiring missional movement between its parts in a spiral form. Van Rheenen explains the missionary's activity using the helix as continuously coiling through its four parts: "theological reflection, cultural analysis, historical perspective, and strategy formation."[5] He further explains that this helical movement is persistent and progressive,

---

3. Van Rheenen, *Missions*, 307.
4. Van Rheenen, *Missions*, 309.
5. Van Rheenen, *Missions*, 308–9.

useful as a "model for theological education."[6] Van Rheenen comprehends the "environment of spiritual formation"[7] not as a goal or result but as the *sine qua non* of the spiraling process. Spiritual formation is the background in which missionaries listen to God and spiritually discern his voice within the MH. The continuous and progressive movement begins with theological reflection, then cultural analysis, followed by the historical perspective, and strategy formation. Then the spiraling reset again with theological reflection. Theological reflection addresses the gods or God, demons, and powers in the kingdom of God. Cultural analysis helps define terms and language usage. Historical perspective aids in worldviews and perceptions contrasting secular and Christian narratives. Lastly, strategy formation fosters Christ-formed ministries, truth, context, and biblical strategies.

FIGURE 1

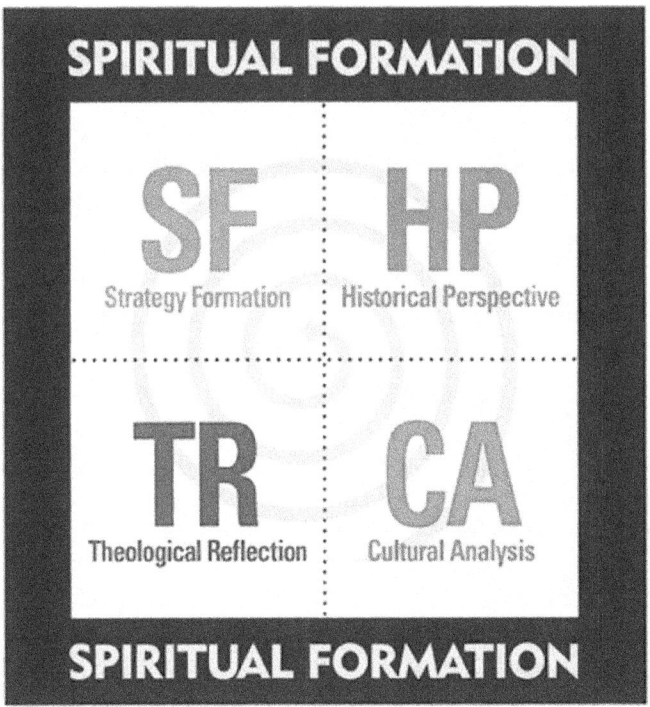

---

6. Van Rheenen, *Missions*, 320.
7. Van Rheenen, *Missions*, 311–12.

Missional Life in Practice and Theory

The Missional Helix in the Environment of Spiritual Formation[8]

Continual movement through the MH brings transformation[9] connected to the biblical image of Christ.[10] It is rooted in the value of the Holy Scriptures as the guide during spiritual formation to begin, but not as the only source for theological comprehension. The essential difference between the MH and other missional interpretations is that the former is not inert like a list or linear steps. Instead, the helix is constantly moving and active. The MH creates ongoing contextual conversations.[11] The intentional movement reflects through its four parts and can shape the "practice of ministry"[12] for an adequate understandings of multiple contexts. Missionaries benefit from the MH, empowering and adjusting their focus on God (theology). In turn, these adjustments help them plant "churches that are rooted in the mission of God rather than in presuppositions of popular culture."[13] Its use benefits intercultural work to form an understanding with intention in the mission of God.[14] The missional reflection is beneficial to missionaries who engage in cultural adjustments in ministry instead of pop culture.[15]

As missionaries serve, their service must be steady and continuous, and the attitude with which they serve can either make or break their best efforts. Missionaries must be able to move missionally from quadrant to quadrant in the MH with a SI attitude within their immediate contexts. When missionaries have this mindset of SI motion, they can appropriately establish, balance, and coordinate spiritual understanding contextually while participating in the mission of God because it improves contextualization.[16] Unfortunately, whether for personal or circumstantial reasons, many LATHIS lack understanding and suffer while serving, neglecting themselves and their families, often leaving them in unhealthy circumstances

---

8. Van Rheenen, *Missions*, 308.

9. Van Rheenen, *Missions*, 317.

10. 2 Cor 3:18a.

11. Stetzer and Putman, *Breaking the Missional Code*, 53.

12. Van Rheenen, *Missions*, 310.

13. Van Rheenen, *Missions*, 311.

14. Horton, *Portable Seminary*, 547.

15. Horton, *Portable Seminary*, 308.

16. Theology is contextual by its very nature. Taking a text seriously isn't just an academic exercise. It's also a social, economic, and political one. David Bosch offers valuable perspicuity into the qualities of the missio Dei. Bosch, *Transforming Mission*, 433.

because they seek to keep a traditional training system to missiology. This neglect of LATHIS theologies repeatedly leads to increased tensions in personal and family relationships. It can produce pressure within the missionary's context and lead to bewilderingly different forms of theological understandings. Therefore, understanding formed by sensible, interdependent, and missional movement can foster a healthy and stable spirit while continually serving God's mission. To develop this notion of *understanding by movement*, I present these fast-growing connections between growing LATHIS theological tensions, and the movement between these considerations using the MH.

OTHER SIMILAR FRAMINGS

The goal is for the missionaries to find a balance and improve LATHIS communities in God's mission. Understanding is found in the spiraling movement of the MH fostering SI. In the MH, one finds that learning is a transformative process of seeking to find meaning with discernment. Some historical approaches to spiritual understanding, like the MH, that have had theologically similar SI movements are:

- The Jewish *PaRDeS* interpretation and its metaphor of being in the garden as the culmination of healthy spirituality found in Genesis.[17]
- Roman Catholic *Quadriga*'s interpretation and the metaphor of the four horses pulling the Greek king's chariot forward.[18]
- Interpretation of the *Wesleyan Quadrilateral* and its four equal parts framework that prioritizes Scripture.[19]
- Urban Holmes's interpretation in his *typology* of spirituality between the mind, the heart, the revealed, and the mystery.[20]

All these interpretations are similar to the MH in that they frame the process of generating understanding by epistemological movements. It is worth noting that none of them unilaterally gives more importance to one part of their respective frameworks over the others. Similarly, Richard Foster offers a more complex metaphor for spiritual formation in his *Six*

---

17. Rotenberg, *Between Rationality and Irrationality*.
18. Leder and Muller, *Biblical Interpretation and Doctrinal Formulation*.
19. Thorsen, *Wesleyan Quadrilateral*.
20. Holmes, *History of Christian Spirituality*.

Streams metaphor.[21] Whatever the number of parts, there is epistemological movement between them. SI is understood when each part is seen as intricately related but not more significant than the whole. It deepens experience amid pain and is always communal. It is a way of conceiving understanding and is ultimately a conscious balance of spiritual tensions and frustrations, creating and seeking a healthy discernment while not falling into excesses or extremes. SI is a condition in that these extremes are kept balanced in the parts of the framings.

TRANSFORMATIONAL AGENCY

Transformation is a method that will help bridge the gap in church growth today by bringing LATHIS theology's capital wealth benefits to the field of missiology. The MH, in its missional helical movement, fosters a mutual relationship between its parts thus reinforcing a SI for the purpose of transformation. This transformation creates agency in missionaries who are being trained and already at work in their ministries. It deals with conflicting interests between theology preceding praxis or praxis preceding theology by the continual spiraling movement providing practical understanding. Furthermore, the movement does not have a specific spiraling left to right or vice versa, nor does it address whether it is getting closer to the center. What needs to be clarified is that if Van Rheenen has the goal of the response to the MH, there ought to be an intentional spiraling movement with SI. Incorporating this movement provides the transformation needed vocationally and/or in biblical training in the LATHIS preparation to deal with potential tensions.[22]

Three of the skills used through the MH (theological reflection, cultural analysis, and historical perspective) have not been considered in training missionaries in Latin America, and as a result, preparation is deficient. More specifically, for the *Restoration Movement* (RM), strategy formation with SI for missionaries preparing to work in Latin America has been non-existent because theological reflection, cultural analysis, and historical perspective have been mostly ignored in the search for restoring the New Testament Church. Missionaries are not taught enough about the historical types of liberation and integral doctrines in Latin America. They are not skilled enough to analyze culture, nor do they accept or understand

21. Foster, *Streams of Living Water*.
22. Van Rheenen, "What Is Missiology?"

the history, context, or pain of Latin America; therefore, they have little to no perspective, analysis, or reflection. Since they do not have these skills, missionaries' SI is paralyzed. Seeking understanding with SI in LATHIS provides an agency lacking in the RM. It is vital to learn about this agency with the numerical growth happening among LATHIS.

LATINIZATION GROWTH

In today's world (especially in the United States), LATHIS is increasing numerically and the way this community is confronted requires to be transformed. This blossoming is referred to as *Latinization*.[23] Because of this change, more work has been undertaken to explore the use of the Bible among LATHIS theologians.[24] Even so, a gap remains in the literature, and this deserves more attention in the future. SI may guide the historical, theological, and cultural aspects of the work. It will bring strategies to enrich the missionaries' spiritual experience with this movement within the MH. Lucas Magnin elaborates on Luther's influence on the Reformation and challenges theology in Argentina and Costa Rica to consider imitating the Reformation in moving from praxis to theology and vice versa. Magnin writes, "Luther's theology was made from life [*desde la vida*] (because it dialogued directly with the neuralgic conflicts of his time) and was projected towards life [*hacia la vida*] (because it was not an abstract reflection on the divine but a relevant, significant explanation with immense implications for faith and reality)."[25] Magnin is proposing that LATHIS makes theology (like the MH) move from life (*desde la vida*) towards life (*hacia la vida*) dealing with the conflicts (or tensions) of the time instead of an abstract reflection or paralysis—a good sensible posture.[26] LATHIS theology is rooted in the perspectives of individuals in diverse social, ethnic, and cultural contexts. Further, LATHIS theology comes from a plural, communal, emancipatory reality. For example, mysticism and celebration are two

---

23. Benitez and González, *Latinization and the Latino Leader*.
24. Lozada and Segovia, *Latino/a Theology and the Bible*.
25. Magnin, "De la Justificación a la Justicia," 77.
26. An example coming out of the Latino and Hispanic Community is RedET (*Red de Entidades Teológica*), a network for theological entities. Their website states: "RedET is a community of people and entities created for mutual support, collaboration and the solution of common problems in theological education." https://www.redet.us/.

defining aspects that create a union reflecting the people of Latin America.[27] In a similar vein, Ada María Isasi-Díaz explains that LATHIS theology in *Mujerista*[28] theology comes from *lo cotidiano* (everyday actions).[29] Such roots nurture the heart of LATHIS theology, which is the admiration of the mystery, revealed in Jesus and guided by the Spirit actively working in the people. Moving between the parts with SI becomes profitable when sensibility is understood in terms of the *mestizo* theologies *en conjunto*[30] as it will be explained next.

THEOLOGICAL CULTURE

LATHIS theology finds its *locus theologicus*[31] in interaction born out of *mestizaje* (miscegenation).[32] The concept of being LATHIS in Christ and finding fulfillment in ethnic identity has its roots in living between two worlds as a *mestizo* but should be based on reconciliation with God in Christ.[33] *Mestizo* Christianity seeks a SI within its origins and seeks praxis by contextually considering people with empathy in the in-between spaces. Among LATHIS, theologians have connected with base communities, defining academic, pastoral, and organic growth characteristics in their contexts, seeking dialogue between received theologies and practical

---

27. Medina, *Christianity, Empire and the Spirit*; Valentín, *In Our Own Voices*.

28. Mujerista theology begins with personal experience and moves toward a theology that advances the dignity and liberation.

29. Isasi-Díaz, *La Lucha Continues*.

30. Rodriguez and Martell-Otero, *Teología en Conjunto*.

31. This is a term made classic by Melchior Cano (d. 1560) in *De locis theologicis*, published 1563. An argument from authority is essential to theology since theology is a derivative of supernatural faith. Cano's treatise studies the loci (places) in which this authority may be found. Cano enumerates ten loci. Seven are proper to theology: (1) Sacred Scripture, (2) apostolic traditions, (3) the universal Church, (4) Church councils, (5) the Papal Magisterium, (6) the Church Fathers, and (7) theologians and canonists. Three are borrowed by theology: (8) natural reason, (9) philosophers and jurists, and (10) history and human tradition. Among these proper loci he distinguishes those that are fundamental, containing the deposit of revelation (1, 2), from those that are declarative, articulating the content of the fundamental loci in successive ages. Declarative loci may provide an efficacious argument, since they involve the infallible magisterium (3, 4, 5), or they may provide a probable argument (6, 7).

32. Elizondo, "Mestizaje as a Locus of Theological Reflection."

33. Elizondo, "Mestizaje as a Locus of Theological Reflection," 23.

relevance for people or missionaries themselves.[34] Considering the origin of *mestizaje* is beneficial in promoting a SI for praxis[35] by reconciling the cultures combined with Christ and finding spiritual understanding *en conjunto* (combination).[36]

Starting from this *mestizo* origin is necessary. The term *mestizo* is used to indicate a mixture of blood and cultures.[37] It explains how to belong to two realities that at the same time do not belong to either of them.[38] For *Mestizo* Christians, *Mestizaje* refers to the use of words and expressions metaphorically or figuratively.[39] With this mixture of ideas emerged political and social oppression. Two collisions characterize Latin America:

- The clash of the native indigenous peoples of the continent with the European conquerors.
- The more recent shock of the Anglo-American neo-colonial invasion.

Both collisions brought partially successful mission theologies to bear on social change, deep-seated struggles, and interculturalities in order for the gospel to spread. It has historically been difficult for missionaries to be sensible and interdependent because of Anglo-American strategies for evangelization through colonization.

Throughout the decades, good work has been accomplished using various gospel-sharing methods. However, considerable improvement in mitigating the current shortages in Latin America requires significant refinement. The future appears more promising by empowering agencies to imagine a suitable outcome based on mestizo Christianity in Latin America and the United States globalized state. Some advocate the use of *Critical Race Theory* (CRT)[40] to understand developments in *mestizo* society in the

---

34. Aquino, "Mestizaje," 283.

35. A theology *en conjunto* initiative enables Hispanic/Latinx scholars to succeed through practices such as structured writing time, editorial support, and intellectual exchange. It refers to the creation of channels for the transmission of wisdom from generation to generation. Creating such a network requires not only establishing a professional network for mutual advancement but also creating a community that can sustain scholars, body and soul, in hostile environments. Smith, "'Learning from Teología En Conjunto."

36. Isasi-Díaz and Segovia, *Hispanic/Latino Theology*.

37. Medina, *Mestizaje*.

38. González, *Mestizo Augustine*.

39. Aquino, "Mestizaje," 285.

40. Delgado and Stefancic, *Critical Race Theory*.

United States and Latin America.[41] Such approaches have provided practical answers, identified commonly in Liberation Theology, Integral Theology, and, more recently, brown theology. Moving with SI among these theologies provides help in the transformative process of finding understanding for missionaries because they can consider the times sensibly by including people, priorities, practices, and proficiencies included in LATHIS. For this reason, the MH includes historical perspective and cultural analysis to form strategies beginning with theological reflection. Because spiritual understanding does not rely on a monocultural perspective, this MH interpretation of missionaries in the Americas finds understanding by including miscegenation through LATHIS theologies when it is done communally in everyday practices.

THEOLOGICAL TENSIONS

The *mestizaje en conjunto desde lo cotidiano* (miscegenation in combination with everyday actions) of LATHIS perspectives gives rise to many tensions for missionaries. Here is where the two overarching theologies—*Teología de Liberación* (Liberation) and *Misión Integral* (Integral)—would be beneficial if placed in the frame of the MH with SI. Similarities at the center of both theologies are the respect for the value of the Holy Scriptures and the lordship of Jesus as Christ. Table 1 lists eight characteristics of and tensions between the two LATHIS theologies. In themselves, these tensions do not have a positive or negative impact on the enterprise. The difference is that they deal with their respective contexts that foster these understandings rather than prescribing a general practice. An attempt similar to what the Restoration Movement aimed for with their theology in the United States in their days began during the Second Great Awakening (1790–1840) of the early nineteenth century on the American frontier.[42]

---

41. Romero, *Brown Church*, 10.
42. Foster, *Encyclopedia of the Stone-Campbell Movement*.

Understanding by Movement

	Summary of Characteristics and Tensions		
	Liberation Theology	**Integral Theology**	**Related Tensions**
Origin	CELAM Vatican II 1962–1965 Medellin Conference	Lausanne 1970 CLAUDE II 1979 FTL Buenos Aires	Catholic *or* Evangelical
Main Concepts	Oppression Violence Domination Marginalization	Salvation Evangelization Ecclesial Protestant	Outreach *or* Sustain
Perspective	For the Poor by the Poor	Gospel	People *or* Bible
Scripture Focus	Matt 10:34	Micah 6:8	Sword *or* Kindness
Agency	Political Social Change Critique institutions	Dichotomy Gospel Social Networks Partnerships	Work Against *or* Work Along-Side
Scope	Ecumenical	Evangelical/Protestant	*Who* to include?
Jesus	Suffering Servant (Isaiah)	Integral Minister	*How* is it done?
Theology	Free/Liberate	Complete/Make Whole	Free from *or* Free to

The first tension is the tradition of these theologies. The origin is either Roman Catholic (post-Vatican II) or Evangelical Protestant (*The Lausanne Covenant*). End goal: Liberation Theology's main concepts are oppression, violence, domination, and marginalization, while Integral Theology's main concepts are salvation, evangelization, ecclesial, and protestant. Secondly are the sources, either the poor or Bible. The perspectives are either for the poor by the poor or the gospel as understood in the New Testament. In this case, it is not the only source, but it is the point of view of the theology. Next is the approach to reading the text. The scriptural focus of Liberation Theology is the command of bringing peace found in Matt 10:34, engaging socially, while Integral Theology focuses on the justice found in Mic 6:8. Fourth is the location for ministry. According to Liberation theologians, the work includes political and social change and the critique of institutions. Integral Theology seeks to be an agent of the dichotomy of the gospel and social change by sharing networks and partnerships. Fifth, each theology answers differently: Whom to include? The scope of Liberation Theology is ecumenical, building bridges that connect otherness, and Integral Theology is evangelical and focused on their covenant. Sixth is the question: How is it done? The two theologies see Jesus differently. In Liberation Theology, he is seen as a suffering servant; in Integral Theology, he is seen as a minister to all. So, Liberation Theology sees suffering to change, while Integral Theology sees serving as the means. Lastly, there is a tension of being free from or free to. In summary, Liberation Theology seeks to free or liberate, and Integral Theology aims to complete or make whole. These tensions are not necessarily opposing each other, but they are complementary to what their traditions value.

Both Liberation and Integral Theologies found in Latin America and the United States have tensions in their contexts, interpretations, and outcomes. Contextual tensions originate at the beginning of these theologies and how they have been interpreted over the years, specifically by the Roman Catholic church and the evangelical church. Hermeneutically, both theologies use the same biblical stories; tensions arise when interpretations change through the two theologies. Both theologies have tension in their final approach to dealing with suffering or pain. The Liberation outcome seeks to free and listen to the people in pain, while Integral Theology is about salvation while in pain.

The missionary who works in the LATHIS community ought to understand these differences and the tensions between them. Understanding comes from seeking SI in the missional movement of the MH. At the core, these theologies are Christ-centered and driven by the mission of God commanded by the Creator, so they both complement each other. Nuance perpetually exists from the differences and similarities and learning how to deal with these is vital for the missionary laboring interculturally. Several tensions exist in LATHIS that are greater than those in Liberation and Integration. There are over 500 years of theologies, each from a unique perspective.

SENSIBLE INTERDEPENDENCE— A 500-YEAR ALIGNMENT

For over 500 years LATHIS theology has offered many great assets to Christianity and if the missionaries would be trained with SI using the MH for all that is found in this theology there are benefits that can be drawn from this capital wealth to the field of missiology. It would benefit the missionaries in dealing with the tensions and frustrations found in the LATHIS theologies producing growth in the church today. Prospective missionaries are discouraged by seeing returning missionaries who cannot cope with tensions and frustrations. For example, some spend less time in the mission field than it took them to prepare academically. This discouragement contributes to a lack of workers willing to enter the mission field and fewer churches engaged in missions. Many people have participated in educational systems to prepare for missionary work, yet they seem to lack a healthy and stable spirit as they serve God's mission without SI.

For LATHIS *sensibility* is a word that contains a variety of possible understandings. In English, the two terms *sensitive* and *sensible* are entirely different words with different meanings. Sensitiveness relates to an emotional response or physical pain or reaction, such as light sensitivity. *Sensible* is different because it relates to the cognitive realm. The colloquial English use of *sensibility* means disposition, capacity, faculty, or aptitude to feel, perceive, value, and even produce action.[43] An English speaker can often use and comprehends sensibility by associating it with common sense or knowledge. At the same time, a more empathic approach is typical among Spanish speakers because the word is used to describe fuller emotions and perspectives than sensibility (i.e., empathy) does in English. Consequently, SI implies that empathy is inevitably accompanied by interdependent affinity.

Soledad Sánchez Flores explains that there was no use of the word *sensibility* related to the spiritual realm in Spanish before the eighteenth century.[44] Instead, Flores found that it was only associated with the physical body in medical cases. After the eighteenth century, it becomes associated with the spiritual realm, with feelings such as love, sadness, or melancholy. For example, for Santa Teresa of Ávila in 1573, this word is still within its

---

43. More specifically, *Meditations and Other Metaphysical Writings* (Descartes) establishes a set of comparisons between the cognitive role assigned to sensitivity and the cognitive role assigned to intelligibility. *Critique of Pure Reason* (Kant et al.) present his conception of *"sensitivity"* to us as part of the conditions for the appearance of representations or as the ability to receive representations according to the way objects affect us. While maintaining the distinction between sensible and intelligible knowledge, some rationalists and some empiricists recognized a certain continuity between the two. Sensitivity was an inferior kind of knowledge for these rationalists, while for the empiricists, it was the fundamental starting point of all possible intellectual operation.

44. Flores, *Concepto de Sensibilidad*.

sensitive and non-emotional connotation, even though the theme, ascetic and mystical, is closely associated with the world of feelings and passions. From this example is seen that older use of the word referred to feelings and the other to the senses. *Sensibilidad* is a word that is sometimes translated into English as sentimentality, and it refers to sentiments, the soul, and morals. *Sensibilidad* is apprehended and perceived as a better advanced literary and philosophical term because it includes physical and spiritual.

To give an example, for Saint Ignatius of Loyola, *sensibility* represents how subtleties and internal movements of feelings lay deep in the concept it describes, as seen in his autobiography and the *Spiritual Exercises* used by the missionary Society of Jesus.[45] St. Ignatius encountered spirituality not as distant and removed but as a teacher subjectively (with *sensibility*) immersed in his everyday life. For Argentine Nora Kviatkovski, Ignatian *sensibility* is the point of confluence of the bodily senses and the effects of knowledge, all of them summoned on an inner plane, a unifying resonance of the sensible, affective, and cognitive realms, which includes the intangible plan of the Spirit and everyday feelings.[46] Similarly, Arturo Bañuelas notes how *sensibility* helps in moments of tension and frustration since it is indisputable because it means profound experiences during pain.[47] For Urban Holmes, with his Circle of Sensibility, *sensibility* is conceiving (in the sense of giving birth to) spirituality.[48] In other words, *sensibility* is a human perception that intensifies with pain and improves spirituality.

Sensibility requires interdependence as an essential component for missionaries in Latin America because of the communal condition found in the culture. The concept of interdependence is a reciprocal link for the social order that helps theologians discern, amalgamate, and develop healthy relationships.[49] Biblical interdependence arises from the interdependent nature of the body of Christ. It is a universal gift of the Holy Spirit, leading Christians to act generously and responsibly while promoting the dignity of another person.[50] Recently in the United States, Robert Chao Romero in his book *Brown (Morena) Theology* has advocated for uniting

---

45. Jamut and González Rivera, *Ejercicios Espirituales*.

46. Kviatkovski, interview by Daniel A. Rodriguez, Buenos Aires, Argentina, Mayo 2020.

47. Bañuelas, *Mestizo Christianity*, 1.

48. Holmes, *History of Christian Spirituality*, 4.

49. Holmes, *History of Christian Spirituality*, 4.

50. Costas, *Christ outside the Gate*, 3.

interdependence with *sensibility*.[51] Interdependence takes place through the lens of oppression and marginalization in the Christian community, recognizing that it is only fulfilled in the love of God through the neighbor in times of stress and frustration. This recognition of a deep communal condition is what SI offers the missionary.

The lack of substantial SI can often undermine a missionary's well-intentioned efforts and overshadow an otherwise positive experience. Such lack ignores context, history, and theology already present in their lives. Having this, SI can create spiritual well-being and a healthy and stable spirit oneself, while continually serving the mission of God connects the dots of the missing gaps in the mission. Among missionaries to LATHIS in the RM, SI is what seems to have lacked in the quest to restore the New Testament Church, especially regarding the claim to have all truth in autonomy from the rest of Christendom. Specifically for Latin America, the RM ignored the *Teología de Liberación* (Liberation) and *Misión Integral* (Integral) doctrines were born out of these same contexts by focusing only on first-century Christianity.

FIGURE 2

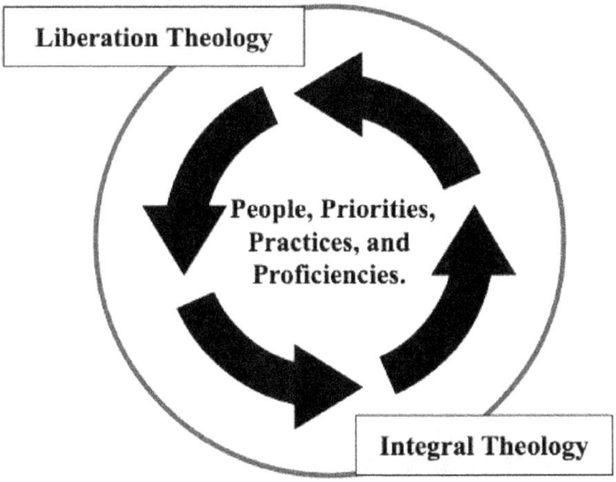

Liberation Theology → People, Priorities, Practices, and Proficiencies. → **Integral Theology**

Latino and Hispanic 500-Year Alignment

---

51. Romero, *Brown Church*, 11.

Missionaries will not function effectively in their Latino Spanish-speaking contexts if they lack a SI in God's call in their mission, shaped by and through spiritual formation. Such dysfunctionality and lack of spiritual health in missionaries and their families reveals a more profound need than most missionary training institutions recognize.[52] To bring alignment to the 500-year LATHIS theologies, SI will promote movement for understanding with people, priorities, practices, and proficiencies found in historical development. Some work has already been done with Justo Gonzáles and Ondina González in *Nuestra Fe*.[53] This is especially so since the future of LATHIS is becoming more Pentecostal in its theology. This essay does not consider such, but the capacity of SI is the same in welcoming new tensions and frustrations because it is again transformational.

Moreover, as Liberation Theology and Integral Theology expand in Latin America, missionaries must respond to uncertainties created by these theologies in their training and ministries. These tensions exist between themselves (missionaries) and the backgrounds (contexts) in which they find themselves. The lack of substantial SI undermines a missionary's well-intentioned efforts and often overshadows an otherwise positive experience.

SENSIBLE INTERDEPENDENCE AS RECONCILIATION

It is not the first time that someone has advocated for contextual theology. Other missiologists such as Bevans, Newbigin, and Bosch have appealed to similar SI in their approach to the mission of God. As part of Van Rheenen's model, MH supposes circumstances by which it can move between its components and considers spiritual formation an essential environmental condition. God's command of reconciliation is only possible if outsiders empathize with the context of the culture through SI. In the development of Latinization theologies over five hundred years, tensions are growing with divisiveness instead of unity. There is disunity within the missionaries due to the competitive, individualistic, and dogmatic practices that may be used to move between the MH parts. As these quadrants are used to indoctrinate or impose theologies that do not consider the context, tensions increase to the point of placing unnecessary stress on the missionary.

---

52. The concept of sensible interdependence (SI) is a reflection I have taken from my dissertation at Fuller Theological Seminary. A following study is also an extract from my thesis (Palafox, "Seeking Sensible Interdependence.")

53. González and González, *Nuestra Fe*.

Understanding by Movement

Van Rheenen's MH calls for movement but does not prescribe the type of movement required for this framing to be successful for reconciliation. As a result, the MH may be used as a weaponized surveying tool rather than a tool for appreciating others if interdependence and a sense of responsibility are lacking. What SI does is insists that theology flows from a particular culture. For O. Ernesto Valiente, it means an "appreciation of the historicity of human existence and of the impact that historical realities exercise on human consciousness."[54] Traditional approaches to missionary training have often ignored the context for reconciliation. In other words, LATHIS are not *mestizo en conjunto en lo cotidiano* (mixed together in every day) enough. Valiente reminds us to consider Jon Sobrino and Gustavo Gutiérrez's drive to undertake a journey grounded in, sustained, and transformed by a reflection of human dignity. He is advocating for reconciliation to be done with a "willingness to welcome all, even the former perpetrators," because this is the "effectiveness and the gratuitousness of God's love."[55] Insensible independence imparted to missionaries renders them lacking a deeper understanding of the contexts they serve with indifference. The independence imparted by the RM to missionaries does not allow them to gain a deeper understanding of the contexts in which they operate. It is specifically related to the RM training curriculum focused on the New Testament, ignoring many years of tradition and rich spiritual capital in Latin America. The exact circumstances are occurring in the United States as brown theology expands. For Samuel Escobar Christians aren't traveling all over the world, but the growth of Christianity in Latin America, Africa, and parts of Asia is eclipsing that of the Western church.[56] Reconciliation theology addresses the problems of underdevelopment and economic justice.[57] We must find a just and effective answer to poverty in LATHIS. A new paradigm in training needs to happen to consider what is imported without consideration of context. Most importantly, fewer tensions and frustrations among LATHIS missionaries.

---

54. Valiente, *Liberation through Reconciliation*, 51.
55. Valiente, *Liberation through Reconciliation*, 196.
56. Escobar, "New Global Mission."
57. Foroohar, "Liberation Theology," 37–58.

CONCLUSION

In the crest growth of *Latinization*, most Latin American missionaries receive their training at Anglo-American Bible institutes with a preference for contextualizing their mission. They expect that doctrines already established as truth will stick when transplanting them to these individuals. Because Latino missionaries are not Anglo-Americans, they often experience frustration and stress. For LATHIS, it is imperative to locate their *locus theologicus* within their context. In this epistemological place, key ideas such as *mestizaje, en conjunto, lo cotidiano*, and others promote engagement lessening tensions. In addition, the differences between *Teología de Liberación* and *Misión Integral* are consequential in fostering frustration. When considering the impact of theologians on training others to be missional, there is a growing awareness of the vast wealth of 500 years of LATHIS perspectives. All these practical theologies can be aligned if this Spanish-speaking era is placed in the MH seeking understanding. To complete this task, one must consider all related theories of knowledge, particularly regarding their methods, validity, and scope. In addition, one must be able to distinguish between justified beliefs and opinions. Van Rheenen has created a helical movement in missiology and the spiral moment in its parts of the MH provides tools that help understand the context. LATHIS theology has been characterized by individuals, priorities, practices, and competencies for over 500 years. To acquire competency in establishing a balanced spiritual experience in a context-appropriate manner while participating in God's mission, LATHIS missionaries can utilize this MH frame to intentionally frame a missional understanding of Latino SI with missional perspicacity and continuously. When importing theology that ignores context, like the RM, the most apparent reason is that the frame used is functional in its context, but it has a predicament relating to the LATHIS. For LATHIS, spiritual capital wealth can expand in Latin America and the United States. For this reason, an epistemological movement with SI in a missional frame like the MH is beneficial in training missionaries. Nuestra Fe (our faith) has plenty of people who are examples, priorities that explain why they acted the way they did, practices that are justified to be done, and proficiencies that can bless the immediate culture and beyond. Seeking understanding by movement must occur with an anointed Christ-like attitude of sensible interdependency.

8

Love, Joy, and Grace

Formation Together in the Life of God

P. KENT SMITH

THE MISSION OF GOD is the life of God. The mission of Jesus is the life of God on earth as it is in heaven. The mission of the community of Jesus is the life of God on earth here and now. This all follows from the reality that God is love. Love seeks and evokes more love. By nature, love is regenerative, creating more of itself with each expression.

These truths, when taken seriously, deeply shape the ways we think about mission and the formation of those who want to share in God's mission. This essay explores a process of human formation that centers in God's life of love. From this understanding of formation follows an outline of what it actually means for us to participate in God's regenerative life together—and to see particular expressions of that life take form in an expanding ecosystem of God's grace.[1]

Answering the question of how we participate in God's life requires that we develop a working understanding of who God is, the process by which God includes people in what God is doing, and how we in our particular situations can engage this process. This essay overviews such a

---

1. In what follows I adopt a broadly understood definition of "ecosystem" as an interdependent community of shared resources.

working understanding. It is presented as a progress report based on decades of work with people seeking to participate in the mission of God. The aim here is to invite a conversation among those who share in this work.

THE LIFE OF GOD

God is love (1 John 4:8). This core claim of the Christian faith can be fully understood only by experience.[2] In practical terms, we experience the love of God and of others as a gift—whether it is a smile, a comforting presence, a new ball glove, a compliment, or a wedding ring.

The ancient Greek language captures this flow of love in the intriguing relationship of a constellation of words rooted in joy:

- *Chara*—joy
- *Charis*—a gift, a grace: that which brings joy
- *Eucharistia*—gratitude, thanks: joy returned

A thoughtful gift, intended to bless, evokes joy in the receiver. The receiver, in joy, then expresses gratitude to the giver. So, the gift of love, expressed by one, is now experienced and expressed by two. In this simple process, love expands. To put it differently, love grows in the dance of joy between gift and gratitude. Love is, by nature, regenerative.[3]

Two conditions are essential here. There must be a basic correspondence between the giver and receiver that appreciates the value of the gift—a basic unity of intent. At the same time there must be a difference in what the giver has to offer and what the receiver already has—a basic diversity.

For love to flow, for gift-giving to flourish, unity and diversity—differentiated integration—must exist between the lovers. These essential conditions find their foundational expression in the life of God, understood in Christian tradition as the shared life of God in the Father, Son, and Holy Spirit.

This ever-expanding life of love—God's life—is the wellspring of history. From a Christian perspective, the great story can be told simply in three lines:

---

2. James K. A. Smith helpfully summarizes why the case for this claim must currently be made in *Desiring the Kingdom*, 37–88.

3. Love itself, of course, does not require reciprocation, as new parents routinely demonstrate. "While we were still rebels, Christ died for us" (Rom 5:8; New Testament translations are the author's). The question here is how love grows.

- In the beginning was joy
- In the end will be deeper joy
- In between is an astounding invitation: "Come, share in Our Joy!"[4]

For the purpose of this overview, two scenes bookend this narrative. In the first verses of Scripture, we learn that even before God said, "Let us make humankind in our image," even before God planted a garden of joy, "Eden," for that first family, even before the eternal Word spoke, even before the Spirit brooded over the watery chaos—there was a communion of love, a fellowship of overflowing joy.[5]

If we fast forward through Scripture to the last verses of the last book, here again we find the fellowship of joy. The Father is present, the Son is present, the Spirit is present. But there is another. She, along with the Spirit, invites the reader to "come" (Rev 22:17).

This beautiful Bride of Christ is made up of a diverse multitude of humans descended from the original family bearing the divine image—every tongue, tribe, and people. This Bride, bearer of God's regenerative life, is the companion made for the ever-expanding celebration of the God who is love. Deeper joy lies ahead.

PARTICIPATING IN THE LIFE OF GOD

How are we to accept the invitation that the Father, Son, Spirit, and Bride extend to join the coming celebration that is already underway—to "come and share in our joy?" A key is to recognize that the love which is God's life is not only regenerative by nature, but also relentlessly revelatory by nature. Love is self-disclosing. This insight is key to our understanding of the process by which God includes people in what God is doing.

---

4. This simple telling of the Christian metanarrative is just one of many ways of framing the master story. But everyone has such a frame, implicit or explicit. As philosopher Max Scheler observed, "Man [sic] is not free to choose whether or not he wants to develop [an idea of ultimate reality]. . . . Man necessarily and always, consciously or unconsciously, *has* such an idea, such a feeling acquired by himself or inherited from tradition. All he can choose for himself is a good and reasonable or a poor and unreasonable idea of the absolute" (*Philosophical Perspectives*, 2).

5. Gen 1:26. All Old Testament Scripture references are from the New English Translation.

Missional Life in Practice and Theory

Revelation

Throughout Scripture, from the very first verses, God speaks, God self-discloses. "And God said," is a recurring refrain, because self-expression is the fundamental gift a lover has to offer the beloved. Revelation is the seed of God's loving initiative that awakens and invites the grateful love and participation of the beloved.

Unsurprisingly, then, in the teaching of Jesus, the seed is the Word of God, where the inbreaking reign of God gets underway in human hearts. For Jesus, this was not simply an abstract claim about the nature of God, but rather, the dominant reality that shaped his daily life: "I do nothing of my own initiative but only speak what the Father has revealed to me" (John 8:28).

When this radical dependence on God's revelation is put to the test in the wilderness by the Adversary, Jesus's response is to quote Moses, "People do not live by bread alone but by every spoken word that continues to flow from the mouth of God" (Matt 4:4).[6] Here Jesus calls to mind the imagery that Moses used to remind the Israelites that God fed the people with manna, day by day, so they could learn not to depend on their own ideas or resources but on God's continuing, daily revelation of care and provision.

Jesus further makes clear to his followers that this radical dependence on God's guidance is to be their new normal life as well. "My sheep keep hearing my voice. I know them and they follow me" (John 10:27).

With the outpouring of the promised Holy Spirit on Pentecost, the long-awaited Counselor is given to all of God's people. Early Christian writers continually affirm their confidence that God's people in this new age can and must learn to be led by, to keep in step with, the Spirit who is now our intimate, day-by-day Guide.

Attention

Here is the pivotal intersection between God and people, between God's life and ours. Perhaps the most precious human asset is our attention. If so, our most important stewardship resides in where we invest or pay, that attention.[7]

---

6. This verse is a quote from Deut 8:3.

7. Accumulating evidence in the field of neuroscience underscores the mind/life-shaping influence of focused attention, of "attention density." So, for example, Schwartz,

Love, Joy, and Grace

Our word "attention," derived from the Latin word for "to reach toward" (*attendere*), signifies more than the objects of our mental focus. Attention is not mere awareness. Rather, as the idea of reaching suggests, it is an act that engages our desire, or to use biblical imagery, our heart, the seat of our desire.

Like a person with a flashlight in a dark attic, we are surrounded by realities we cannot see until we direct the beam of our attention to them. This act of directing where we place the focus of our awareness is the act of attention-paying. In the bustle of life, many things may "grab" for our attention, but where our attention comes to rest is an act of will.[8]

Attention-paying, then, is a whole-hearted, whole-brained process. It involves those aspects of our mind/heart that include rational thought as well as the centers where emotion, desire, and relationship reside.[9] The great commandment of both the Hebrew and Christian Scriptures makes clear that God's desire is for our full-dimensioned love, heart, soul, mind, and strength.[10]

In this light, God's ongoing revelation comes to us as an invitation to give God our ongoing attention. Ultimately, we give our attention to what we value and want, so the focus of our attention is a telling marker of our true desire, the state of our heart.

Underscoring this, in the pivotal teachings of Jesus about how the life of God comes to us, we are called to be "very careful about how you listen" (Luke 8:18; Mark 4:24)—that is to say, how we direct our attention calls for great care. In the parable of the soils, for example, the seed of God's

---

Mind and the Brain, 369, says, "the truly important manifestation of will, the one from which our decisions and behaviors flow, is the choice we make about the quality and direction of attentional focus."

8. James, *Works of William James*, 1168, says that "attention is the fundamental act of the will," drawing distinctions between passive attention and the active, effortful attention that is the focus here.

9. Ian McGilcrist chronicles the essential function of the relational dimensions of mind/heart in attention and its suppression in Western civilization. See *Master and His Emissary*.

10. See, for example, Mark 12:29–30 and Deut 6:4–5. These two passages highlight the ancient distinction between the Hebrew understanding of "heart" as inclusive of the functions of thought, desire and choice and the Greek addition of "mind" as a separate category for thought. Although contemporary neuroscience may map these functions more in terms of "whole brain" functioning, the categories remain important, and distinct.

revelation falls in many places. Only where it falls on the soil of an "honest and good heart" (Luke 8:4–18), however, does it come to bear fruit.[11]

Paying attention is a critical point of intersection between God's life and ours. Here the ongoing initiatives of God's revelation invite us to participate in God's life.

Reception

Closely related but different than our attention is the matter of accepting God's revelation—of saying "yes" to the revelation we have discerned. Once, my toddler son, responding to a request he did not like, stood up, looked me in the eyes, placed his hands over his ears, and said, "What did you say, Daddy? I can't hear you!"

Like this child, it is entirely possible for us to hear what God says, understand what God says, and yet refuse to receive what God says. William James puts it this way: "The effort to attend is only a part of what the word 'will' covers; it covers also the effort to consent to something to which our attention is not quite complete . . . so that although attention is the first and fundamental thing in volition, *express consent to the reality of what is attended to* is often an additional and quite distinct phenomenon."[12]

Reception, like attention, is a work of the whole mind and heart. In biblical teaching, it is the essential marker of the quality of a person's heart. Routinely we are called to avoid a hard heart, a heart of stone, a sinful heart (Exod 7:14, Ezek 11:19, Ps 66:18), all of which reveal opposition to God's revelation. Instead, we are called to a good heart, a heart of flesh, a pure heart (Luke 8:15, Ezek 36:26, Matt 5:8), that is ready to receive what God reveals to us.

Summarizing this point, the writer of Hebrews repeats the call of the psalmist: "Today, if you hear his voice, do not harden your hearts" (Heb 3:7, 15). Whole-hearted, whole-brained reception of God's present revelation, then, is a vital aspect of our coming to participate in the life of God.

---

11. The teaching of Jesus here echoes a key theme in the wisdom literature: "Guard your heart with all vigilance, for from it are the sources of life" (Prov 4:23).

12. James, *Principles of Psychology*, 569 (emphasis added).

Vocation

The word "vocation" has its roots in the Latin word *vocare*, "to call." Those who receive the gift of God's revelation are called to participate in God's life. This calling comes in two forms: the call that all of God's people receive, our universal grace, and the particular callings that come to us as individuals and as community that are specific to our situations.

The writer of Ephesians unpacks this distinction between universal and particular calling as he urges his readers to "therefore, live a life aligned with the calling to which you have been called" (Eph 4:1). What follows is a reminder that these gifts are received together in love, in unity, and then they are summarized. The author names first the universal gifts all God's people have received: "one Body, one Spirit, one hope, one Lord, one faith, one baptism, one God and Father of all" (Eph 4:4–6).

At this point, the focus shifts to the particular calling of each person. "But to each one of us a grace has been given as distributed by Christ" (Eph 4:7). Certain gifts of influence are given, but these are for the explicit purpose of calling forth, drawing out the gifting of each member of the body.[13]

As this every-member gifting is released, the eternal purposes of God in Christ are realized: "From Christ the whole body is joined and held together . . . by means of the distributed divine energy of every single growing part of the body working to build up his body in love" (Eph 4:16).

This idea of a grace as the particular calling of individual people is a dominant, but often overlooked, New Testament theme in Western Christianity. Paul routinely refers to the grace he has been given as his unique calling to bring the gospel message to the non-Jewish peoples. But as we have just seen in Ephesians, such a distinctive grace has been distributed by Christ to every part, every person in the body.[14]

Clearly, much hangs on our acceptance not only of God's *universal* calling, but of the *personal* call of God on our lives. However, if the stories of Scripture are a reliable indicator, people routinely find receiving the call of God challenging. Whether that call is unexpected and puzzling (think of Mary, or of Abraham and Sarah) or fundamentally disorienting and

---

13. This whole constellation of thought concerning vocation stands in contrast to the widely held American notion that "you can be anything you want to be."

14. The grace (*charis*) that each disciple receives, along with the corresponding equipment to fulfill that grace (*charismata*) is a repeated, commonly assumed theme elsewhere in the New Testament. See, for example, Rom 12:3–8 and 1 Pet 4:10.

frightening (think of Moses, Jonah, Peter, and Paul), God's calling brings change. We often perceive that called-for change as a threat.

And yet, if God is love and God's revelation comes as gift, then the vocation that makes us a gift of God is also an invitation into God's joy, however reluctantly we receive this at first. Calling is an invitation to God's joy, for our joy and for the joy of the world. It is not only grace *by* which we are saved but also grace *for* which we are saved. As Frederick Buechner put it, "The place God calls you to is the place where your deep gladness and the world's deep hunger meet."[15]

Our vocation, then, as an expression of the life of God, holds universal dimensions we share with all, as well as differentiated dimensions unique to us. Whatever that specific gift is, and whatever assignments attend that gift, it carries a call to a relationship—to a family.

Communion

Our unique graces, called together by God in a specific time and place, create a unique ecosystem of grace that expresses the life of God. According to Ephesians, the coming of this ecosystem, inaugurated by Jesus Christ, is the hinge of history.

This ecosystem of God's grace is the pre-ordained system for the summing up of all things into God by way of Christ.[16] Here is how the idea is introduced in the first chapter: "making known to us the mystery of his will, in accordance with his good pleasure that he purposed in himself, leading to the *ecosystem* of the fullness of times, to head up all things in Christ—the things in heaven and the things on the earth" (Eph 1:9–10).

This ecosystem is the object of God's self-purposed pleasure, something revealed in the fullness of times, that has been a mystery but has now been made known. These ideas are taken up and developed more in chapter 3: "To me, less than the least of all saints, was this grace given: to announce to the non-Jewish peoples the boundless riches of Christ and to enlighten all that they may see what the *ecosystem* of the mystery is, which throughout the ages has been hidden in God, who created all things, so that now, to the rulers and authorities in the heavenlies, the multifaceted wisdom of God might be made known through the *ekklesia*. This aligns with the eternal purpose which God made in Christ Jesus our Lord" (Eph

---

15. Buechner, *Wishful Thinking*, 119.
16. I present a case for translating *oikonomia* as ecosystem in "Ecosystems of Grace."

3:8–11). In the *ekklesia*—the called-together people of God—God reveals this finally disclosed "ecosystem of the fullness of time." The *ekklesia* is the divinely appointed means of displaying God's multifaceted wisdom to the heavenly powers.

The "many, multiple forms" of God's wisdom are on display in the *ekklesia*, precisely because each person who makes up that ecosystem bears a distinctive grace-gift of God. Such ecosystems of God's grace are full yet unique expressions of the life of God and bearers of God's in-breaking reign in history here and now. As the letter to the little band of people in Colossae puts it, "In Christ, the fullness of Deity is *presently living in bodily form*—and you [Colossians, together among yourselves] have the fullness of Christ" (Col 2:9).

Here, the life of God is fully present in a small, God-called community, an ecosystem of God's grace. Such household community, according to early Christian thought, is God's plan for the consummation of history, culminating in a Bride who shares God's life.[17]

The process we have surveyed—from revelation, attention, and reception through vocation and communion—broadly describes the way people come to participate in the life of God. The flow, however, is not merely linear. Like the love that undergirds this process from start to finish, this flow is regenerative. As individuals and communities receive and enact the life of God, they become agents of further revelation themselves, and so the cycle continues and grows. The life of God regenerates in love.

SHARING THE LIFE OF GOD TOGETHER HERE AND NOW

How, practically speaking, do people individually and together continue to bring their attention to God's revelation and, so, come to live as active participants in the community of Jesus—this life of love which is God's life? In whatever ways we begin to answer that question, we know our response will need to address the full experience of human love: heart, soul, mind, and body.

---

17. Anglo-Americans face a particular challenge in engaging or even imagining the kind of deep interdependence such community calls for, in part because we are usually generations away from actually experiencing extended family. David Brooks surveys this development in "Nuclear Family Was a Mistake."

To direct our attention to this broad spectrum of human experience is to explore the fundamental challenge the life of God presents to all humans in all cultures. God's invitation to God's life comes as a calling to be a contrast culture in a suffering world where people's attention is not directed to God. At the same time, because God is love, the call of God always attends deeply to the real situation of those being called. Love is incarnational; it reaches to people where they are even in their inattention.

In this light, training for a way of life that centers in ongoing attention to God calls for the capacity to enter culture as it is *and* to nurture culture change. Personal and systemic change at this level is possible through new understandings, skills, and habits in three key dimensions of human experience: story, setting, and system.

These three elements, story, setting, and system, together form a typology that has proven helpful for individuals and teams seeking to understand and address the complexities of culture, whether their own or that of others. In this typology, culture can be seen as an ecosystem of interdependent dimensions in which story and setting are connected by a system.

What follows is an outline of the kinds of questions that individuals and communities address as they attend to God's calling in these three dimensions. Coming to shared conviction in response to these questions and then working out the implications of those convictions in a shared way of life is the ongoing work of God's called-forth, called-together family.

The outline below serves as a broad framework for those seeking to heed that call.[18] It includes key questions in each dimension of story, setting, and system that every community addresses, either with intention or by inherited default. The questions are followed by sample conviction statements to illustrate how a community might answer each question.

The Story Dimension

Attending to the meaning-making *stories* a community shares. All people live within a framework of meaning that is shaped by their understanding of four stories they inhabit.

---

18. *Finding Regenerative Culture: A Journey Together into Four Living Stories* is a portfolio guide that assists individuals and groups in working through these questions. It is available through the Eden Center for Regenerative Culture.

Love, Joy, and Grace

The Story

Question: What is the story God is telling?

Conviction: In the beginning was joy. In the end will be deeper joy. In between is an astounding invitation: "Come, share in our joy."

My Story

Question: What is the story God is telling in and through me? How am I being invited to participate in the master story God is telling?

Conviction: Each person, made in the image of the God who is love, is a gift—a grace designed by God in advance to share uniquely in God's life.

Our Story

Question: What is the story God is telling in and through us? How are we being invited to participate in the master story God is revealing?

Conviction: Each community called out and called together by God is a whole ecosystem of God's grace—designed and prepared to uniquely demonstrate and carry out God's life of love.

This Story

Question: What is the story God is telling in this place at this time? How are we together being invited here and now to participate in the story God is telling?

Conviction: Each community called together by God is invited to join in the specific work of seeing God's kingdom come and God's will done in their present setting.

The Setting Dimension

Attending to the land-use and build design of the community—the place in which the community interacts among itself and with its wider environmental context. From the days of Eden on, God's life intersects with human life in specific places. Whether in an Egyptian palace, the Judean wilderness, or the streets of New York, place profoundly, unavoidably shapes the stories that unfold there—and, in turn, is shaped by those stories.

Natural Environment

Question: What are the realities of the climate, context, and biome in which we live, and how are we called to be good stewards of this place?

Conviction: As creatures in God's good creation, our calling is to nurture, enjoy, and steward this great gift upon which we and all living creatures depend.[19]

Built Environment

Question: In what homes, buildings, and human structures does God call us to live and work?

Conviction: Our homes and the structures in which we gather and work should reflect our love for the Lord, one another, our neighbors, and our world through proximity, simplicity, functionality, and beauty.[20]

The System Dimension

Attending to the *connection* of those stories to those places through realigned commitments, communication patterns, decision-making, and rhythms of attention in the community. As noted above, the consummation of history, according to the New Testament, hinges on the revelation of God's ecosystem of grace in the fullness of time. This *economia*, or household operating system, takes distinctive form as particular, called-forth communities join God in their specific place to bear witness to the life of God. Several key questions help communities develop a way of life that aligns their unique calling to their unique context.

---

19. For a constructive overview of the ways our call to love intersects with the natural environment, see Raworth's *Doughnut Economics*.

20. An introduction to some of the ways our housing and built environment impact relationships can be found in Roberts, "How Our Housing Choices Make Adult Friendships More Difficult."

Covenant

Question: What is our shared commitment as individuals and community?

Conviction: Jesus is Lord, so we will follow him as we discern the leading of his Spirit together.

Communication

Question: How will we nurture a culture where the whole community is developing its communication skills, and where we engage the conflict that arises constructively?

Conviction: Communication, as the process of revelation, is the lifeblood of the community of God. When conflict surfaces, an opportunity for learning, growth, and deeper care beckons us.

Governance

Question: How will we practice attention to God in and with one another so that our life together is governed by the Lord Jesus through the Holy Spirit?

Conviction: The children of God have been promised a Counselor who guides God's people as a community. Our practice is to seek that guidance steadily as we attend to God's voice in and with one another.

Rhythms of Attention

Question: What routine practices are we fostering to ensure that our attention continues to be drawn to God, to one another, and to God's ongoing call on our lives?

Conviction: Every community is formed and sustained by a more or less explicit *regula* or rule of life. We will be explicit about our *regula*, always holding ourselves open to the Spirit's guidance on how to revise these practices as our situation changes over time.[21]

---

21. Historically, communities of faith have developed these rhythms of attention or rules of life—*regula*—as their response to the kinds of *story* and *setting* questions raised

CONCLUSION

We have surveyed a process of human formation that centers in God's life of love. Love is regenerative, revelational, and incarnate. This overview and outline can help individuals and communities undertake the vital work of discerning and engaging the specific ways God's life is underway among them.

Joy, along with all the fruits of God's Spirit, naturally flows in this ecosystem that is God's life of love. Conversely, a steady lack of joy or the other spiritual fruits marks an incomplete ecosystem of grace.

By attending to the process of human formation that centers in God's life, we together engage in the journey of discovery that draws us individually and collectively into the grace to which we are called. From that place of discovered design and joy, we bear witness to the good news of God's life here and now.

As Jesus said, "Love one another as I have loved you. In this people will know you are my disciples—by this quality of your love for one another" (John 13:34–35). This love, sourced in God's life, becomes the unmistakable marker of our lives and future in joy together.

---

here. This constitutes a robust and specific answer to theologian James K. A. Smith's provocative questions about the kind of liturgy that will be powerful enough in our time to capture and hold the attention of God's people. See *Desiring the Kingdom*, 70–88.

9

Contemplative Mission

The Interplay of Spirituality and Missional Practice in Mission Alive Church Planters

Tod K. Vogt and Charles Kiser

Shortly before leaving his missions post at Abilene Christian University (ACU), Gailyn Van Rheenen developed a framework called "the missional helix" in order to describe "the process of effective ministry formation."[1] The missional helix consists of four internal elements: (1) theological reflection; (2) cultural analysis; (3) historical perspective; and (4) strategy formation.[2] Faithful missionaries, Van Rheenen suggests, cycle through each of these elements as they engage their contexts in the mission of God. This framework became a response to the popular Church Growth Movement, which Van Rheenen critiqued for its dry pragmatism and results-focus to the neglect of theological reflection.[3] When Gailyn and Becky Van Rheenen left ACU to found Mission Alive (MA), a North

---

1. Van Rheenen, *Missions*, 308.

2. Van Rheenen, *Missions*, 308.

3. Van Rheenen used the helix to propose a reformist view of church growth in Engle and McIntosh, *Evaluating the Church Growth Movement*, 167–89; cf. Van Rheenen, *Missions*, 308n3.

American church planting ministry, they built its church planter training upon the elements of the missional helix.

The missional helix includes a fifth element, which Van Rheenen describes as the "environment of ministry formation" and the most critical component of the helix: spiritual formation. "This shaping of ministry," reflected by the helix's four internal elements (theology, culture, history, strategy), "takes place within the environment of spiritual formation as Christian servants humbly submit their lives to a covenant relationship with God as Father and enthrone Christ as their King."[4] Van Rheenen's commitment to spiritual formation as the center of church planting was made manifest both in the personal and ministerial equipping MA provided church planters. Since its inception, MA has equipped church planters personally by connecting them to therapists and spiritual mentors to support their own spiritual formation while in the trenches of mission. As part of ministerial equipping in MA, church planters develop a process of spiritual formation by which the people they reach can grow as disciples of Jesus.

FIGURE 3

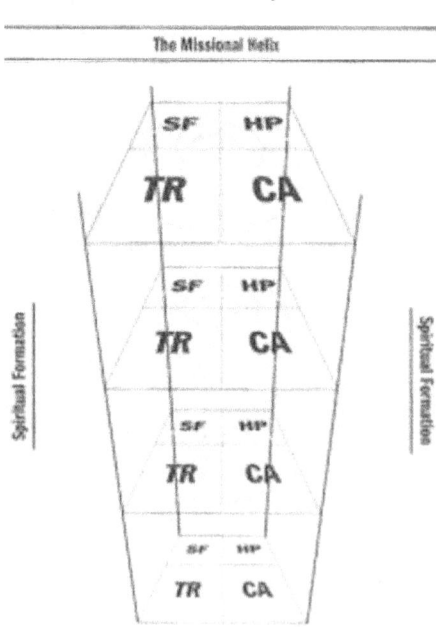

4. Van Rheenen, *Missions*, 316.

The Missional Helix

We (Tod and Charles) have been coworkers of the Van Rheenens in Mission Alive for many years and could think of no better way to honor their legacy of mission than to conduct a research project among Mission Alive's church planters that focuses on the impact of their spirituality upon their missional practice and vice versa. In this paper, we share our findings from this research in three moves. First, we describe the methodology and design of our project. Second, we share observations and analysis of the interviews we conducted with thirteen Mission Alive church planters. Third, we explore the implications we see for Mission Alive, and perhaps other church planting ministries, as it continues to equip church planters for mission in an environment of spiritual formation.

METHODOLOGY AND DESIGN

Research Participants

We chose thirteen Mission Alive church planters to participate in our project. We selected them based on our personal knowledge of them and their ministries, their connection to Mission Alive (through assessment and/or training), and their ongoing participation in church planting ministry. Nine were male; four were female. All were of white/European descent. The average age of research participants was forty-five, with one cluster between the ages of forty to forty-four and another around age fifty-five. Participants averaged twenty-two years of ministry experience in general and eight years of church planting experience. All had some connection or identification with the Stone-Campbell tradition, specifically Churches of Christ. All participants were the founding and leading planters in their churches. Four were employed full-time in church planting; nine were bi-vocational, receiving part or all of their income from a job in their communities. Most participants' church planting experience was located in a single church planting geography—ranging from 1.5 years for the newest church to 13.5 years for the oldest. Their contexts of church planting were spread over the United States and Canada: some contexts were urban, others suburban, and others semi-rural.

Social Location

The presence of researchers among research participants impacts what takes place in that context and the perspective from which information is gleaned. "No field researcher can be a completely neutral, detached observer who is outside and independent of the observed phenomenon."[5] Because of this dynamic, it was vital to explore our own social location as researchers, how we were perceived by others, and our limits within the context.

Both of us are or have been in staff positions within Mission Alive and have assessed, trained, mentored, and counseled all of these church planters in their ministry. We recognize this power dynamic and the possibility it may create for these participants to skew their responses because of our roles. At the same time, the depth of relationship we share with these planters may also create more transparency and honesty in the interviews. Further, given our role within Mission Alive, we recognize our own bias to cast Mission Alive and its church planters in a favorable light and obscure more critical data. Yet, we also remain committed to sharing the truth of these planters' stories, believing that even critical feedback and discoveries will help us grow and deepen our collective participation in the mission of God.

Research Questions

Our primary research questions were "How does the spirituality of Mission Alive church planters impact their missional practice?" and "How does that inform the equipping of future church planters?" Subsidiary questions were "What is the nature of Christian missional spirituality?," "What is the relationship between spirituality and mission?," "Where do these planters see God amid their spiritual and missional experiences?," "What theological imagination about spirituality or mission do participants' stories create?," "What strengths and limitations have participants experienced in their equipping by Mission Alive?," and "What are the implications of their experiences for how Mission Alive trains future church planters?" These questions informed and shaped the interviews and cultural learning that were part of our research method.

---

5. Emerson et al., *Writing Ethnographic Fieldnotes*, 4.

Contextual Method

Our methodological framework was influenced by Robert Schreiter's *Constructing Local Theologies*, who suggests that contextual spiritual and theological imagination are developed through the interplay of the church's spiritual/theological tradition and culture(s).[6] In this paper, we implemented Schreiter's insight in four steps: (1) opening culture; (2) opening our spiritual/theological tradition; (3) opening dialogue between culture and spiritual/theological tradition; (4) opening the future through contextual theology and practice.[7]

In this project, the church planters and their contexts reflected the cultures we sought to open. They represented both *a culture* (of the Mission Alive network) and the *cultures* of their various ministry contexts. Our approach to opening culture(s) was "grounded theory," whereby through semi-formal interviews with church planters we analyzed qualitative data by giving priority to developing categories directly from the data rather than from preconceived theory or concepts.[8] We acknowledge, however, the degree to which we bring frameworks of understanding about spirituality and mission to our research that impact how we listen in the interviews and how we interpret the data we glean. This culture-opening work is reflected in the observations in the section that follows.

The analysis element of the next section reflects our second and third steps: to open our spiritual/theological tradition and to open dialogue between our spiritual/theological tradition and culture. We did this by interacting with our Stone-Campbell tradition as well as relevant traditions that shape us from broader orthodox Christianity in light of the themes and theologies that emerge in our interviews. Finally, we open the future through contextual theology and practices in the implications section, where we reflected on the impact our observations and analysis have upon Mission Alive's ongoing equipping of church planters for mission in the United States and Canada.

---

6. Schreiter, *Constructing Local Theologies*, 25–29.

7. These steps are strongly influenced by Fitch, "Biblical/Theological Method."

8. Emerson, *Writing Ethnographic Fieldnotes*, 172. Our interview questions are also informed by the framework of appreciative inquiry, wherein we seek to draw out from participants their strengths, hopes, and life-giving experiences in an attempt to imagine and innovate a better future, as in Branson, *Memories, Hopes, and Conversations*.

Design

This research project was built upon in-depth interviews of thirteen Mission Alive church planters. Interviews create space to listen deeply and learn about the spirituality and missional practice of the participants. Following ethical research standards, we gained formal permission to conduct the study through informed consent documents signed before the interviews.[9] The informed consent document outlines the voluntary nature of participation, potential risks and benefits, confidentiality/anonymity, and our intentions in conducting the research. All the interviews were conducted via video conference. Interviews began with basic intake questions about themselves and their church planting ministry. The main questions were arranged according to three themes: (1) spirituality; (2) the intersection of spirituality and missional practice; and (3) equipping church planters. The interview format was flexible and semi-structured to allow for additional probes and inquiries in the midst of the interview. We recorded the interviews and took notes on our observations and learnings. We transcribed the interviews using a transcription service, read all the transcripts thoroughly, and coded them for common themes and insights. Finally, we met to discuss and identify the major observations that emerged in both of our reading and coding processes.

OBSERVATIONS AND ANALYSIS

Three major themes emerged from our interviews related to the spirituality and missional practice of MA church planters. First, church planters often experienced mission as a crucible that spiritually broke, shaped, and refined them. Second, planters described their participation in mission in terms of spiritual discernment—identifying God's activity around them and collaborating with God. Third, planters expressed both an experience of and deep longing for community in their spirituality and mission. We explore each of these themes in what follows, narrating them with church planters' comments, and offering analysis by comparing their comments with frameworks for spirituality and mission from our spiritual/theological tradition.

---

9. See Moschella, *Ethnography as a Pastoral Practice*, 86–103.

The Crucible

Tony described the sense of overwhelming terror often experienced by missionaries when they realized that the plans they made for ministry would not work in their context, and they had no idea what to do next.

> Okay, I know what's *not* going to work. I don't know what to do next. And so, in some ways, to go back to my own personal spirituality . . . I felt like was formed in the crucible of just trying to be like, "I don't have a clue and I'm scared to death. What's next?" Because I don't want to write a report that says I don't know what to do. (Tony)[10]

This experience, Tony remarked, was not without meaning or benefit—it was a crucible of formation. A crucible is "a place or situation in which concentrated forces interact to cause or influence change or development," originating in reference to materials like porcelain being used to heat items within it to a melting point.[11] The majority of MA planters alluded to feeling the heat of this church planting crucible, particularly when they experienced failure, when outcomes did not occur as they expected, or when they were not able to accomplish what they hoped to accomplish.

When asked about how church planting impacted his spiritual life, John described his spiritual life as "an incomplete system" that "needs challenges to help build its capacity and to change me and to make me better and to make me into someone who is more like Christ. And church planting has done that." God used church planting to "burn off the impurities," John says—the exact function of a crucible—and "to make you into something more pure and stronger."[12] Beth, reflecting on the weight of her leadership in church planting, acknowledged that throughout her life "growth has come through difficult times, and that's okay. I've come to accept that. That's how I think it happens."[13]

Several church planters described the voices of the crucible, either within themselves or from others in their context. James, for instance, reveals a sampling of the internal voices that pipe up in the planter's mind: "There come days where you think you're crazy, like, 'I'm a failure. This isn't working. I've done it all wrong. The ups and downs of emotions that come

---

10. Zoom interview by Tod K. Vogt and Charles Kiser, January 28, 2021.
11. "Crucible (*n*.)."
12. Zoom interview by Tod K. Vogt and Charles Kiser, January 28, 2021.
13. Zoom interview by Tod K. Vogt and Charles Kiser, February 26, 2021.

with the nature of this work is too hard. I can't do this anymore.'" These internal voices also include false narratives or beliefs that church planters carried with them into planting that were deconstructed by the crucible. For example, Matt described the way his beliefs about God's financial provision were challenged by perceived failure in ministry: "If you're doing what God wants, you're going to be blessed. And when you're having to scrape by [financially], then you question if you're doing the right thing . . . That's what you're taught, right? If you're doing it right, it's going to take care of itself."[14]

Church planters not only contended with the voices of their own insecurities but also with the spoken and implicit voices of their post-Christian contexts. Tony warned future church planters to brace themselves for this aspect of the crucible: "Most of the people you encounter aren't going to give two craps about you and what you're trying to do here. So, get ready to feel irrelevant ninety-five percent of the time. That's just the way it is."[15]

In the case of church planting, the heat of uncertainty, unmanageability, and perceived failure kindled change and development in the inner being of the church planter. The church planting crucible shaped the church planter's mind, heart, and soul. Three interior effects caught our attention: (1) the crucible leads planters to trust God; (2) the crucible leads them to ground themselves in their spiritual identity; (3) the crucible leads them to release the outcomes of their work to God.

Trusting God

First, the crucible led church planters to trust God. Church planting helped Tony realize he would have to trust God because his previous skills for "running a program" in an established church were not effective in his church planting context. James shares the way church planting stretched him—"stretched my vision, stretched my capacity, stretched my thinking, my comfortability and probably ultimately my need for God's presence in my life for ministry to be effective."[16] John recalled times he felt stuck, not knowing what to do, and how that forced him to ask God for help and listen for direction: "I cannot put it in cruise control over here. I have to work

---

14. Zoom interview by Tod K. Vogt and Charles Kiser, February 2, 2021.
15. Zoom interview by Tod K. Vogt and Charles Kiser, January 28, 2021.
16. Zoom interview by Tod K. Vogt and Charles Kiser, January 28, 2021.

hard at [trusting God]."[17] Church planters mentioned a variety of practices in which they engaged as the crucible led them closer to God: silence, meditation, lament, nature walks, prayer walking, intercession, spiritual retreat, Scripture reading, and study.

Grounding Identity

Second, the crucible led church planters to ground themselves in their spiritual identity. Kara admitted that in hindsight she did not have a very good understanding of who she was as a child of God before church planting. She described entering the crucible when her new church experienced a significant decline in growth due to transience. It devastated her and led her to ask God what she was doing wrong and if God approved of her. Through experiences like these, she came to believe that "Jesus is for us. He's for me. He's always rooting for me . . . and that is very grounding."[18] She called this realization of her own belovedness the "anchoring core" of her spirituality. With the help of a mentor, she learned to differentiate her own personal well-being from the well-being of her church planting ministry. Kara observed: "I feel like my contemplative journey began as a pursuit of those kinds of moments where I rested in my belovedness and in the presence of God in a way that grounded me and centered me and sustained me for all of the ups and downs and all of the demands and all of the challenges and uncertainties of church planting."[19] She wondered if she would have been open to such connection to God through contemplative practices had it not been for the crisis she experienced in church planting.

Releasing Outcomes

Third, the crucible led church planters to release the outcomes of their work to God. Jill recounted that on some level she could never have prepared for church planting—she just had to learn by doing it. She was sometimes tempted to take responsibility for the results of her ministry, except that the size, complexity, uncertainty, and volatility of church planting led to her

---

17. Zoom interview by Tod K. Vogt and Charles Kiser, January 29, 2021.
18. Zoom interview by Tod K. Vogt and Charles Kiser, February 26, 2021.
19. Zoom interview by Tod K. Vogt and Charles Kiser, February 26, 2021.

realize that "if I try to take responsibility for that, I'm going to go insane."[20] It was through her experience in the crucible of a previous ministry, in which she did assume full responsibility and felt like a failure, that God began to loosen her grip on the outcomes. The crucible of church planting was teaching her to have a better sense of where she did have responsibility but also to "give more responsibility to God for the success of those things and understand that I'm free to engage and try to join him without feeling the responsibility of success or failure."[21]

Jill's perspective was shared by several other church planters. Jack, for instance, while admitting he did not realize how much he was not in control of the outcomes when he was younger, offered an exhortation to his fellow planters: "We need to get our mind off the grand end result and let God do the grand end result. Let God give the increase."[22] Keith reflected this same wisdom in his advice to future church planters about their own spiritual care: "Don't strategize everything. Don't try to do it yourself. Give God space to help you. I guess that's the big lesson I feel like I have learned over my ministry is that God does it better than I do."[23]

The Wall and the Crucible

This crucible theme intersected significantly with a framework Mission Alive has used for training in the past: Janet Hagberg and Robert Guelich's six stages of faith development.[24] Mission Alive has offered these stages most often as a resource to planters developing spiritual formation processes in their churches. However, Hagberg and Guelich's concept of "the wall" resonates with church planters' own experience of the crucible. The wall is part of the fourth stage, "the journey inward," and "represents our will meeting God's will face to face. We decide anew whether we are willing to surrender and let God direct our lives."[25] The wall often accompanies crisis—a moment that brings a person to the end of their rope. Some come to the wall only once; others come to it repeatedly. While some may try to avoid it, go around it, over it, or under it, the wall remains until one goes

20. Zoom interview by Tod K. Vogt and Charles Kiser, March 4, 2021.
21. Zoom interview by Tod K. Vogt and Charles Kiser, March 4, 2021.
22. Zoom interview by Tod K. Vogt and Charles Kiser, January 28, 2021.
23. Zoom interview by Tod K. Vogt and Charles Kiser, January 27, 2021.
24. Hagberg and Guelich, *Critical Journey*.
25. Hagberg and Guelich, *Critical Journey*, 114.

through it. In order to move through the wall, individuals must deeply accept God's unconditional love and acceptance of them—similar to the ways the crucible leads church planters to ground themselves in their spiritual identity (i.e., as a beloved child of God). Another aspect of the wall is surrender: those who go through the wall give something up to God. They release and detach from something central to their identity. In our findings, one form of surrender was the invitation to release outcomes to God, which are often central to church planters' identities. Interestingly, Hagberg and Guelich describe the wall as a place of melting and molding, the very activity of the crucible: "The melting and molding with fire and wax are excellent analogies of the Wall experience. Before filling and using comes the time of melting and molding."[26] The intersection of these two concepts reveals that church planting, in the testimony of almost every person we interviewed, inevitably creates a wall experience. Those who persist in church planting meet the wall (or crucible) and go through it, or are at least in the process of going through it.

Spiritual Discernment

> Sometimes it's jarring, and all we do is sit and listen in community and discern what we hear from God based on what we see and experience in mission. (Kara)

In some way or another, most of Mission Alive's church planters expressed what Kara noted above. They find themselves in circumstances beyond their training, beyond their seminary degrees, and beyond Mission Alive's equipping. In those moments, they find themselves turning to God for wisdom and guidance, similar to the apostle Paul's prayer for the Ephesian Christians: "I pray that the God of our Lord Jesus Christ, the Father of glory, may give you a spirit of wisdom and revelation as you come to know him." (Eph 1:17). Mission Alive church planters described practicing spiritual discernment regardless of age, gender, length of ministry, church planting experience, or educational level.

In general, Mission Alive church planters recognized the practice of spiritual discernment either: (1) in relation to the preparation and guidance they received as they were becoming church planters; or (2) in relation to their missional practices as church planters. Those who recognized

---

26. Hagberg and Guelich, *Critical Journey*, 123.

spiritual discernment as part of their becoming church planters most often used the language or description of "calling" to describe their experience. For example, Adam noted: "What I was doing as a full-time minister wasn't what I felt I was called to do." Ann recalled: "I was just willing to go where I was being sent. And to not buck the system."[27] In these cases, their practice of spiritual discernment focused on their vocational calling.

Spiritual discernment played a significant role in the missional practice of Mission Alive church planters. Note what John said: "I have to listen [to God]. I cannot put it on cruise control."[28] Ann said: "If I have a hunch to message someone, I try to follow that hunch like there's a reason."[29] Keith, speaking more broadly, shared: "God has been at work, and he's been revealing himself and nudging me here and there."

More surprising was the practice of spiritual discernment in relationship to unbelieving neighbors. Kara, Tony, and Keith in varying ways described how they each saw God moving in their neighborhood among their neighbors. In one particularly insightful comment, Tony observed the inbreaking of the kingdom of God in the context of a summer children's day camp that they helped the local residents host: "Part of the Eschaton is the renewal of all things. There's something about people in poverty cultures being empowered to attend to and meet their own needs that speaks to the end times."[30] Such comments are surprising in their recognition of God's movement among unbelieving neighbors and in mediating the church planters' relationships with them.

Assessment as Spiritual Discernment

Several church planters mentioned how MA's Assessment Retreat (formerly called Discovery Lab) played a significant role in discerning their call into church planting. The Assessment Retreat helps individuals and MA determine their readiness for church planting. James: "I think the Discovery Lab for me was a really foundational, pivotal, critical—whatever adjective you want to use—experience of calling and affirmation."[31] Mission Alive church planters understand that the assessment process is as much about

---

27. Zoom interview by Tod K. Vogt and Charles Kiser, January 27, 2021.
28. Zoom interview by Tod K. Vogt and Charles Kiser, January 29, 2021.
29. Zoom interview by Tod K. Vogt and Charles Kiser, March 4, 2021.
30. Zoom interview by Tod K. Vogt and Charles Kiser, January 28, 2021.
31. Zoom interview by Tod K. Vogt and Charles Kiser, January 28, 2021.

spiritual discernment as assessing their competencies. For some of Mission Alive's church planters, the period of assessment proved to be one of the most transformative experiences of their life. Keith makes a similar comment: "The preparation for church planting, I would say, is what impacted my spirituality most, that season of discernment of what God actually wanted us to do."

Community as Spirituality

Ruth Haley Barton, in her book *Pursuing God's Will Together*, suggests that spiritual discernment is not only an individual discipline, but a discipline that should be practiced in community.[32] While MA church planters practice communal spiritual discernment, they seem to do so with less intentionality. Note Kara's comment: "I think it was the first time I really felt like we have people in this who love us, who are in this, who are listening to God with us."[33] In the interview, she spoke with a spirit of relief as she remembered the experience of others joining them in listening to God. Tony more intentionally attempted to model the practice of spiritual discernment for those in his gathering: "When we do our Bible studies, when we do gatherings, I don't teach [the meaning of the passage], I teach them practices for listening to God on their own with Scripture and then we do it communally."[34]

Prayer-Walking as Spiritual Discernment

Mission Alive church planters shared that they regularly practiced prayer-walking and described how prayer-walking was a practice of spiritual discernment. Tony described it in detail: "Prayer-walking has been really, really good because it combines a few different things for me. Number one, just going on a long walk helps me clear my mind, but it's also helped me to have eyes for the neighborhood and to pray with awareness when I'm in front of specific houses, specific blocks, a school here, that sort of thing."[35] We see prayer-walking as a practice of spiritual discernment when Tony

---

32. Barton, *Pursuing God's Will Together*.
33. Zoom interview by Tod K. Vogt and Charles Kiser, February 26, 2021.
34. Zoom interview by Tod K. Vogt and Charles Kiser, January 28, 2021.
35. Zoom interview by Tod K. Vogt and Charles Kiser, January 28, 2021.

says it helped to give him "eyes for the neighborhood" and helped him "pray with awareness."[36]

Scripture and Spiritual Discernment

Christians have discovered the association between the Christian Scriptures and spiritual formation, including spiritual discernment, as early as the writing of the Christian Scriptures themselves. Consequently, there is no surprise that Mission Alive church planters found that the more they read Scripture, the better they were at recognizing God's voice when they were away from Scripture. Keith said: "The more scripture I read, the more I feel like I'm in tune with, you know, when God does say something, it helps to recognize it."[37] This current study serves to reinforce the effective association between spending time in the Scriptures and learning to hear God more clearly.

Missional Theology and Spiritual Discernment

Mission Alive's commitment to missional theology is embedded in its name. From its inception, missional theology has been taught as part of Mission Alive's equipping of church planters. Resources such as the *Missional Church: A Vision for the Sending of the Church in North America*, and Michael Frost and Alan Hirsch's *The Shaping of Things to Come: Innovation and Mission for the 21st Century Church* have played seminal roles in Mission Alive's equipping.[38] Consequently, Mission Alive has trained church planters to see God and not themselves as "the primary agent of mission."[39] In adopting this perspective, Mission Alive church planters have been trained to "seek to participate in God's already-in-motion mission."[40] Yet this pursuit raises the question, How? How do church planters identify God's mission, and how do they determine their role?

Mission Alive church planters, as evidenced by the observations above, have identified a practice that allows them to recognize "what God is doing"

---

36. Zoom interview by Tod K. Vogt and Charles Kiser, January 28, 2021.
37. Zoom interview by Tod K. Vogt and Charles Kiser, January 27, 2021.
38. Guder, *Missional Church*; Frost and Hirsch, *Shaping of Things*.
39. James, *Church Planting in Post-Christian Soil*, 141.
40. James, *Church Planting in Post-Christian Soil*, 141.

and "how they will join in." Through the practice of spiritual discernment, they listen and watch for indications of how God is already moving in the community and pay attention, seeking evidence of divine guidance as to how they can engage with the divine activity. We find this noteworthy given that, while Mission Alive has subscribed to missional theology and the idea that God is already at work in each respective community where church planters reside, Mission Alive has never overtly taught church planters how to identify God's work or more specifically how they can participate in it. Furthermore, while Mission Alive has occasionally suggested prayer-walking, we have not suggested it as a specific practice of spiritual discernment to help church planters identify how to participate in God's mission. Planters have discovered that on their own.

Community

> Having a strong support system or community that isn't just helping you troubleshoot things that are logistically going wrong with the church, but are really, in the middle of those hard times, anchoring you to what we know to be true about God. (Kara)[41]

Throughout the interviews, Mission Alive church planters expressed—in a considerable number of ways—how they longed for greater community with fellow church planters and the broader Mission Alive community as well as with local community members. In the above comment, Kara reflected on how crucial it was to have a community of support when in the crucible. She indicated that one of the roles community plays in the life of a church planter is to be an anchor during those seasons when everything has become disoriented, and planters need to be reminded of "what we know to be true about God."[42] James hungered "to be in community with other church planters who have walked in those shoes."[43] Beth may have said it most clearly: "I think, as the wife of a church planter, I think the camaraderie of Mission Alive, just knowing there's other people doing some of those same things as you are, experiencing some of those same things, and then that helps you maybe feel understood."[44] Their desire for community, we

---

41. Zoom interview by Tod K. Vogt and Charles Kiser, February 26, 2021.
42. Zoom interview by Tod K. Vogt and Charles Kiser, February 26, 2021.
43. Zoom interview by Tod K. Vogt and Charles Kiser, January 28, 2021.
44. Zoom interview by Tod K. Vogt and Charles Kiser, February 26, 2021.

will show, connected directly to both their spirituality and their practice of mission. Our observations fall into three categories: (1) outside of their ministry context; (2) inside their ministry context; and (3) general desire for community.

Outside Their Ministry Context

Mission Alive church planters expressed a desire for greater camaraderie with people outside the immediate context of their ministry. In many cases they desire community with their fellow Mission Alive church planters. Others longed for regular access to the Mission Alive staff, mentors, counselors, or spiritual directors. In several cases, like Adam's, they mentioned having an annual retreat for Mission Alive church planters: "A Mission Alive retreat, once a year, where we get together, play games, talk, and laugh. We're going to cry. We're going to pray."[45] Matt also expresses his desire for "a retreat to build connections."[46] Similarly, other planters express a desire to be part of a larger network of church planters, like when James says: "The ups and downs of emotions that come with the nature of this work is too hard. 'I can't do it anymore.' If you're in a network with people, I think you are in a greater position to [say], 'Oh. This is normal!' . . . At least for me, the greatest encouragement [is when] someone says, 'Oh man, let me tell you my war story.' Having those kinds of conversations is the value of being in a church planting network."[47]

Inside Their Ministry Context

Tony expressed a hunger for a greater sense of local community when he conveyed his desire for a team: "One of the things I wish we had done before we came was gather a team, at least one other family to come with us."[48] He goes on to caution future church planters: "Don't even get started unless you have a team and that team is committed together to discerning God's voice through Scripture and prayer. . . . If you have a team of folks that are committed to praying and reading the Bible and talking together and

---

45. Zoom interview by Tod K. Vogt and Charles Kiser, January 27, 2021.
46. Zoom interview by Tod K. Vogt and Charles Kiser, February 2, 2021.
47. Zoom interview by Tod K. Vogt and Charles Kiser, January 28, 2021.
48. Zoom interview by Tod K. Vogt and Charles Kiser, January 28, 2021.

discerning God's will, I think you'll have a far better chance of succeeding."[49] It is easy to recognize in Tony's comments the connection he saw between having a team helping with the mission and spiritual discernment.

General Desire for Community

Other church planters expressed their desire for community in more general terms. Some expressed a longing for greater accountability, like James and Jill. James said simply, "You need accountability."[50] Jill deepened this perspective by explaining that as an introvert she did not necessarily crave relationships and accountability but knew she needed them. Jill expressed a desire for a community with greater transparency. She said, "I am trying to create a culture of transparency and confession and openness that flow out of my own walk."[51] Jill imagined a community of people that together shared those qualities. She explained that it was the kind of community her new church was hungering for but had not been able to find in traditional churches: "They want something that requires a lot more transparency than you can get away with in a traditional church."[52]

Others hungered for a greater sense of communal spirituality and encouragement. Tony shared that he has been trying to grow to be more open with his spiritual life and share it with those in his community. He confessed, "I'm trying to move to more of a communal spirituality."[53] Jack expressed his desire for a church planter retreat or a retreat for ladies for the sake of encouragement.

Perhaps the most poignant desire for community came from two of Mission Alive's female church planters. Kara shared, "I think there's a sense, without sounding too fragile, of isolation and loneliness in this place of spirituality."[54] Ann revealed a bit more when she said, "I need to find a woman to talk to that's been through this because I've got nobody . . . I've just really had nobody to talk to."[55] In these comments we observe the deep

---

49. Zoom interview by Tod K. Vogt and Charles Kiser, January 28, 2021.
50. Zoom interview by Tod K. Vogt and Charles Kiser, January 28, 2021.
51. Zoom interview by Tod K. Vogt and Charles Kiser, March 4, 2021.
52. Zoom interview by Tod K. Vogt and Charles Kiser, March 4, 2021.
53. Zoom interview by Tod K. Vogt and Charles Kiser, January 28, 2021.
54. Zoom interview by Tod K. Vogt and Charles Kiser, February 26, 2021.
55. Zoom interview by Tod K. Vogt and Charles Kiser, March 4, 2021.

connection between their desire for community, their spirituality, and the mission to which they have committed themselves.

Through the church planters we observed a desire for deeper community with one another to combat loneliness and isolation and to provide assurances that what they experience is common. They craved authentic fellowship within their local ministry context so that they have others with whom to practice spiritual discernment for the sake of the mission. We also heard a desire to have access to other helping professionals to assist them as they process their unique experiences. All of these observations illustrate the need for a multi-layered community working in support of Mission Alive church planters.

Communal Spirituality

As far back as Pseudo-Dionysius in the late fifth century, three states (or stages) of Christian perfection have been widely accepted: the purgative way, the illuminative way, and the unitive way.[56] While these descriptions of how people experience spiritual formation have served Christians for over 1,500 years, they imagine the epitome of spiritual maturity as individual union with the divine. It is beyond the scope of this project to speculate how appropriate that imagination was in earlier centuries. In the twenty-first century, amidst the acute individualism that dominates Western culture and popular conceptions of spirituality in North American Christianity, Mission Alive's church planters imagine a different spirituality, one that has both individual and communal dimensions. Tony expressed it this way: "I began thinking about this more communal dimension of spirituality because of my missional practice of trying to engage with people, engage with groups. It caused me to think there is something more to spiritual growth than just sitting in a room by myself with a Bible and a journal."[57] While the three states described by Pseudo-Dionysius involve considerably more than sitting in a room with a Bible and journal, both Pseudo-Dionysius' method and the early twenty-first century popular approach to spirituality share an individualistic approach to spirituality. Matt spoke specifically of prayer in relation to this communal dimension: "Communal prayer . . . is heavier for me than individual prayer and so we have three prayer times throughout

---

56. See "State or Way (Purgative, Illuminative, Unitive)."

57. Zoom interview by Tod K. Vogt and Charles Kiser, January 28, 2021.

the week with people."[58] While Mission Alive's church planters maintain personal aspects to their spirituality, they discovered a hunger for a more communal expression to their spirituality, usually after they experienced a difficult season like the crucible. They longed for these communal expressions of spirituality with fellow church planters, with Mission Alive staff and board, other helping professionals (especially mentors and spiritual directors), and with both Christian and unbelieving neighbors in their immediate community. It seems, for Mission Alive church planters, that their spirituality was not so much epitomized by an individual union with God but by incarnating God within the community and enjoying his presence together. For these church planters, spirituality is both missional (spiritual discernment) and communal.

IMPLICATIONS

Upon reflection on these observations and analyses, the clearest implication is that the single most defining element to fruitful participation in God's mission is the spirituality of the practitioner. This is consistent with Van Rheenen's missional helix, which places all other elements of the helix within the sphere of spiritual formation. The Mission Alive church planters interviewed for this project repeatedly illustrated that more than cultural analysis, historical perspectives, theological reflection, or strategy formation, it was their own life of faith that allowed them to hear God's call into church planting ministry. Furthermore, it was their spiritual practices of prayer, Scripture reading, journaling, fasting, and ultimately spiritual discernment that provided them with what they needed to stay in the ministry of church planting when they struggled with loneliness and feelings of failure. It was also the practice of spiritual discernment that fueled their imaginations when their experience and equipping was inadequate. As Bart put it, "The most important thing Mission Alive can do is tend to who the church planters are becoming."[59]

Additional implications surfaced for Mission Alive. In light of the hunger expressed by the church planters for greater communal spirituality, Mission Alive must provide them with easier access to counselors and spiritual directors. Mission Alive must develop a network of church planters and empower them to connect as they desire and also renew a periodic

58. Zoom interview by Tod K. Vogt and Charles Kiser, February 2, 2021.
59. Zoom interview by Tod K. Vogt and Charles Kiser, January 26, 2021.

retreat experience for them. Mission Alive must develop an intentional mentoring program that will partner veteran church planters with new ones. Perhaps the most valuable goal to help church planters experience greater community is to encourage future church planters to form a team prior to launching their church planting ministry.

CONCLUSION

As we drew this project to a close, we were compelled to recognize again the central role Gailyn Van Rheenen's work played in its design. Van Rheenen's recognition that the work of mission described in the missional helix exists within the milieu of spiritual formation makes him unique among missiologists and more specifically among North American church-planting network leaders. At a time when most church planting network leaders pay far more attention to the development of strategy, Van Rheenen recognized that excellent strategy offers little promise for a successful church plant if spiritual depth is not formed in the practitioner.

We also want to recognize the dynamic perspective on spirituality that our church planters reveal. They demonstrate that spirituality is personal and interior as well as communal. It is expressed in spiritual practices and through spiritual listening. Perhaps most surprising, they show us that Christian spirituality, while expressed in many ways within the Christian community, is also expressed outside the Christian community and in relationships with unbelieving neighbors. Their spiritual experiences both broaden and deepen our own spirituality. We conclude this project by repeating the primary implication to which this research leads: the single most central element of fruitful participation in God's mission is the spirituality of the practitioner. Our prayer is that this truth will motivate North American church planting ministries, as it has Mission Alive, to invest far more deeply in the spiritual formation of emerging and veteran church planters. We further pray that, beyond North American church planting organizations, other organizations and institutions will recognize the tremendous importance the spiritual life of the practitioner plays in the success of their ministry and continue to develop classes, groups, and other means to deepen the spirituality of future practitioners.

CONTEMPLATIVE MISSION
CHURCH PLANTER INTERVIEW GUIDE

We are conducting interviews to explore how Mission Alive church planters' personal spirituality impacts their missional practice, and how that informs Mission Alive's equipping of future church planters. After getting basic intake information, the questions will follow in three sections, the first on spirituality; the second on spirituality and missional practice; and the third on equipping church planters.

INTAKE

- How old are you?
- How long have you been in ministry?
- How long have you been a church planter?
- From where do you receive your personal income?

CHURCH PLANTING MINISTRY

- At what stage of development is your church presently?
- How many years ago did you start the church?
- On a scale of 1–10 how difficult has your church planting ministry been? (1=not at all; 10=extremely difficult)

SPIRITUALITY

- Describe your personal spirituality.
- How would you describe your current personal spiritual health?
- On a scale of 1–10 how would you rate your contemplative life?
- On a scale of 1–10 how would you rate your activist life?
- How has church planting ministry impacted your personal spirituality?
- What spiritual practices do you find most helpful for sustaining your ministry?

SPIRITUALITY + MISSIONAL PRACTICE

- How does your spirituality impact your missional practice?
- How does your missional practice impact your spirituality?

EQUIPPING CHURCH PLANTERS

- In what ways were you well-equipped spiritually for mission?
- What spiritual formation do you wish you had received before church planting?
- What are the most important lessons about personal spirituality that you would want to pass on to future church planters?
- What suggestions do you have for Mission Alive as it seeks to spiritually nurture church planters for church planting work?

CONCLUSION

- What responses do you have to questions we haven't thought to ask?

10

The Impact of Diaspora Mission and the Shift to a Mission Paradigm in the North American Church

Jared Looney

My personal journey into urban mission unfolded at a relatively brisk pace during my college years. In February of 1991, I had the experience of feeling called into Christian ministry during my senior year in high school. A few months later, I left the Rio Grande Valley and entered Abilene Christian University as a youth ministry major. Within weeks, I was recruited by a classmate, a missionary kid who grew up in Kenya, to volunteer with a church program that was reaching teens from the poorest neighborhoods around town. During my second semester in college, I went on a short-term mission trip to volunteer in some of Houston's toughest center-city neighborhoods After that, I felt compelled to serve as an urban minister. During my second year in college, I took an Introduction to Missions course, required of all Bible and Ministry majors at the time, taught by Gailyn Van Rheenen. Halfway through that Intro to Missions class, it occurred to me that what I was pursuing was actually cross-cultural missions. Since the ministry context that I was stepping into did not require a passport, it had not been obvious to me until that point that urban ministry could be thought of as "missions." Yet, it was cross-cultural in more ways than one. The work was evangelistic, and I was beginning to catch a vision for church multiplication in cities. All of the theological underpinnings and practical issues in missions that I was learning about in the classroom I was also discovering on city streets and in urban neighborhoods. I was beginning to realize how the intersection of global missions, city life, and understanding the context of North America as "mission field" would take center stage in my own journey.

Nearly a decade later, I was a part of a small mission team in New York City gathering a new faith community in a ground floor apartment in the East Bronx. Our first meetings included people from Puerto Rico, Colombia, Jamaica, Ghana, The Gambia, Vietnam, Mexico, and even a few native New Yorkers. There were only a few who were already Christians. Most were on the margins of faith, and still others who had a long way to go. As a young missionary, I had stepped into the deep end of the pool of global mission in a quintessential urban context. There was, as my missiology professor had cautioned some years earlier, much yet to learn. In the years that followed, everyday activities looked like sitting at the dinner table of my Russian neighbor, helping newly arrived refugees from Liberia, facilitating a bilingual house church among both first- and second-generation Dominicans, or starting a gospel conversation with a Muslim cab driver from Northern Ghana. As friends visiting from elsewhere marveled at the dizzying diversity of the city, this multicultural cacophony had become my normal life rhythm.

I had read stacks of church-growth and church-planting texts, but few seemed to address the multicultural world I had come to know. There were important lessons I discovered in my studies; however, I had found little that addressed the emerging realities of multicultural contexts. Reading in church growth led me to assumptions that did not take into account the constancy of change in urban settings, and while cultural anthropology continues to be a helpful resource for understanding cross-cultural encounters, I knew of few resources at the time for grasping the continuums of cultural change taking place in diverse neighborhoods in global cities. As Ray Bakke points out, "urban neighborhoods are now infinitely more complex than tribal cultures."[1] As I experienced hands-on ministry, I essentially found myself running on parallel educational tracks. While I had pursued my traditional bible college and seminary courses and poured myself into practical ministry situations, I had also initiated self-education by diving into related fields such as urban studies, ethnic studies, and the personal accounts of urban practitioners to complement what I was learning in the

---

1. Bakke, "Urbanization and Evangelism," 233.

classroom. I wanted to make sense of what I was experiencing in practical, on-the-ground ministry in light of missiological theory.

I continued to research the trends that appeared to impact my everyday ministry and rhythms of life in the city. Meanwhile, issues such as immigration and trauma, culture and language, ethnicity and tribalism, displacement and assimilation, and globalization and urbanism all played out in regular ministry practice with considerable complexity. The intersection of these issues became apparent in both daily life-on-life ministry and multidisciplinary research in pursuit of a missiological grasp of a global city.

I also began to realize that this type of ministry context was not limited to historical gateway cities like New York or Los Angeles. I began to learn of international communities in places like Dallas, Seattle, and Atlanta. I realized that the multifaceted encounter of global mission and well-established cultural diversity that I was sorting out in daily ministry was in fact the emerging reality in communities throughout North America—some more recent than others and in both city centers and suburbs. As I leaned in more intentionally, I heard stories of Somalis in Kenya, Bengalis in London, South Americans in Japan, or Iranians in Berlin. I also learned that the context of diversity and global mobility in which I was ministering had a name—diaspora. I was serving in a city of global cultures and peoples constantly on the move. I was laboring in diaspora communities. As the Lausanne Committee and many others have instructed, diaspora mission is a global phenomenon. In fact, mission among diaspora communities is increasingly a reality to varying degrees in specific regions, cities, and communities throughout the world. Both by forced displacement and by choice, many people today are on the move.

The term *diaspora* was previously used by academics to describe the Jewish experience of becoming scattered across the Mediterranean world, especially during the period of the Roman Empire. In contemporary social sciences, the term has come to be applied to ethnic groups throughout the world that are experiencing global relocation.[2] As global migration has become a normative experience for many families and communities around the world, mission among diaspora communities has emerged as an important area of focus within missiology. Furthermore, diaspora mission will have an important place in mission efforts within North America

---

2. Cohen, *Global Diasporas*, 21–22.

both through local engagement and as a learning resource for the broader church.

Sadiri Joy Tira explains that diaspora missiology is essentially "a missiological framework for understanding and participating in God's redemptive mission among people living outside their place of origin."[3] Voices within North America such as J. D. Payne, Enoch Wan, and others have helped advocate for a greater emphasis on diaspora mission. Mission organizations including Global Gates, International Project, Global Frontier Missions, GoTen, and Global City Mission Initiative have worked to mobilize mission laborers among diaspora communities in American cities.

While migration, multidirectional globalization, urbanization, and various other issues are having an inevitable impact on what we have traditionally thought of as mission contexts, North America—or specifically the United States and Canada—is, in the minds of many Christian leaders, becoming a context for mission. It may be a stretch to suggest that missiological principles are being applied in a widespread way in American ministry contexts. Many ministers at the helm of Christian congregations may recognize patterns of diversity in their neighborhoods but mistakenly assume that the same messaging, methods, structures, symbols, or rhythms apply universally to all subcultures. However, there does seem to be an increasing awareness that the West is not as won as we once might have thought. Due to the decades-long decline in church membership, Christian leaders have increasingly begun to view locations both near and far in North America as places in need of missional engagement. (A notable exception is Assemblies of God, which has steadily grown as a denomination.[4]) To be clear, North America was always in need of a missionary perspective and of the application of missiological principles and practices. Ladep Gwamzhi points out:

> The American church has held a prominent place in missions from the nineteenth to the early twenty-first century. This has changed as the church in the United States and Canada continues to witness a decline in membership and impact. This consequence stems from a misconception of mission as God intended it to be. Traditional missions had concentrated on foreign lands while leaving

---

3. Tira, "Diaspora Missiology."

4. The reasons for continued growth are undetermined, but some distinctives highlighted by a 2021 *Christianity Today* article include: Assemblies of God in the US are 44 percent ethnic minorities, actively plant churches, stay outside of political news coverage, and are a Pentecostal tradition. See Burge, "Assemblies of God Growing."

the home turf unattended. This thinking was so pervasive in the age of Christendom when there was the assumption that Europe, North America, and the West were already Christian in culture, thought, policy, and government, without need of evangelism and mission.[5]

The emergence of diaspora mission especially as applied to the US and Canada—two of the largest receiving nations of global migrants worldwide—may finally force the Western church to dissolve the dichotomy of "home" and "mission field." Samuel Escobar is correct in arguing that, in contrast to this unhelpful distinction of "home" and "mission field," the mission of the church involves "everyone going everywhere."[6]

While the Christian movement has continued to grow in the Global South, North American churches—specifically historically Anglo-American versions of Christianity—appear to be grappling with a missional insecurity. In their private moments, many church leaders may be more likely to confess their struggle with the status quo. Many believers only associate with like-minded Christian peers, leaders see the average age of their congregations increasing in years, and arguably some church planters appear content to develop new congregations through transfer growth. Publicly, voices such as Michael Frost, Stuart Murray, Lesslie Newbigin, and several others have addressed the challenges of ministry in a post-Christendom society.[7] Countless papers citing a statistical decline in overall church participation simply give way, year after year, to a new set of statistics showing a continued decrease in church participation in general or in some segment of Western society. Following the COVID-19 pandemic, it appears that these religious trends were only accelerated. In a March 2021 article, Gallup Survey indicated that involvement in religious institutions in the United States, including churches, mosques, and synagogues has fallen below 50 percent for the first time since Gallup initially asked the question eighty years ago.[8]

I have spent many hours training churches in relational approaches to evangelism and speaking with church leaders about the need to equip their churches. Much like international migrants who form ethnic enclaves (e.g.,

---

5. Gwamzhi, "Contextualization in Diaspora Mission," 2–3.

6. Escobar, *New Global Mission*.

7. Helpful resources may include: Frost, *Exiles*; Murray, *Post-Christendom*; Newbigin, *Foolishness to the Greeks*.

8. Jones, "U.S. Church Membership Falls."

Chinatown, Little Saigon, Koreatown, El Barrio, etc.), many churches—often with the best of intentions—have essentially formed religious enclaves. Constructing these social worlds impacts Christian witness. Perhaps a lack of Christian mission led to the formation of religious enclaves. Or maybe forming a more isolated social world diminished the ability to see missional opportunities beyond their own walls. Regardless, it certainly does not encourage incarnational ministry. To make an impact on the world around us, deep engagement with the unreached in our communities beyond the comfort of one's own religious enclaves will require learning the "language," worldview, and patterns of foreign social worlds. In many cases, however, the first step is simply learning to be friends with the "other." If we are to engage the emerging North American context, a missionary footing is required, and there may be helpful examples for living out our newfound minority status just across town or down the street.

Whether from Thailand, El Salvador, or Nigeria, newly arrived migrants must learn how to navigate a dominant culture different from their homeland. Many migrants have crossed an ocean originating from a collectivist culture to make a new home in a society with the highest degree of individualism on the globe.[9] Many new international migrants must learn to live in their new cultural world while simultaneously attempting to hold on to what they value from their homeland. At least metaphorically, immigrants are a model for the Christian life. It is no accident that 1 Pet 2:11 teaches us to live as foreigners. Many of the first-century Christians were global migrants and understood the significance of this metaphor. For American Christians clinging to native status while adjusting to what is beginning to feel like religious-minority status, diaspora communities provide a model for living between cultural worlds. In addition, a significant portion of global migrants to North America were Christians living as a religious minority long before they relocated to their new country. While it should be said that not every example of national churches in the Global South provides a strong missional model, many of these brothers and sisters represent a valuable resource as consultants for living as Christ's ambassadors in a pluralistic society or as a religious minority. Many have even lived out a Christian witness within societies hostile to Christian faith.

The reality facing the church in North America is multifaceted. First, diaspora mission brings cross-cultural evangelism and church planting into the local context as unreached peoples live or work right down the street.

9. Davis, *Making Disciples across Cultures*, 81; Hofstede, "Individualism."

In addition, diaspora Christians represent a potential new missionary force in North America for what some term *reverse mission*. Furthermore, diaspora mission may also be a stimulus for helping the church reorient to the missionary footing it should have had all along. While the American version of a cultural Christendom steadily gives way to some form of post-Christendom, diaspora mission may serve as an opportunity to help the church orient to a missionary footing in the North American landscape. Addressing the implications of these contextual realities, there are several things to consider to equip the church and prepare a next generation of leadership. I will outline a few of those themes here.

ADAPTABILITY

When speaking on the need for adaptability in contemporary urban ministry, I frequently share a pair of stories. In the first, I was speaking with a North African Muslim, and our conversation was exactly what one might expect. Our discussion involved bridging between the Qur'an and the Bible, and he was what we might consider traditional in his worldview as a Muslim from Northwest Africa. It was a textbook example of what I was taught in my Introduction to Islam course during my graduate school years. On another occasion, I was speaking to a man from the same region. However, he had previously spent a short season of his life as an atheist, read French postmodern philosophy, and embraced religious relativism. That conversation was not what I had assumed, so I had to engage in a different type of discussion of faith. Globalization and urbanization on a worldwide scale plus increasing pluralism at the local level means that many of our encounters are not one-size-fits-all. Indeed, with the diversity of an urban society, it is common for multiple social or religious trends to exist in parallel and in contradiction at the same time. For example, many new migrants may be open to religious change upon arrival to a new country, and other migrants may embrace their cultural-religious identity more strongly in response to the immigrant experience. Both responses are possible as one encounters new international arrivals, and the responses vary from household to household.

Many of our evangelism tools in the church involve a pre-set template that we tend to "plug and play" as we encounter unbelievers. However, this feels inadequate if we are to recover a missionary footing in the diversity of contemporary North America. The commonplace deployment of one-size-fits-all evangelism templates may be mistaken for apathy or shallow soil when the presentation model itself is what fails to connect. A presentation prepared for Muslim listeners, for example, assumes all Muslims are the same or that Muslim subcultures are somehow untouched by the effects of globalization. As another example, it is common to make a gospel presentation that emphasizes eternal security. "Where will you go if you die today?" Many cultural worldviews simply don't ask this question. That does not mean the question is unimportant, but it does mean it is likely the wrong starting point to launch a spiritual conversation if it is not a primary concern for the listener. Oftentimes, a gospel presentation in an American context assumes there lies a felt need when it comes to dealing with guilt and sin. Rehearsed presentations of the gospel framed around individual guilt predominate in the dominant culture—at least among evangelical churches. Unsurprisingly, this approach misses the mark when presented in a diaspora community where collectivist views of honor and shame often shape ways of thinking.

In culturally diverse contexts, a one-size-fits-all template may overlook people who are open to talking about faith because they do not share the assumptions inherent in the presentation. Instead, this moment in our history requires us to equip Christians with new tools so that we may connect with others in their own cultural locale. Followers of Christ must become adaptable as faithful ambassadors to the variety of worldviews inherently present in a society as pluralistic as North America. As multicultural settings expand, learning to share the gospel of Christ from different cultural lenses will be a crucial factor in Christian witness. Of course, no one person will become an expert in every culture or subculture they encounter. Yet, each person can cultivate sufficient humility to learn from others and form friendships based on respect. We must learn to listen well and connect relationally. If we are preparing to communicate the truth of the gospel to a variety of worldviews, listening to others' stories will help us know where to begin rather than assume every person starts at the same point. Essentially, we cannot presuppose a generally Christian orientation. Nor can we assume every individual asks the same existential questions. We must allow the full breadth of the gospel to fill our evangelistic discourses. We must learn to think like missionaries *in diaspora*.

The Impact of Diaspora Mission

LOCAL CONTEXTUALIZATION

Frequently, when American Christians address contextualization, we apply it "over there." Stemming from our colonial history, we often employ a contextual approach solely for distant places where we imagine life looks different than what we expect "here at home." By uncritically authorizing only Western forms of church and theology, too often our foreign mission efforts have lacked critical contextualization. Contextualization is a mission practice oriented around specificity and meaning—*not* limited to geography. Contextual missions center around cultures and subcultures of ministries in every location, not just those that require a passport. As we form ministries among specific ethnic or language groups, multiethnic neighborhoods, unreached peoples, post-Christendom populations, or other cultural environments, we are stepping into dynamic contexts. Diaspora communities will likely represent a continuum that exists between the culture of homeland and the culture of the host country—not to mention various Western influences such as media, travel, and other factors. In addition, cultural hybridity is commonplace as representatives of different cultures both share the same media and live in proximity in global cities. The resulting hybridity is different ethnic communities that begin to think similarly and similar ethnic communities that begin to think differently. In such dynamic and hybrid circumstances, a renewed understanding of contextualization necessitates our attention.

To advance contextualization across the diverse cultures and pockets of unreached peoples represented in North American cities, seminaries and other training programs must equip those preparing for pastoral leadership *locally*. Too often, our Christian preparatory institutions reserve trainings on culture and contextualization for missionary candidates in foreign fields, while American church planters default to their assumed ecclesiology, standardized gospel presentation, or default leadership structures. While future congregational leaders may not be preparing to face the exact same issues as families that navigate life in a foreign land, they will need to gain similar ministry skills and cross-cultural competencies to put the church on a missional footing across the American landscape. A basic grasp of ethnography, critical contextualization, folk religion, honor and shame frameworks, and cross-cultural communication are increasingly important when training American pastors. At the very least, congregational leaders must develop a keen awareness toward the needs and opportunities of diaspora communities in their cities.

Western church growth models typically elevate normative church experiences based on popular religious culture. Anyone who equips emerging congregational leaders must train them to think contextually about both the dominant culture and the variety of subcultures encountered through Christian witness. A variety of approaches, strategies, and communication styles is expected when global diversity and social change are compacted in shared urban space.

MULTICULTURAL, MULTIETHNIC, AND ETHNIC CHURCHES

When speaking at a seminary, Bible college class, conference, workshop, or any other ministry setting, one question frequently comes up: What about multicultural churches? Most people from the dominant culture actually mean *multiethnic* rather than *multicultural* when framing this question. In our contemporary global society, multiethnic churches meet an important need. Any number of people from a variety of ethnic backgrounds may be drawn to multiethnic churches that represent what they hear on Christian radio or see on religious television or online streaming, or that reflect their experience in an international church or Christian school overseas.

Forming faith communities and developing disciples in an increasingly complex and pluralistic society requires multifaceted perspectives. Multiple methods, philosophies, and strategies within the same communities or even people groups. In this chapter I am advocating for an acknowledgment of God's mosaic of people and human expressions of faith in Jesus as Lord. Let us grow in understanding the various cultural and missiological dynamics at play as we form communities of faith in dynamic contemporary contexts.

Multiethnic churches may include many participants from different backgrounds and different ethnicities and cultural heritages, but they are still, for the most part, operating within one dominant culture frame. By contrast, multicultural churches are heterogenous in cultural expression as well as ethnic identity. Multicultural churches express a plurality of voices, styles, influences, social structures, and expressions. They realize that giving voice to a variety of cultures equals more than what takes place on stage. Differences in decision-making, community rhythms, conflict resolution, communication styles, and many other factors must be taken into account.

Those arguing for saturation church planting might suggest that there is not time for this type of deep ecclesiological development work considering the urgency of the task. Saturation church planting means many churches are being planted as quickly as possible in an area. It is an effort to fill an area with Christian communities that a Christian witness is within easy access of every person. Advocates for this approach are not wrong. To cultivate a fully multicultural community, it takes time. Saturation church planting requires both ethnic and multiethnic churches to multiply at an increasing pace. Multicultural churches will represent only a minority of church planting efforts. Still, these churches provide an opportunity for deep collaboration across otherwise divisive boundaries, and they may emerge as models for loving our neighbors in multicultural neighborhoods where inter-ethnic conflict is not uncommon. They model self-emptying as an essential component of community life.[10] They are intercultural pioneers that will help navigate the way forward in pluralistic contexts and develop communities of mutual sharing, leadership, and variety of expression. Such churches provide a space where the global nature of heaven is experienced on earth. While they will not be the most common church experience, we need the courage and humility to plant multicultural churches too.

In many cities, there are at least a handful of churches that include a variety of ethnicities while largely operating under a dominant cultural expression—typically one of the dominant Anglo-American church paradigms. However, global metro areas feature a continuum of culture and cultural change. That continuum includes individuals and families that prefer a religious expression that reflects the dominant culture or a popular Christian tradition. Many people have been digesting religious media, attended a Western-style private school in their home country, or have previously participated in a church modeled after American or European culture before migrating. Others find the dominant religious expressions to be culturally strange, but they prefer to connect with a body that they view as "mainstream." Still others may have adopted Christian faith in an ethnic church within their own community but as they assimilate into the dominant culture in other areas of their life, they are drawn to a church experience that reflects the dominant culture as well. Multiethnic churches were previously the celebrated exception, but in recent years these types of churches are becoming increasingly common. In an age of globalization,

---

10. Oh, "Cultural Pluralism and Multiethnic Congregation."

multiethnic churches will grow and flourish, and they provide a space between multicultural and ethnically homogenous churches.

Ethnic churches are frequently planted by either cross-cultural workers or by global migrants themselves. These churches are incredibly important in the advance of God's mission in globally diverse cities and regions. In these spaces, the gospel is fully expressed in a group's heart language, community rhythms, and cultural practices. They are where a subculture can forge a Christ-centered identity incarnationally in terms of their specific cultural commitments and practices. They are the settings where the communities can develop deeply contextualized expressions of the gospel that make sense to members of those cultures. Ethnic leaders may wrestle with Scripture to develop theologies that speak the truth of God's word clearly to diaspora enclaves and perhaps resonate in their homeland. Indeed, for church planters who desire to evangelize an unreached people in their diaspora context with the intention of bridging the gospel to their homeland, local contextualization among a specific ethnic culture must be a critical consideration. Naturally, critics of single-ethnicity church planting might ask: What about unity across these ethnic boundaries? Yes, unity is essential. However, does unity mean that everyone must be in the same room generally opting to submit to a dominant culture other than their own? How might we encourage Christian unity without assuming a single religious monoculture? As a start, multi-congregational summits and retreats, decentralized church networks, leadership forums, shared celebrations, and other platforms can forge unity across the wider multicultural body of Christ while celebrating contextualized church planting among different cultures and subcultures in a city.

NEW PIONEERS

Participation in the mission of God, specifically through the practice of forming disciples and planting churches, requires new missionary pioneers. In Global City Mission, we regularly articulate that we are a pioneering ministry, but not because we are laboring in geographically remote places historically walled off from gospel proclamation. Rather, it is a pioneering ministry because a new world has emerged in our midst. In this hour, the church urgently needs cross-cultural workers who will navigate the type of missionary practice I have outlined here in that new world. Mission pioneers are needed to apply missional principles and practices at the intersection of globalization, urbanization, and the implications that these realities bring—including the multidimensional perspective of diaspora mission—as well as the challenges of post-Christendom in the West. Meanwhile, as seminary halls continue to echo with discussions of postmodernity, much of the rest of the church outside the West is wrestling with the realities of a postcolonial faith.

Even as the dominant culture around us was changing, diaspora mission taught us that we must operate from a mission paradigm in our proverbial backyard. In reality, we always should have labored on a missionary footing, but now it is a practical necessity. New pioneers must pursue grassroots church planting and contextual evangelism in North American cities. These efforts will provide a space for equipping the body of Christ to recover a missionary identity through relational practice. One may argue, as I have here, that ministry in the emerging "post-" landscape of North America and the practice of diaspora mission share overlapping concerns. In fact, diaspora mission may be the stimulant that churches rooted in the dominant culture have needed all along.

CONCLUSION

Diaspora mission and the emerging context of post-Christendom is generally treated as two separate issues. However, from the standpoint of a practitioner in pluralistic urban communities, we should treat the underlying principles for each of these two areas as inherently missionary. Many diaspora Christians possess evangelistic zeal but need to be equipped to adjust to a secularized and increasingly post-Christendom society. For many American Christians, learning to offer a Christian witness from the margins represents uncharted waters. Both post-religious settings and diaspora peoples require a missionary framework.

We see a theme weaving itself into the goals of those reimagining ministry in North America and Christian workers laboring among diaspora communities. Applying a missiological lens for discerning ministry practices plays a principal role in each context. Among some churches or church networks, ministers are encountering both the changing North American religious scene and global peoples in the same local context. While the answers to critical questions will likely differ based on specific encounters, the starting questions may be remarkably similar as we apply a missiological lens, listen and learn from our diaspora neighbors, and adapt to the dynamic diversity embodied in our contemporary environment.

Forming faith communities and developing disciples in a complex and pluralistic society requires multifaceted perspectives. Leaders may employ a spectrum of methods, philosophies, and strategies within the same communities or people groups. In this chapter, I have sought to advocate for an acknowledgment of God's mosaic of people and human expressions of faith in Jesus as Lord. As we form communities of faith in dynamic contemporary contexts, let us grow our understandings of the various cultural and missiological dynamics at play.

Bibliography

Addison, Steve. "Rapid Mobilization: How the West Was Won." *Mission Frontiers*, Mar 2020. https://www.missionfrontiers.org/issue/article/rapid-mobilization1.
Adkins, A. W. H. "Theoria versus Praxis in the Nicomachean Ethics and the Republic." *Classical Philology* 73 (1978) 297–13.
Allen, Leonard. *Poured Out: The Spirit of God Empowering the Mission of God*. Abilene, TX: Abilene Christian University Press, 2018.
Allison, Fieldon. "God's Work among the Kipsigis." In *Church Planting, Watering, and Increasing in Kenya: The Study of Church Growth among Churches of Christ in Kenya, 1965–1979*, edited by Kenya Mission Team, 75–80. Austin, TX: Firm Foundation, 1980.
Aquino, Jorge A. "Mestizaje: The Latina/o Religious Imaginary on the North American Racial Crucible." In *The Wiley Blackwell Companion to Latino/a Theology*, edited by Orlando O. Espín, 283–312. Oxford: John Wiley & Sons, 2015.
Arlund, Pam, and Warrick Farah. "Discussing and Catalyzing Movements: An Invitation to Research, Sacrifice, and Commitments." *Global Missiology* 19 (2022). http://ojs.globalmissiology.org/index.php/english/article/view/2691/6623.
Bacon, Michael. *Pragmatism: An Introduction*. Malden, MA: Polity, 2012.
Baker, Dwight P. "Missiology as an Interested Discipline—And Is It Happening?" *International Bulletin of Missionary Research* 38 (2014) 17–20.
Bakke, Raymond J. "Urbanization and Evangelism: A Global View." *Word and World* 19 (1999) 225–35.
Balaban, Oded. "Aristotle's Theory of Πρᾶξις." *Hermes* 114 (1986) 163–72.
Bañuelas, Arturo J., ed. *Mestizo Christianity: Theology from the Latino Perspective*. Maryknoll, NY: Orbis, 1995.
Barrett, David B. *Schism and Renewal in Africa: An Analysis of Six Thousand Contemporary Religious Movements*. Nairobi: Oxford University Press, 1968.
Barton, Ruth Haley. *Pursuing God's Will Together: A Discernment Practice for Leadership Groups*. Downers Grove, IL: InterVarsity, 2012.
Bass, Dorothy C., and Craig Dykstra, eds. *For Life Abundant: Practical Theology, Theological Education, and Christian Ministry*. Grand Rapids: Eerdmans, 2008.
Bauerlein, Mark, and Adam Bellow, eds. *The State of the American Mind: 16 Leading Critics on the New Anti-Intellectualism*. West Conshohocken, PA: Templeton, 2015.
Benitez, Cristina, and Marlene González. *Latinization and the Latino Leader: How to Value, Develop, and Advance Latino Professionals*. Ithaca, NY: Paramount Market, 2011.

Bibliography

Bernasconi, Robert. "The Fate of the Distinction between *Praxis* and *Poiesis*." *Heidegger Studies* 2 (1986) 111–39.

Bernstein, Richard J. *The Pragmatic Turn*. Malden, MA: Polity, 2010.

Boff, Clodovis. *Theology and Praxis: Epistemological Foundations*. Translated by Robert R. Barr. Maryknoll, NY: Orbis, 1987.

Boring, M. Eugene. *Disciples and the Bible: A History of Disciples Biblical Interpretation in North America*. St. Louis, MO: Chalice, 1997.

Bosch, David. *Transforming Mission: Paradigm Shifts in Theology of Mission*. 25th anniversary ed. American Society of Missiology Series 16. Maryknoll, NY: Orbis, 2011.

Bourdillon, M. F. C. *The Shona Peoples: An Ethnography of the Contemporary Shona, with Special Reference to Their Religion*. Rev. ed. Gweru, Zimbabwe: Mambo, 1976.

Branson, Mark Lau. *Memories, Hopes, and Conversations: Appreciative Inquiry and Congregational Change*. Herndon, VA: Alban Institute, 2004.

Brooks, David. "The Nuclear Family Was a Mistake." *The Atlantic*, Mar 15, 2020. https://www.theatlantic.com/magazine/archive/2020/03/the-nuclear-family-was-a-mistake/605536.

Brown, Anna, and Renee Stepler. "Statistical Portrait of the Foreign-Born Population of the United States." Pew Research Center, Apr 19, 2016. https://www.pewresearch.org/hispanic/2016/04/19/2014-statistical-information-on-immigrants-in-united-states.

Budiman, Abby, et al. "Facts on U.S. Immigrants, 2018: Statistical Portrait of the Foreign-Born Population in the United States." Pew Research Center, Aug 20, 2020. https://www.pewresearch.org/hispanic/2020/08/20/facts-on-u-s-immigrants.

Buechner, Frederick. *Wishful Thinking: A Seeker's ABC*. New York: Harper and Row, 1984.

Bujo, Benézét. *African Theology in Its Social Context*. New York: Orbis, 1992.

Burge, Ryan P. "Assemblies of God Growing with Pentecostal Persistence." *Christianity Today*, Aug 11, 2021. https://www.christianitytoday.com/news/2021/august/assemblies-of-god-grow-us-council-denomination-decline-poli.html.

Casey, Michael W. "The First Graduate Theological Education in the Churches of Christ, Part 1: Jesse Sewell's and George Klingman's Audacious Synthesis of Spirituality and Academic Excellence at Abilene Christian College." *Restoration Quarterly* 44 (2002) 73–92.

———. "The First Graduate Theological Education in the Churches of Christ, Part 2: The Controversy over Webb Freeman's 'Modernism' and the Resulting Collapse of Sewell's Dream." *Restoration Quarterly* 44 (2002) 139–57.

Castor, Trevor. "Mapping the Diaspora with Facebook©." In *Diaspora Missiology: Reflections on Reaching The Scattered Peoples of the World*, edited by Michael Pocock and Enoch Wan, 21–35. Evangelical Missiological Society Series 23. Pasadena: William Carey Library, 2015.

Cheong, John. "Reassessing John Stott's, David Hesselgrave's, and Andreas Köstenberger's Views of the Incarnational Model." In *Missionary Methods: Research, Reflections, and Realities*, edited by Craig Ott and J. D. Payne, 39–60. Pasadena: William Carey Library, 2013.

Clinton, Bobby. *Interpreting the Scriptures: Figures and Idioms*. Coral Gables, FL: Learning Resource Center–West Indies Mission, 1977.

Cohen, Robin. *Global Diasporas: An Introduction*. Seattle: University of Washington Press, 1997.

Bibliography

Coleman, Jules L. "Legal Theory and Practice." *The Georgetown Law Journal* 83 (1995) 2579–617.

Coles, Dave, and Don Little. "Church Planting Approaches in Tension: Traditional versus Movements." Missio Nexus Mission Leaders Conference. Orlando, FL, September 19–21, 2019. Debate, 02:12:14. https://youtu.be/G5cvuFg1VVE.

Corbett, Steve, and Brian Fikkert. *Helping without Hurting in Short-Term Missions: Participant's Guide*. Chicago: Moody, 2014.

Costas, Orlando E. *Christ outside the Gate: Mission beyond Christendom*. 1982. Reprint, Eugene, OR: Wipf & Stock, 2005.

"Crucible." https://www.merriam-webster.com/dictionary/crucible.

Crouch, Andy. *Culture Making: Recovering Our Creative Calling*. Downers Grove, IL: InterVarsity, 2013.

Daneel, M. L. *The God of the Matopo Hills: An Essay on the Mwari Cult in Rhodesia*. The Hague: Mouton, 1970.

———. "Review of Marshall W. Murphree Christianity and the Shona. London School of Economics; Monographs on Social Anthropology." *Bijdragen Tot de Taal-, Land- En Volkenkunde* 127 (1971) n.p.

Davis, Charles A. *Making Disciples across Cultures: Missional Principles for a Diverse World*. Downers Grove, IL: InterVarsity, 2015.

DeHart, Scott M. "The Convergence of Praxis and Theoria in Aristotle." *Journal of the History of Philosophy* 33 (1995) 7–27.

Delgado, Richard, and Jean Stefancic. *Critical Race Theory: An Introduction*. 3rd ed. New York: New York University Press, 2017.

Dent, Don. "Decisive Discipleship: Why Rapid Discipleship Is Preferable and How It Is Possible." *Global Missiology—English* 1 (2015). http://ojs.globalmissiology.org/index.php/english/article/view/1818/4029.

Descartes, René. *Meditations and Other Metaphysical Writings*. London: Penguin, 2003.

Dogbe, Korsi. "Concept of Community and Community Support Systems in Africa." *Anthropos* 75 (1980) 781–98.

Doriani, Dan. "Why I Don't Think You Must Vote for the Lesser of Two Evils." *The Gospel Coalition*, Sept. 6, 2016. https://www.thegospelcoalition.org/article/why-i-dont-think-you-must-vote-for-lesser-two-evils.

Downes, Stan. "Mission by and beyond the Diaspora: Partnering with Diaspora Believers to Reach Other Immigrant Groups and the Local People." In *Diaspora Missiology: Reflections on Reaching the Scattered Peoples of the World*, edited by Michael Pocock and Enoch Wan, 77–88. Evangelical Missiological Society Series 23. Pasadena: William Carey Library, 2015.

Eden Center for Regenerative Culture. https://www.edencenter.org.

Editor. "An African Village." *Gospel Advocate* (October 17, 1878) 41.

Elizondo, Virgilio. "Mestizaje as a Locus of Theological Reflection." In *The Future of Liberation Theology: Essays in Honor of Gustavo Gutiérrez*, edited by Marc H. Ellis and Otto Maduro, 358–74. Maryknoll, NY: Orbis, 1989.

Emerson, Robert M., et al. *Writing Ethnographic Fieldnotes*. 2nd ed. Chicago: University of Chicago Press, 2011.

Engle, Paul E., and Gary L. McIntosh, eds. *Evaluating the Church Growth Movement*. Grand Rapids: Zondervan, 2004.

Escobar, Samuel. "A Movement Divided: Three Approaches to World Evangelization Stand in Tension with One Another." *Transformation* 8 (1991) 7–13.

Bibliography

———. *The New Global Mission: The Gospel from Everywhere to Everyone.* Downers Grove, IL: InterVarsity, 2013.

Espín, Orlando O., ed. *The Wiley Blackwell Companion to Latino/a Theology.* Hoboken, NJ: Wiley, 2015.

Espinosa, Gastón. *Latino Pentecostals in America.* Cambridge, MA: Harvard University Press, 2014.

Evans-Pritchard, E. E. "The Study of Kinship in Primitive Societies." *Man* 29 (1929) 190–93.

Farah, Warrick. "Motus Dei: Disciple-Making Movements and the Mission of God." *Global Missiology—English* (January 2020). http://ojs.globalmissiology.org/index.php/english/article/view/2309/5306.

Farrell, B. Hunter. "Re-Membering Missiology: An Invitation to an Activist Agenda." *Missiology: An International Review* 46 (2018) 37–49.

Fensham, Charles, ed. "Group Discussion Conclusions on the Future of the Discipline of Missiology: Annual Meeting of the American Society of Missiology." *Missiology: An International Review* 42 (2013) 80–86.

Ferguson, Everett. *Baptism in the Early Church: History, Theology, and Liturgy in the First Five Centuries.* Grand Rapids: Eerdmans, 2009.

———. "Catechesis, Catechumenate." In *The Encyclopedia of Early Christianity*, edited by Everett Ferguson et al., 223–25. New York: Routledge, 1999.

———. *The Early Church at Work and Worship.* Vol. 2, *Catechesis, Baptism, Eschatology, and Martyrdom.* The Early Church at Work and Worship. Cambridge: James Clarke, 2014.

Fiorenza, Francis Schüssler. "Theory and Practice: Theological Education as a Reconstructive, Hermeneutical, and Practical Task." *Theological Education Supplement* (1987) 113–41.

Fitch, David. "Biblical/Theological Method." Seminar at Northern Seminary, Lombard, IL, January 8–12, 2018.

Flanders, Christopher L., ed. "The Beginning of Missionary Training in Churches of Christ (Part 1)." *Restoration Quarterly* 61 (2019) 27–38.

———. "The Beginning of Missionary Training in Churches of Christ (Part 2)." *Restoration Quarterly* 61 (2019) 65–76.

———. *Devoted to Christ: Missiological Reflections in Honor of Sherwood G. Lingenfelter.* Eugene, OR: Pickwick Publications, 2019.

Flores, Soledad Sánchez. *Concepto de Sensibilidad en la Ilustración.* Pensamiento Ilustrado. Granada: Universidad de Granada, 2017.

Foroohar, Manzar. "Liberation Theology: The Response of Latin American Catholics to Socioeconomic Problems." *Latin American Perspectives* 13 (1986) 37–58.

Fortes, Meyer. *Kinship and the Social Order: The Legacy of Lewis Henry Morgan.* Chicago: Aldine, 1969.

Foster, Douglas A., ed. *The Encyclopedia of the Stone-Campbell Movement: Christian Church (Disciples of Christ), Christian Churches/Churches of Christ/Churches of Christ.* Grand Rapids: Eerdmans, 2004.

Foster, Richard J. *Streams of Living Water: Celebrating the Great Traditions of Christian Faith.* San Francisco: Harper, 1998.

Franke, John R. *Missional Theology: An Introduction.* Grand Rapids: Baker Academic, 2020.

Frost, M. *Exiles: Living Missionally in a Post-Christian Culture.* Grand Rapids: Baker, 2006.

Bibliography

Frost, Michael, and Alan Hirsch. *The Shaping of Things to Come: Innovation and Mission for the 21st-Century Church*. Peabody, MA: Hendrickson, 2003.

Garrison, David. *Church Planting Movements: How God Is Redeeming a Lost World*. Midlothian, VA: WIGTake Resources, 2004.

Gelfand, Michael. *The Genuine Shona: Survival Values of an African Culture*. Gwelo, Rhodesia: Mambo, 1973.

Global Migration Data Analysis Center, 2021. https://www.migrationdataportal.org/international-data?i=stock_abs_&t=2020.

González, Justo L. *The History of Theological Education*. Nashville: Abingdon, 2015.

———. *The Mestizo Augustine: A Theologian between Two Cultures*. Downers Grove, IL: InterVarsity, 2016.

González, Ondina E., and González, Justo L. *Nuestra Fe: A Latin American Church History Sourcebook*. Nashville: Abingdon, 2014.

Goodenough, Ward H. "Rethinking 'Status' and 'Role': Toward a General Model of the Cultural Relationship." In *The Relevance of Models for Social Anthropology*, edited by Michael Banton, 1–24. London: Routledge, 2004.

Graham, Billy. "Why Lausanne?" First International Congress on World Evangelization. Lausanne, Switzerland, 1974. https://www.lausanne.org/content/why-lausanne-print.

Guder, Darrell L., ed. *Missional Church: A Vision for the Sending of the Church in North America*. The Gospel and Our Culture Series. Grand Rapids: Eerdmans, 1998.

Gustavo, Jamut E., and Diego A. González Rivera, eds. *Ejercicios Espirituales de San Ignacio de Loyola: Texto Modernizado y Adaptado a Nuestro Tiempo por el P. Gustavo Jamut, OMV, y el P. Diego Gonzalez*. Argentina: Editorial Claretiana, 2022.

Gutiérrez, Gustavo. *On Job: God-Talk and the Suffering of the Innocent*. Translated by Matthew J. O'Connell. Maryknoll, NY: Orbis, 1987.

Gwamzhi, L. N. "Contextualization in Diaspora Mission: An African Christian's Perspective of the Mission Agenda in the US." *Global Missiology* 4 (2013) 2–3.

Hagberg, Janet O., and Robert A. Guelich. *The Critical Journey: Stages in the Life of Faith*. 2nd ed. Salem, WI: Sheffield, 2005.

Hallett, Jeff, and Lindsay Hallett. *Kipsigis Kalenjin in Kenya*. https://joshuaproject.net/people_groups/12709/KE.

Hammar, Anna Nilsson. "Theoria, Praxis, and Poiesis: Theoretical Considerations on the Circulation of Knowledge in Everyday Life." In *Circulation of Knowledge: Explorations in the History of Knowledge*, edited by E. Sandmo Östling et al., 107–24. Lund, Sweden: Nordic Academic, 2018.

Hanciles, Jehu. "The Future of Missiology as a Discipline: A View from the Non-Western World." *Missiology: An International Review* 42 (2014) 121–38.

Hartwell, Jay. "The Seoul Declaration on Diaspora Missiology." Lausanne Movement, Sep 22, 2014. https://lausanne.org/content/statement/the-seoul-declaration-on-diaspora-missiology.

Hatch, Nathan O. "The Christian Movement and the Demand for a Theology of the People." *Journal of American History* 67 (1980) 545–67.

———, ed. *The Democratization of American Christianity*. New Haven: Yale University Press, 1989.

Hiestand, Gerald, and Todd Wilson. *The Pastor Theologian: Resurrecting an Ancient Vision*. Grand Rapids: Zondervan, 2015.

Bibliography

Hofstede, Geert. "Individualism." Clearly Cultural. https://clearlycultural.com/geert-hofstede-cultural-dimensions/individualism/.

Holmes, Urban T. *A History of Christian Spirituality: An Analytical Introduction*. New York: Seabury, 1980.

Horton, David. *The Portable Seminary: A Master's Level Overview in One Volume*. 2nd ed. Minneapolis: Bethany, 2018.

Horton, Robin. "African Conversion." *Africa: Journal of the International African Institute* 41 (1971) 85–108.

Hove, Musavengana. "Muslims Court Varemba Community." *The Herald*, Jul 29, 2016. https://www.herald.co.zw/muslims-court-varemba-community.

Huffard, Evertt W. "When Scholarship Goes South: Biblical Scholarship and Global Trends." *Restoration Quarterly* 48 (2006) 65–72.

Hughes, Richard T., and C. Leonard Allen. *Illusions of Innocence: Protestant Primitivism in America, 1630–1875*. Chicago: University of Chicago Press, 1988.

Hsu, Francis. L. K. *Clan, Caste, and Club*. Princeton: Van Nostrand, 1963.

———. "The Effect of Dominant Kinship Relationships on Kin and Non-Kin Behavior: A Hypothesis." *American Anthropologist* 67 (1965) 638–61.

———, ed. *Kinship and Culture*. Chicago: Aldine, 1971.

Isasi-Díaz, Ada María. *La Lucha Continues: Mujerista Theology*. Maryknoll, NY: Orbis, 1996.

Isasi-Díaz, Ada María, and Fernando F. Segovia, eds. *Hispanic/Latino Theology: Challenge and Promise*. Minneapolis: Fortress, 1996.

Jacoby, Susan. *The Age of American Unreason in a Culture of Lies*. 2nd ed. New York: Vintage, 2018.

James, Christopher B. *Church Planting in Post-Christian Soil: Theology and Practice*. New York: Oxford University Press, 2018.

James, William. *Principles of Psychology*. New York: Henry Holt, 1890.

———. *The Works of William James*. Vol. 13, *Essays in Psychology*. Edited by Frederick H. Burkhardt et al. Cambridge, MA: Harvard University Press, 1983.

Johnson, Todd M., et al. "Christianity 2018: More African Christians and Counting Martyrs." *International Bulletin of Mission Research* 42 (2017) 1–12.

Jones, Jeffrey M. "Presidential Moral Leadership Less Important to Republicans." Gallup, May 29, 2018. https://news.gallup.com/poll/235022/presidential-moral-leadership-less-important-republicans.aspx.

———. "U.S. Church Membership Falls below Majority for First Time." Gallup, Nov 20, 2021. https://news.gallup.com/poll/341963/church-membership-falls-below-majority-first-time.aspx.

Jones, Robert P. "Donald Trump and the Transformation of White Evangelicals." *Time*, Nov 19, 2016. https://time.com/4577752/donald-trump-transformation-white-evangelicals.

———. *The End of White Christian America*. New York: Simon and Schuster, 2016.

Kachapova, Farida. "On the Importance of Pure Mathematics." *Journal of Mathematics and Statistics* 10 (2014) 421–22.

Kant, Immanuel, et al. *Critique of Pure Reason*. New York: Penguin, 2007.

Kenya Mission Team, eds. *Church Planting, Watering, and Increasing in Kenya: The Study of Church Growth among the Churches of Christ in Kenya, 1965–1979*. Austin, TX: Firm Foundation, 1980.

Bibliography

Kim, Eun-Young Julia. "Born Again with Trump: The Portrayal of Evangelicals in the Media." *Journal of Religion and Society* 21 (2019) 1–30.

Kim, Hyun-Sook. "The Hermeneutical-Praxis Paradigm and Practical Theology." *Religious Education* 102 (2007) 419–36.

Kim, Kirsteen. *The Holy Spirit in the World*. Maryknoll, NY: Orbis, 2007.

Klingman, George A. "John Sherriff in Toronto, Ontario, Canada." *Gospel Advocate* 6 (March 1924) n.p.

Lamola, Malesela. "Marx, the Praxis of Liberation Theology, and the Bane of Religious Epistemology." *Religions* 9 (2018) 13.

Langmead, Ross. "What Is Missiology?" *Missiology: An International Review* 42 (2013) 67–79.

Larkin, Ernest E. "The Three Spiritual Ways." http://carmelnet.org/larkin/larkin092.pdf.

Latourette, Kenneth Scott. *A History of the Expansion of Christianity*. 7 vols. Contemporary Evangelical Perspectives. Grand Rapids: Zondervan, 1970.

Leder, Arie C., and Richard A. Muller. *Biblical Interpretation and Doctrinal Formulation in the Reformed Tradition: Essays in Honor of James A. De Jong*. Grand Rapids: Reformation Heritage, 2014.

Leedy, Todd H. "History with a Mission: Abraham Kawadza and Narratives of Agrarian Change in Zimbabwe." *History in Africa* 33 (2006) 255–70.

LifeWay Research. "New Hispanic Churches Often Do More with Less." Jul 24, 2019. https://lifewayresearch.com/2019/07/24/new-hispanic-churches-often-do-more-with-less.

Livermore, David A. *Serving with Eyes Wide Open: Doing Short-Term Missions with Cultural Intelligence*. Grand Rapids: Baker, 2012.

Lopez, Mark Hugo, et al. "Who Is Hispanic?" Pew Research Center, Sep 15, 2022. https://www.pewresearch.org/fact-tank/2020/09/15/who-is-hispanic.

Lopez, Mark Hugo, et al. "Key Facts about the Changing U.S. Unauthorized Immigrant Population." Pew Research Center, Apr 13, 2021. https://www.pewresearch.org/fact-tank/2021/04/13/key-facts-about-the-changing-u-s-unauthorized-immigrant-population.

Loy, Allan W. "Praxis: Karl Marx's Challenge to Christian Theology." *St. Mark's Review* 113 (1983) 7–14.

Loyola, Ignacio de. *Ejercicios Espirituales de San Ignacio de Loyola: Texto Modernizado y Adaptado a Nuestro Tiempo por el P. Gustavo Jamut, OMV, y el P. Diego González*. Edited by Jamut E. Gustavo and Diego A González Rivera. Argentina: Editorial Claretiana, 2022.

Lozada, Francisco, Jr., and Fernando F. Segovia, eds. *Latino/a Theology and the Bible: Ethnic-Racial Reflections on Interpretation*. Lanham, MD: Lexington, 2021.

Lukianoff, Greg, and Jonathan Haidt. *The Coddling of the American Mind: How Good Intentions and Bad Ideas Are Setting Up a Generation for Failure*. New York: Penguin, 2018.

Magnin, Lucas. "De la Justificación a la Justicia." *Escuela de Ciencias Teológicas, UBL*, Aportes Teológicos 1 (2021) 77.

Makunde, Mirimi. Personal notes, n.d. Pindukai Makunde, personal library, Two Streams Farm, Virginia, Macheke, Zimbabwe.

Malinowski, Bronislaw. *Argonauts of the Western Pacific*. New York: Dutton, 1922.

———. *Sex and Repression in Savage Society*. London: Routledge & Kegan Paul, 1927.

Bibliography

Markey, John J. "Praxis in Liberation Theology: Some Clarifications." *Missiology: An International Review* 23 (1995) 179–95.

Martinez, Juan Francisco. *The Story of Latino Protestants in the United States*. Grand Rapids: Eerdmans, 2018.

———. *Walk with the People: Latino Ministry in the United States*. 2008. Reprint, Eugene, OR: Wipf & Stock, 2016.

Masondo, Sibusiso. "Indigenous Conceptions of Conversion among African Christians in South Africa." *Journal for the Study of Religion* 28 (2015) 87–112.

Matthews, A. "Person of Peace Methodology in Church Planting: A Critical Analysis." *Missiology: An International Review* 47 (2019) 187–99.

Maxwell, David. "'Delivered from the Spirit of Poverty?' Pentecostalism, Prosperity and Modernity in Zimbabwe." *Journal of Religion in Africa* 28 (1998) 353.

McCaleb, J. M. "On The Trail of the Missionaries." Nashville: *Gospel Advocate*, 1930.

McGavran, Donald A. *The Bridges of God: A Study in the Strategy of Missions*. 1955. Reprint, Eugene, OR: Wipf & Stock, 2005.

———. *Understanding Church Growth*. Edited by C. Peter Wagner. 3rd ed. Grand Rapids: Eerdmans, 1990.

———. "Will Uppsala Betray the Two Billion?" In *The Eye of the Storm: The Great Debate in Mission*, edited by Donald McGavran, 233–41. Waco, TX: Word, 1972.

McGilcrist, Ian. *The Master and His Emissary: The Divided Brain and the Making of the Western World*. 2nd ed. New Haven: Yale University Press, 2018.

McKinzie, Greg. "All Things in Relation to God's Mission (Editorial Preface to the Issue)." *Missio Dei: A Journal of Missional Theology and Praxis* 12 (2021). https://missiodeijournal.com/issues/md-12-1/authors/md-12-1-preface.

———. "The Hermeneutics of Participation: Missional Interpretation of Scripture and Readerly Formation." PhD diss., Fuller Theological Seminary, 2022.

———. "Missional Hermeneutics as Theological Interpretation." *Journal of Theological Interpretation* 11 (2017) 160–69.

McNeel, Bekah. "Latino Immigrants Are Evangelizing America." *Christianity Today*, July 24, 2019. https://www.christianitytoday.com/news/2019/july/hispanic-church-planting-survey-immigration-evangelism.html.

Medina, Néstor. *Christianity, Empire and the Spirit: (Re)Configuring Faith and the Cultural*. Theology and Mission in World Christianity 11. Leiden: Brill, 2018.

———. *Mestizaje: Remapping Race, Culture, and Faith in Latina/o Catholicism*. Studies in Latino/a Catholicism. Maryknoll, NY: Orbis, 2014.

Melloni, Javier. *Éxodo y Éxtasis en Ignacio de Loyola: Una Aproximación a Su Autobiografía*. Maliaño Cantabria, España: Sal Terrae, 2020.

Merritt, John Dow. *The Dew Breakers*. Winona, MS: Choate, 1980.

Miller-McLemore, Bonnie. "The Theory–Practice Distinction and the Complexity of Practical Knowledge." *HTS Teologiese Studies / Theological Studies* 72 (2016). http://www.hts.org.za/index.php/HTS/article/view/3381.

Morgan, Lewis Henry. *Ancient Society*. New York: Word, 1877.

Moschella, Mary Clark. *Ethnography as a Pastoral Practice: An Introduction*. Cleveland, OH: Pilgrim, 2008.

Mulder, Mark T., et al. *Latino Protestants in America: Growing and Diverse*. Lanham, MD: Rowman & Littlefield, 2017.

Murray, Stuart. *Post-Christendom: Church and Mission in a Strange New World*. Eugene, OR: Cascade Books, 2018.

Nehrbass, Kenneth. "Does Missiology Have a Leg to Stand On? The Upsurge of Interdisciplinarity." *Missiology: An International Review* 44 (2016) 50–65.

Newbigin, Lesslie. *Foolishness to the Greeks: The Gospel and Western Culture*. Grand Rapids: Eerdmans, 1988.

———. *The Gospel in a Pluralist Society*. Grand Rapids: Eerdmans, 1989.

———. *The Open Secret: An Introduction to the Theory of Mission*. Rev. ed. Grand Rapids: Eerdmans, 1995.

Nichols, Tom. *The Death of Expertise: The Campaign against Established Knowledge and Why It Matters*. New York: Oxford University Press, 2017.

Nishioka, Billy. "Rice and Bread: Metaphorical Construction of Reality: Toward a New Approach to Worldview." PhD diss., Fuller Theological Seminary, 1997.

Nock, Arthur Darby. *Conversion: The Old and the New in Religion from Alexander the Great to Augustine of Hippo*. Brown Classics in Judaica. Lanham, MD: University Press of America, 1988.

Noll, Mark A. *The Scandal of the Evangelical Mind*. Grand Rapids: Eerdmans, 1994.

Oh, Mark Edward. "Cultural Pluralism and Multiethnic Congregation as a Ministry Model in an Urban Society." DMin diss., Fuller Theological Seminary, 1988.

Okesson, Gregg. *A Public Missiology: How Local Churches Witness to a Complex World*. Grand Rapids: Baker Academic, 2020.

Olbricht, Thomas H. "The Coming of Ph.D.'s in Churches of Christ Colleges." *Restoration Quarterly* 51 (2009) 193–201.

———. "Hermeneutics in the Churches of Christ." *Restoration Quarterly* 37 (1995) 1–24.

———. "The Invitation: A Historical Survey." *Restoration Quarterly* 5 (1961) 6–16.

———. "Religious Scholarship and the Restoration Movement." *Restoration Quarterly* 25 (1982) 193–204.

Ortiz, Manuel. *The Hispanic Challenge: Opportunities Confronting the Church*. Downers Grove, IL: IVP Academic, 1994.

Paas, Stefan. "The Discipline of Missiology in 2016." *Calvin Theological Journal* 51 (2016) 37–54.

Padilla, C. René. *Raíces de un Evangelio integral*. Ediciones Kairós. Buenos Aires: Fraternidad Teológica Latinoamericana, 2020.

Palafox, Omar. "Seeking Sensible Interdependency for Missionaries Coming from the Church of Christ in Latin America." DMiss diss., Fuller Theological Seminary, 2020.

Peterson, Roger, et al. *Maximum Impact Short-Term Mission: The God-Commanded, Repetitive Deployment of Swift, Temporary, Non-Professional Missionaries*. Minneapolis: STEMPress, 2003.

Pew Research Center. "Facts on Latinos in the U.S." Sep 19, 2021. https://www.pewresearch.org/hispanic/fact-sheet/latinos-in-the-u-s-fact-sheet.

———. "Facts on U.S. Immigrants, 2018." https://www.pewresearch.org/hispanic/2020/08/20/facts-on-u-s-immigrants.

Pike, Kenneth L. *Language in Relation to a Unified Theory of the Structure of Human Behavior*. The Hague: Mouton, 1967.

Pocock, Michael, et al. *The Changing Face of World Missions: Engaging Contemporary Issues and Trends*. Grand Rapids: Baker Academic, 2005.

"Populist." https://www.merriam-webster.com/dictionary/populism.

Priest, Robert J., ed. *Effective Engagement in Short-Term Missions: Doing It Right!* Evangelical Missiological Society Series 16. Pasadena: William Carey Library, 2008.

Bibliography

PRRI. "Backing Trump, White Evangelicals Flip Flop on Importance of Candidate Character." PRRI/Brookings Survey. Oct 19, 2016. https://www.prri.org/research/prri-brookings-oct-19-poll-politics-election-clinton-double-digit-lead-trump.

Radcliffe-Brown, A. R. "A Mother's Brother in South Africa." *South Africa Journal of Science* 21 (1924) 542–55.

Radcliffe-Brown, A. R., and Daryll Forde, eds. *African Systems of Kinship and Marriage.* New York: Oxford University Press, 1967.

Raworth, Kate. *Doughnut Economics: Seven Ways to Think Like a 21st Century Economist.* White River Junction, VT: Chelsea Green, 2018.

Reed, James E., and Ronnie Prevost. *A History of Christian Education.* Nashville: Broadman and Holman, 1993.

Rhodes, Matt. "Advancing Conversations about Proclamational and Movements Methodologies." *Global Missiology* 19 (2022). http://ojs.globalmissiology.org/index.php/english/article/view/2692/6656.

———. *No Shortcut to Success: A Manifesto for Modern Missions.* 9Marks. Wheaton, IL: Crossway, 2022.

Rivers, W. H. R. "The Genealogical Method of Anthropological Inquiry." *The Sociological Review* 3 (1910) 1–12. Reprinted 1968 in *Kinship and Social Organization.* Monographs on Social Organization. London: London School of Economics.

Roberts, David. "How Our Housing Choices Make Adult Friendships More Difficult." *Vox*, Dec 27, 2018. http://vox.com/2015/10/28/9622920/housing-adult-friendship.

Rodriguez, Daniel A. *A Future for the Latino Church: Models for Multilingual, Multigenerational Hispanic Congregations.* Downers Grove, IL: IVP Academic, 2011.

———. "Hispanic Youth Ministry in the USA." In *Pentecostals and Charismatics in Latin America and Latino Communities*, edited by Nestor Medina and Sammy Alfaro, 127–39. New York: Palgrave MacMillan, 2015.

———. "Multigenerational Hispanic Ministry." In *The Hispanic Evangelical Church in the United States: History, Ministry, and Challenges*, edited by Samuel Pagán, 11–35. Elk Grove, CA: National Hispanic Leadership Conference, 2016.

Rodriguez, José David, and Loida I. Martell-Otero, eds. *Teología En Conjunto: A Collaborative Hispanic Protestant Theology.* Louisville, KY: Westminster John Knox, 1997.

Romero, Robert Chao. *Brown Church: Five Centuries of Latina/o Social Justice, Theology, and Identity.* Downers Grove, IL: InterVarsity, 2020.

Rotenberg, Mordechai. *Between Rationality and Irrationality: The Jewish Psychotherapeutic System.* New York: Routledge, 2017.

Roth, Wolff-Michael, et al. "The Theory-Practice Gap: Epistemology, Identity, and Education." *Education + Training* 56 (2014) 521–36.

Roxborogh, John. "Missiology after 'Mission'?" *International Bulletin of Missionary Research* 38 (2014) 120–24.

Scheler, Max. *Philosophical Perspectives.* Translated by O. A. Haac. Boston: Bacon, 1958.

Schneider, David. *American Kinship.* Englewood Cliffs, NJ: Prentice-Hall, 1968.

———. "Introduction: The Distinctive Features of Matrilineal Descent Groups." In *Matrilineal Kinship*, edited by David M. Schneider and Kathleen Gough, 1–20. Los Angeles: University of California Press, 1961.

Schreiter, Robert. *Constructing Local Theologies: 30th Anniversary Edition.* Maryknoll, NY: Orbis, 2015.

Bibliography

Schusky, Ernest L. *Manual for Kinship Analysis*. 2nd ed. New York: University Press of America, 1983.

Schwartz, Jeffrey. *The Mind and the Brain: Neuroplasticity and the Power of Mental Force*. New York: HarperCollins, 2009.

Shaw, R. Daniel. *Transculturation*. Pasadena: William Carey, 1988.

Sherriff, John. "Forest Vale Mission, Bulawayo, Rhodesia/Fifth Annual Report." *Christian Leader and the Way* 7 (1913) 13.

———. "From South Africa." *Christian Leader and the Way* 23 (1915) 4.

———. "South Africa, Seventh Annual Report." *Christian Leader and the Way* 5 (1915) 12–13.

Shewmaker, Jimmy (J. C.). *Memoirs of J. C. and Joyce Shewmaker*. Filed at Mutare School of Preaching and African Christian College, 1985.

Shweder, Richard A. *Why Do Men Barbecue? Recipes for Cultural Psychology*. Cambridge, MA: Harvard University Press, 2003.

Sinnott-Armstrong, Walter. "Consequentialism." In *Stanford Encyclopedia of Philosophy*. https://plato.stanford.edu/entries/consequentialism.

Smith, James K. A. *Desiring the Kingdom: Worship, Worldview and Cultural Formation*. Vol. 1 of *Cultural Liturgies*. Grand Rapids: Baker Academic, 2009.

Smith, Kent. "Ecosystems of Grace: An Old Vision for the New Church." *Missio Dei: A Journal of Missional Theology and Praxis* 7 (2016). https://missiodeijournal.com/issues/md-7/authors/md-7-smith.

Smith, Ted A. "Learning from Teología En Conjunto." https://perspectivasonline.com/downloads/learning-from-teologia-en-conjunto/.

S.O.E. "7 Standards of Excellence: A Code of Best Practice for Short-Term Mission Practitioners." https://soe.org/wp-content/uploads/SOE_Booklet.pdf.

Squires, Geoffrey. "Praxis: A Dissenting Note." *Journal of Curriculum Studies* 35 (2003) 1–7.

"State or Way (Purgative, Illuminative, Unitive)." https://www.newadvent.org/cathen/14254a.htm.

Stetzer, Ed, and David Putman. *Breaking the Missional Code: When Churches Become Missionaries in Their Communities*. Nashville: B&H, 2006.

Sundkler, Bengt G. *Bantu Prophets in South Africa*. 2nd ed. Toronto: Oxford University Press, 1970.

Temba, Chikonye. Interview by Linda F. Whitmer, Gweru, Zimbabwe, March 31 and April 7, 1998.

Thiemann, Ronald F. "Praxis: The Practical Atheism of Karl Marx." *Journal of Ecumenical Studies* 22 (1985) 544–49.

Thorsen, Don. *The Wesleyan Quadrilateral: Scripture, Tradition, Reason and Experience as a Model of Evangelical Theology*. Lexington, KY: Emeth, 2005.

Tira, Sadiri Joy. "Diasporas from Cape Town 2010 to Manila 2015 and Beyond: The Lausanne Movement and Scattered Peoples." *Lausanne Global Analysis*, Mar 9, 2015. https://lausanne.org/content/lga/2015-03/diasporas-from-cape-town-2010-to-manila-2015-and-beyond.

———. "Diaspora Missiology." *Global Missiology* 2 (2011) 1.

Tracy, David. "Theoria and Praxis: A Partial Response." *Theological Education* 17 (1981) 167–74.

Trousdale, Jerry. *Miraculous Movements: How Hundreds of Thousands of Muslims Are Falling in Love with Jesus*. Nashville: Thomas Nelson, 2012.

Bibliography

———. "Simple Churches: Dramatic Transformations, Rapid Replication." *Mission Frontiers*, 2015. https://www.missionfrontiers.org/issue/article/simple-churches.

Trousdale, Jerry, and Glenn Sunshine, with Gregory Benoit. *The Kingdom Unleashed: How Jesus' 1st-Century Kingdom Values Are Transforming Thousands of Cultures and Awakening His Church.* Murfreesboro, TN: DMM Library, 2018.

Trull, Richard E., Jr. *The Fourth Self: Theological Education to Facilitate Self-Theologizing for Local Church Leaders in Kenya.* New York: Peter Lang, 2013.

Tylor, Edward. "On a Method of Investigating the Development of Institutions; Applied to the Laws of Marriage and Descent." *Journal of the Royal Anthropological Institute* 18 (1889) 245–72.

Udall, Jessica A. "The Ethiopian Diaspora: Ethiopian Immigrants as Cross-Cultural Missionaries: Activating the Diaspora for Great Commission Impact." In *Diaspora Missiology: Reflections on Reaching the Scattered Peoples of the World*, edited by Michael Pocock and Enoch Wan, 183–195. Evangelical Missiological Society Series 23. Pasadena: William Carey Library, 2015.

United States Census Bureau. "About the Foreign-Born Population." https://www.census.gov/topics/population/foreign-born/about.html.

Valentín, Benjamín, ed. *In Our Own Voices: Latino/a Renditions of Theology.* United States: Orbis, 2010.

Valiente, Orfilio Ernesto. *Liberation through Reconciliation: Jon Sobrino's Christological Spirituality.* New York: Fordham University Press, 2015.

Van Engen, Charles. *Mission on the Way.* Grand Rapids: Baker, 1996.

Van Gelder, Craig. "The Future of the Discipline of Missiology: Framing Current Realities and Future Possibilities." *Missiology: An International Review* 42 (2013) 39–56.

———. *The Ministry of the Missional Church: A Community Led by the Spirit.* Grand Rapids: Baker, 2007.

Vanhoozer, Kevin, and Owen Strachan. *The Pastor as Public Theologian: Reclaiming a Lost Vision.* Grand Rapids: Baker Academic, 2015.

Van Rheenen, Gailyn. *Biblically Anchored Missions.* Austin, TX: Firm Foundation, 1983.

———. *Church Planting in Uganda: A Comparative Study.* South Pasadena: William Carey Library, 1976.

———. *Communicating Christ in Animistic Contexts.* Pasadena: William Carey Library, 1991.

———. "Introducing the Kenya Church Growth Philosophy." In *Church Planting, Watering, and Increasing in Kenya: The Study of Church Growth among Churches of Christ in Kenya, 1965–1979*, edited by Kenya Mission Team, 5–10. Austin, TX: Firm Foundation, 1980.

———. *Missions: Biblical Foundations and Contemporary Strategies.* Grand Rapids: Zondervan, 1996.

———. "Review of *Church Planting Movements* by David Garrison." *Restoration Quarterly* 44 (2002) 128.

Van Rheenen, Gailyn, with Anthony Parker. *Missions: Biblical Foundations and Contemporary Strategies.* 2nd ed. Grand Rapids: Zondervan, 2014.

Vassiliadis, Petros. "Mission and Theology: Teaching Missiology on the Basis of Together towards Life." *International Review of Mission* 106 (2017) 51–58.

Verkuyl, Johannes. *Contemporary Missiology: An Introduction.* Translated and edited by Dale Cooper. Grand Rapids: Eerdmans, 1978.

Bibliography

Verster, Pieter. "Missiology: Rise, Demise and Future at the University." *Nederduitse Gereformeerde Teologiese Tydskrif* 55 (2014) 879–93.

Vilaça, Guilherme Vasconcelos. "Why Teach Legal Theory Today?" *German Law Journal* 16 (2015) 781–819.

Volf, Miroslav. "Doing and Interpreting: An Examination of the Relationship between Theory and Practice in Latin American Liberation Theology." *Themelios* 8 (1983) 11–19.

Volf, Miroslav, and Dorothy C. Bass, eds. *Practicing Theology: Beliefs and Practices in Christian Life.* Grand Rapids: Eerdmans, 2002.

Wan, Enoch. "Diaspora Missiology." *Global Missiology* 4 (2007). http://ojs.globalmissiology.org/index.php/english/article/view/303.

———. "Global People and Diaspora Missiology." In *Tokyo 2010 Global Mission Consultation Handbook*, edited by Yong J. Cho and David Taylor, 92–100. Pasadena: Tokyo 2010 Global Mission Consultation Planning Committee, 2010.

———. "The Phenomenon of Diaspora: Missiological Implications for Christian Missions." *Global Missiology* 4 (2012). http://ojs.globalmissiology.org/index.php/english/article/view/1036/2416.

Wan, Enoch, et al. *Diaspora Missiology: Theory, Methodology, and Practice.* 2nd ed. Portland, OR: Institute of Diaspora Studies of USA, Western Seminary, 2014.

Watson, David L., and Paul D. Watson. *Contagious Disciple Making: Leading Others on a Journey of Discovery.* Nashville: Thomas Nelson, 2014.

West, Earl. "James A. Harding and Christian Education." *Restoration Quarterly* 24 (1981) 65–79.

———. "Ministerial Education in America: A Survey." *Restoration Quarterly* 17 (1974) 65–84.

Williams, D. Newell, et al. *The Stone-Campbell Movement: A Global History.* St. Louis, MO: Chalice, 2013.

Wilson, Todd, and Gerald Hiestand, eds. *Becoming a Pastor Theologian: New Possibilities for Church Leadership.* Grand Rapids: IVP Academic, 2016.

Winter, Ralph. "The Highest Priority: Cross-Cultural Evangelism." *First International Congress on World Evangelization.* Lausanne, Switzerland, 1974. https://www.lausanne.org/content/the-highest-priority-cross-cultural-evangelism.

———. "Momentum Is Building! New Discussion on Completing the Task." *International Journal of Frontier Missions* 3 (1986) 67–78.

Wolfe, Stephen. "A Consequentialist Theory of Voting." *Mere Orthodoxy*, Dec 14, 2017. https://mereorthodoxy.com/consequentialist-theory-voting.

Wolterstorff, Nicholas. "Theory and Praxis." *Christian Scholar's Review* 9 (1980) 317–34.

World Population Review. "Zimbabwe 2022." https://worldpopulationreview.com/countries/zimbabwe-population&sa=D&source=docs&ust=1671647029702383&usg=AOvVaw3sbe1ov7iCubzVJkMRXiZZ.

Yip, George. "The Contours of a Post-Postmodern Missiology." *Missiology: An International Review* 42 (2014) 399–411.

Yong, Amos. *The Missiological Spirit: Christian Mission Theology in the Third Millennium Global Context.* Eugene, OR: Cascade Books, 2014.

www.ingramcontent.com/pod-product-compliance
Lightning Source LLC
Chambersburg PA
CBHW070313240426
43663CB00038BA/2225